ɔ

www.hert
L32

KIWI SPITFIRE ACE

KIWI SPITFIRE ACE

A GRIPPING WORLD WAR II STORY
OF ACTION, CAPTIVITY AND FREEDOM

Flt Lt J.D. Rae DFC and Bar

GRUB STREET · LONDON

Published by
Grub Street
The Basement
10 Chivalry Road
London SW11 1HT

Copyright © 2001 Grub Street, London
Text copyright © 2001 Jack Rae

British Library Cataloguing in Publication Data
  Rae, Jack
  Kiwi Spitfire ace: a gripping World War Two story of action, captivity and freedom
  1. Rae, Jack 2. Great Britain. Royal Air Force. Squadron 485 – History
  3. World War, 1939-1945 4. World War, 1939-1945 – Aerial operations, British
  I. Title
  940.5'44941'092

ISBN 1 902304 78 0

Typeset by Pearl Graphics, Hemel Hempstead

Printed and bound in Great Britain by
Biddles Ltd, Guildford and King's Lynn

ACKNOWLEDGEMENTS

I wish to thank those who have helped me with the preparation of this book. Bob Molloy for his patience and ability as an editor to convert a jumble of words that were my manuscript into a readable presentation, to aviation historian enthusiast Larry Hill who introduced me to the magic world of the computer, no manuscript would ever have been written without his help.

To the late Laddie Lucas for sharing his friendship over the years and his records of Malta history during those critical, vital first six months of 1942. To John Dyson for his encouragement and help. To my son Grant and his wife Lesley for their constant help and interest. To my daughter Barbara for her encouragement. To David Wisdom for his continued interest as a representative of good old USA. To Chris Widt for his generous help with a copy of John Chrisp's Spitfire painting.

A very special thanks for the encouragement and support from my dear wife Veronique, a Lady steeped in aviation interest through her magnificent late brothers – all three of whom served with distinction in the Royal Air Force.

Contents

	Dedication	iv
	Foreword	vi
I	Salad Days	1
II	Gaining Wings	6
III	Canadian Interlude	9
IV	Reality Dawns	17
V	First Operations	21
VI	People, Pilots and Personalities	26
VII	Redhill to Kenley	32
VIII	Kenley – Into the Thick of It	35
IX	Malta	43
X	Into the Cauldron	52
XI	The Island Battle	56
XII	Operation Hercules	61
XIII	Hercules Abandoned	70
XIV	Back to Red Tape Basics	76
XV	On Operations Again	83
XVI	Biggin Hill	91
XVII	Permanently Grounded	97
XVIII	Enemy Territory	108
XIX	In the Bag	120
XX	Tunnel Mania	126
XXI	The Great Escape	138
XXII	The Long Journey	147
XXIII	Chaos	155
XXIV	The Grand Finale	163
Appendix	Service Record	172
	Successes	174
	Index	176

Foreword

Jack Rae is a friend of many years. Our association dates back to early 1941 when we were both Sergeant Pilots on 485 New Zealand Spitfire Squadron. I have enjoyed reading his memoirs and feel privileged to write a foreword for his book *Kiwi Spitfire Ace*.

This is a story that very nearly remained untold. It is a gripping story of extraordinary experiences and valiant deeds. It takes you into the skies over occupied northern France and above the beleaguered Island of Malta. You feel the constant pressure of operational flying and the full intensity of aerial combat. You experience the close comradeship of the squadron pilots at work and at play and meet many a unique character. Perhaps the greatest trial of all – the numbing despair and bitter experience of becoming a POW and all the harrowing incidents associated with that life.

Shining through it all is a story of great courage and dogged resilience in times of extreme adversity. Jack tells his story clearly, factually and modestly with his underlying sense of humour always apparent. It is completely devoid of heroics. I consider it to be a very worthy addition to the many fine books written about the aerial battles of World War II.

I commend this book to you. You will enjoy it.

Squadron Leader Harvey Sweetman DFC, TP

I

Salad Days

The world changes in seconds. Moments earlier I had been flying a state of the art war machine that was outperforming anything the enemy could produce. Now I was steering a falling brick, dead stick and engine silent, diving almost vertically on to enemy-occupied territory in what promised to be a very hard landing.

True, I was headed for the soft green fields of France but still a bit too hard for the kind of wheels-up landing I had in mind. Of course I could bale out but I'd already figured the odds on that one and felt I had a better chance of escaping capture if I could choose my landing area. Good plan. My problem was that I was doing it blind with the windscreen oiled up and two Messerschmitt 109s on my tail.

I can't say my whole life flashed in front of me. I was too busy trying to shake off the 109s with as much twist and turn as was possible in a falling brick, but I did have a split second to wonder what happened. What I remembered happening was a dogfight involving dozens of aircraft, a Focke Wulf 190 turning only metres in front of me, myself firing until the FW disintegrated and then flying willy-nilly through the rain of debris. One of those pieces must have ripped through my engine cooling system.

Even the finest engines in the world – and the elegantly designed Rolls-Royce engine which powered my aircraft was very high in that category – can take only so much maltreatment. This one coughed, spewed oil over my windscreen and stopped. I switched it off, put the nose down, hoped the airflow would clear the screen and started looking for a piece of France that was flatter than the rest. I didn't need anyone to spell it out. This time I'd drawn the short straw.

Though I didn't realise it then, my career as a fighter pilot had ended. It would be the last time I would ever fly a military aircraft in battle. And not just any military plane, this was a Spitfire, the latest in a long series of superbly engineered fighter aircraft that had already flown themselves into legend. It was a dream machine, based on the design that won the Schneider Trophy for high performance aircraft back in the 1930s. I had spent the best part of the previous three years flying various versions of this incredible aircraft.

At certain moments in our lives we often wonder how we got from there to here. There would be times in the next months I would ponder that very point, going back to my carefree days as a 20-year-old in New Zealand interested only in weekend surfing and girls.

New Zealand then was a far-flung Dominion of the British Empire. As New Zealanders we loved our country and were proud of its achievements. Our forefathers had created a nation from virgin bush. They carved out huge dams for hydropower supplies, set up railroads the length and breadth of main islands and built a network of roads that connected all our main centres. In human rights achievements we believed we led the world, and all this in less than a century.

In the sciences, literature and the arts we also had a proud record. Militarily, too, our short history showed that during World War One our fathers and our Maori cousins had joined as one to help mother Britain in her hour of need. We were proud without knowing it. A kind of unstated and almost unconscious attitude, which back in 1939 translated as supreme confidence. We were quietly pleased to call ourselves British but at the same time feeling a bit sorry for the old-fashioned state of the Britain we knew little about but our grandparents referred to as 'Home'.

Life was just great. I had loving and caring parents, a 14-year-old younger brother and a wonderful grandmother. My days at Auckland Grammar School were behind me but friendships of those days still affected my life strongly. New Zealand, as with nations around the world, was climbing slowly out of the Great Depression of the 1930s. There was little or no unemployment; everyone seemed able to find meaningful work.

For me the summer days were fully involved with the Piha Surf Life Saving Club. My close friend Jim Dyson had moved to Australia to continue his veterinary studies. Max Cleary, who encouraged me to join the Surf Club, was also a close friend and an outstanding swimmer. At one stage he held the Junior, Intermediate, and Senior Over-arm sprint championships at Auckland Grammar.

He was also a powerful breaststroke swimmer, which proved invaluable when making headway pulling a rescue line against raging surf. Max could dive under and continue swimming. Without being driven backwards. We had a standard joke amongst us that if a rescue was imminent our first action was to look around and call out: "Where's Max?"

As a result Max often got some of the most difficult swims but he always took it in good part. During that exciting summer, in a land blessed with a 40-hour working week, everybody I knew was dashing out to Piha on Friday evenings. At that time I was working at the Dargaville Bus Terminal for Percy Laycock.

After leaving Auckland Grammar I took a job with the Westfield Freezing Co, which involved time and motion studies, a relatively new vocation for those days. In fact all the duties there were interesting although the 'hard-cased' cannery and casing girls used to give me hell at times. As a young fellow who blushed easily I became a sure mark.

I'd been working there quite happily until suddenly a clerical union was formed; at least it seemed sudden to me, as I knew nothing about it previously. Prior to this I had just received a raise and my pay was a healthy sum of three pounds fifteen shillings. That was about 1937, I think and the money was quite ample for my needs. Weekend supplies for Piha were ten shillings and board with my parents was ten shillings, which left me with plenty. I didn't smoke and did very little drinking, perhaps an occasional beer.

Life was blissful until I discovered that according to the union wage scale I was grossly overpaid and it would take another five years before I was entitled to a further raise. So for a short period of my life I became very anti-union, particularly when I learnt that I had to belong or else. So why not work as a labourer for the next five years and collect at least seven pounds a week – nearly double my present wage?

The father of one of the girls at Piha got me a job working in a quarry attached to a State Housing Scheme at Mount Albert. The only problem was that I was supposed to be a married man to qualify and have been out of work for a period of time. The stonemasons there were a great bunch of men to work with. They insisted on clubbing together and lending me a couple of pounds, as I must need it for "my Missus" after being out of work.

The situation was embarrassing but it was important that I went along with the pretence. And, would you believe, I had to join the Stone Masons' Union – which shortly afterwards appointed me to be their delegate.

Cutting giant lumps of stone into kerbing blocks was a fascinating job that needed great skill and knowledge of the grain of rock. I was very lucky to have as my companions either a Tasmanian or a Dalmatian. Both were delightful to work with; they would tell where to chip at those giant blocks and when I had gone deep enough. Then they directed me where to put the wedge. One hit with a weighty hammer and those great blocks would open up with a beautiful straight side. The pay was very good and soon I'd traded my BSA motorbike for an old Singer car, a vintage tourer with side curtains.

Things were looking up; it was much easier to get to Piha and a pleasure to take some other of the fellows along. Until then I'd been dependent on Edgar Carew and his front-wheel drive Citroen. However, with sisters Peggy and Nora plus younger brother Dennis it didn't quite like the extra weight. When climbing steep hills the front wheels were notorious for skidding in the loose gravel.

My old car proved great except that the clutch slipped on a few of the steep pinches so the chaps were well trained to jump out and push. The technique worked well. My car did have another snag. It had a long chassis and tended to skid badly on sharp corners – all part of the fun!

The summer of 1939 proved to be one that I would remember for a long time – not for any great happenings but for those wonderful days in this beautiful place that I would recall many times over when living, fighting, yes even killing and at times suffering hardships half a world away.

I remembered vividly one glorious sunny day with an offshore wind. Just off the beach massive swells were breaking vertically in a crushing wall of foaming water. Beyond that were row after row of beautiful tempting swells, promising us long and exciting rides on our surf skis. The big problem was to get out there.

There was one lone swimmer in those swells. He was Tom Pearce, a giant of a man physically who easily handled our powerful West Coast surf. A few of us had tried to get through the break on skis but all had wiped out, given up and opted instead to relax in the sun.

I had looked for a break in the surf for what seemed like hours. Finally the temptation was too much. I just had to try and elected to head off on my favourite 'blue ski' (all wood and fairly heavy – no lightweight skis and surfboards then).

I knew the drill. Ride the surf-ski out just short of the wall of broken sea, choose the moment and then paddle like mad, crash into the rocketing surf, turn over and hold on with all your strength to the paddle which was attached to the ski. On surfacing, pull your ski back, leap aboard quickly, paddle madly again at that churning mass which was now trying to drag you back, crash into the next wall of water, roll over and repeat it all again until you're through into the regular seas beyond.

Halfway through and – horrors – the rope had broken and there was my ski upside down. Very close but could I grab it in time, turn it over, jump on and start paddling before the next wall hit? Thinking back, I don't think I would have ever made it if luck hadn't played a huge part.

Suddenly there was one of those unpredictable lulls in the surf. In seconds I was back on board my ski and heading out beyond the break to ride those beautiful huge swells. Later, with my paddle re-knotted to the ski, Tom and I took turns for an idyllic hour of ski and body surfing.

Afterwards back on the beach I lay in the warm sands, body tingling with pleasure and an immense sense of achievement. That was the memory I was to take with me when thousands of feet in the air over England, over France, Belgium, Holland and again over the blue Mediterranean. And those wonderful memories supported the spirit when tramping over the icy roads of eastern Germany as part of a struggling, cold and weary group of prisoners of war.

There were of course other nostalgic moments to take with me into those appalling war years, exciting times in our Aussie surf boat and the wonderful companionship within our second fifteen Grammar Old Boys rugby team. I had played in the team until September 1940, just before entering the Royal New Zealand Air Force.

In that year we had a tally of 16 games played and 16 games won, with a total of 321 points scored and 79 against. We were justly proud of our games record. Sadly, quite a few from that team did not return at the end of the war. In fact my generation as a whole was to pay a heavy price for a war that had started so far away.

New Zealand then was a small country of about three million people; indeed it is not a great deal larger today. By the time the conflict ended, our cost in human lives was considerable. Army casualties alone were over 33,000 dead and the Air Force lost 4,263. Hardly to be compared with the millions lost by other countries but it amounted to more than 18 per cent of an armed forces total of 205,000.

I guess that what this preamble is all about is to try and paint a picture of what we teenagers and young men were like during those years. I think we were a very fortunate people to be living in such a wonderful country. We had a caring society, there was none of the dog-eat-dog philosophy common today. Food banks were unknown and there was full employment.

We certainly had a lot that was worth fighting for, though the cynics don't see it that way. The revisionists and the rewriters of history would have you believe that the young men went to war to escape their uncertain futures and that patriotism was only a product of propaganda. Nothing could be further from the truth.

A very large part of our motivation was the strong sense of adventure, but there was pride there too and a very real feeling that what we stood for was right. If that sounds a bit crass, so be it. Perhaps the world was simpler then. Simple enough for me to make a clear-cut decision on the issues as I saw them and march up to the recruiting office.

II
Gaining Wings

At the outbreak of war in September 1939 I was 20 years old. Hill Boucher and I applied to the Royal New Zealand Air Force (RNZAF) for training as pilots. From that moment on we waited with increasing impatience to be called up. Meantime we swotted hard with our maths, learnt our Morse code, and studied navigation under the tuition of a thoughtful ex-Navy man who offered the course free of charge – we met in a room at the Ferry Building in Auckland.

Months later we each received that official envelope. We'd been accepted but there was a snag: Hill was to report a month before me. That wasn't quite what I had in mind. An urgent appeal was made and, unbelievably, I was re-drafted to report at the same time, 1 September, 1940, a year after we had first applied.

The thrill of donning that light blue uniform was almost compensation for the month of square bashing that all recruits had to go through at Levin. It was our first taste of military discipline. Then followed what seemed like endless examinations to test our grasp of maths and other skills, all critical to our final selection.

The real excitement and thrills came with posting to our first 'course'. There would be many in my flying career but I don't think any quite evoked the keyed-up feelings we had when ordered to New Plymouth to start basic flying.

In retrospect I now marvel at the incredible efficiency of all of our British air forces, in particular the RAF, RNZAF, RAAF and the RCAF. Our own RNZAF made an outstanding contribution to the training of young men, effectively turning raw recruits into capable air crew. So capable that when Japan entered the war we were able to contribute first class squadrons to support our American allies in the fierce air battles over the Pacific.

From our point of view we felt fortunate to have been given the basic training that helped most of us to stay alive. There would often be circumstances in which no amount of skill could help – we knew that but preferred to ignore such thoughts.

The pace for us was now increasing. We were flying just about every day. The first big step was solo, the moment when the instructor would land the aircraft, step out and invite you to take off on your own. After that it was a blur of various exercises, circuits and bumps, the first attempt to fly cross-country, navigating from point to point and being totally grateful when the plotted destination appeared.

This to me was an amazing achievement. My logbook states it baldly:

> Cross-Country to Hawera .55 (min) Hawera (return) to New Plymouth (.25 min).

There must have been a strong wind blowing off the snowy peak of Mount Egmont that day and the little Tiger Moth would have been struggling on the trip to Hawera.

We also received instruction in what was then known as a Link Trainer, the forerunner of today's highly sophisticated Flight Simulators. It was a ground-based closed unit in the form of a cockpit with all the basic instruments. These could simulate all the flying attitudes, and also stalling and spinning should you be lax enough to allow your speed to fall below safety levels.

I consider this training was one of the most vital parts of our early flying experiences. I enjoyed the challenges they posed. There were many times during later flight operations that I'm sure I wouldn't have survived without the skills acquired in those chubby Link Trainers.

In November we moved to Ohakea. This was crunch time. Which of us would continue training in the single-engined Hawker Hinds as future fighter pilots? And who would fly the twin-engined Oxfords that would fit them for a career in Bomber or Coastal Commands?

Rumour had it that if you wanted to be selected for fighter pilot training you had to operate heavily on the controls. Tend to over-control, the rumour mill said, and you wouldn't be trusted to fly multi-engined aircraft. I doubt if such manoeuvring ever fooled our instructors but it probably boosted our own egos. It certainly fooled us when we flew badly which in those early days was probably quite often.

Whatever the reasons, luck held for Hill and me. We were both chosen to fly those 'extra great' fully aerobatic Hawker Hind biplanes with their powerful Rolls-Royce Kestrel engines. They were magnificent planes to fly. Until then we'd felt lucky to be flying around in the Tiger Moths but those Hawker Hinds – well. For motion freaks like Hill and myself they were the ultimate.

The only chance we had to fly the twin-engined Oxfords was in the 'under the hood' (blind flying) triangular courses, a means of testing our navigation skills. We were most impressed to find that after calculating our drift by means of a bomb sight and then applying the calculations and flying blind under the hood we actually did get where we wanted to – at least most of the time.

Dive-bombing practice was extra fun. Then there was low flying. Every day was a highlight. We also had to study madly: know every part of a

Browning machine gun and be able to dismantle and assemble it at speed, know meteorology and navigation. And always looming ahead were the final exams and the prospect of those coveted 'Wings' – in Air Force parlance our flying badge.

There were sad moments for some as our training time came to an end. A fine young Maori, Johnny Tawhai, on our course seemed to be doing well but just couldn't map-read while travelling over the land at speed. According to his instructor he became disoriented. We were sorry to see him miss out.

Then there was our very popular 'Bottler' Barry who was held back to do 'ground work' for a month. His craziest effort was to take off in a lumbering underpowered Oxford trainer, fly to his girl friend's home in Matamata, beat up the town and the Arapuni Dam, and arrive back at Ohakea with a near empty tank.

I failed to get a commission but Hill did. In some ways the price he had to pay for receiving his commission was high as he was kept back to be an instructor. After I was posted one of my regrets was separating from Hill, who served with distinction in operations in the Pacific. We never met again. He was killed in a flying accident back in New Zealand. His father, a flying pioneer and founder of Radio 1ZB, was also killed while flying.

Then came that unforgettable final leave in New Zealand and the long sea journey to Britain and the war.

III

Canadian Interlude

We had been trained to the highest standard that our Royal New Zealand Air Force could attain. True, our skills had been honed on obsolete aircraft but these were adequate to help us learn the basics of flying. They also provided a basis for the RNZAF to rate our abilities and to recommend to the Royal Air Force in Britain what type of operation would best suit our individual aptitudes. We had no notion what those recommended assessments were but we each had our own secret hopes and excited anticipation.

The three training courses in New Zealand, 5A, 5B and 5C, had each contained 30 potential pilots. One or two from each course were held back in New Zealand to become instructors. One or two were sent to Singapore. Sadly for them, this proved to be a death sentence as they found themselves flying hopelessly outmoded planes against a well-equipped enemy.

It was a cool autumn morning in Auckland in late March 1941, when the balance of us – about 80 pilots – marched up the gangways of the old SS *Monowai*, a converted military transport. From its crowded decks we waved farewell to our loved ones and set sail into the unknown; each of us was burning with excitement, wondering and hoping that very soon we would be flying high performance military aircraft against the enemy. We knew we'd have a short training period but nerves tingled just at the thought of flying in strange skies, of seeing the England we had heard about so often, at the reality of actually being on our way there.

Those of us who had been flying single-engined planes in New Zealand were very confident we would soon be flying fighter aircraft. And not just any fighter aircraft; in our minds there was only one and that was the ultimate aircraft, the fabulous Spitfire. That thought alone was enough to set the adrenalin flowing, though the outcome for those of us who had trained on twin-engined aircraft was less certain.

We had only the vaguest knowledge of what would happen to us when we reached Britain. None of us then knew our individual fates would be decided at a place called Uxbridge, near London. It was there, in that great big RAF melting pot of aspirations, that our appointments with destiny would be made.

Others were scattered all over Britain. The majority, those who had trained on twin-engined planes, went to Bomber Command. Many of these would very soon be flying giant four-engined bombers while others had the unenviable task of flying slow, old Blenheims on daylight raids into Europe. Other New Zealanders I remember who were posted to Heston on the same course were Pilot Officer Reg Baker and Sergeant Pilots Ray Phillips, Jim McIvor, Hughie Dean and Ted Carpenter.

However, when we set sail on the *Monowai* we had little knowledge of what was in store. At that stage the details mattered little. To a man we lived in a tingle of anticipation, thrilled to be part of this massive struggle. We were graded sergeant pilot, not of any great concern to us at that stage of our career. We hardly noticed the difference between ourselves and a small group who had been commissioned and held the rank of pilot officer.

We were soon to find that the difference in living conditions and the opportunities for promotion were vastly different. These differences became obvious from the moment we boarded the *Monowai* for the first leg of our long trip to Britain via Canada. However, we were enjoying service life too much to pay it any serious attention. In fact I ignored the service hierarchy throughout my service career as an NCO though every now and again the ridiculous demarcation rankled.

The trip to Britain was an adventure in itself. Apart from the new pilots of 5 Course, self-consciously but proudly wearing our brand new Wings, there was a large contingent of aspirant aircrew and pupil pilots. They were the first group to commence their training under the Empire Training School in Canada.

This was a scheme destined to produce thousands of aircrew, firstly to catch up with the Luftwaffe and then to vastly outstrip them. Those who conceived and administered this vast organisation gave an invaluable service to the Allied cause.

We soon discovered the *Monowai* had other duties to perform apart from taking us to Canada. Our first call was at Christmas and Fanning Islands, delivering supplies. No chance of us going ashore. Orders were that we remained cooped up aboard, so for the entire stop of several days we stared at those white beaches and sapphire blue waters. We were of a generation that never ventured beyond our shores and the sight of those islands of paradise shimmering in the heat left us awe-struck.

When off-loading was complete we headed off again, this time for Vancouver, Canada. To us it was fascinating to sail along the distant coast of California – the sea was incredibly blue and in the deep gentle swells the flying fish gave us a demonstration of superbly executed low flying. We had them as an escort for many miles up that coast.

At last we arrived at our port of disembarkation. This was it, we thought. Vancouver here we come – silk stockings to buy for the girl friends back home, and how about those Canadian girls? The entire contingent on board was vibrant with anticipation. Then the blow fell. The military machine had ideas other than allowing a bunch of eager youngsters to gum up the works with unsupervised trips around the city. Orders came through that we were to march from the ship directly to transport trucks. And so it was that our only glimpse of one of the world's most beautiful cities was from a crowded dockside.

The trucks, canvas canopies denying us any chance of sightseeing but for a fortunate few at the rear, whisked us across town to the main railway station. It was a slick operation. Within hours we were travelling across Canada on the Canadian Pacific Railways. Our destination wasn't disclosed but there were strict orders not to leave the train during stops at stations.

The new recruits accepted such orders with reluctance. The atmosphere among the sergeant pilots was quite different, almost mutinous. We questioned the whole deal. Why? Who do they think they are? We've been through all that discipline stuff! This isn't meant to apply to us, is it?

As we were to demonstrate in the next few weeks, we were on an understandable ego trip (at least I like to think it was understandable). After all, weren't we fully trained? We knew it all. Weren't we seen as responsible enough? The answers we gave ourselves added up to one thing – the intention to defy such orders at the first opportunity. Our learning curve was just beginning.

The train journey took us through the magnificent snow-peaked Rocky Mountains and finally stopped at Banff. Here all the troops were allowed off the train to stretch their legs. For a few short hours we mingled and milled about, staring at the beauty of this scenic area and drinking in every nuance. It was interesting to see some of the local Mounties in their famous red uniforms, and then it was off again across the endless plains of that great country.

Information filtered through to us that our next stop would be Calgary, site of the famed annual stampede and rodeo show. The train would be there for at least one hour but as we approached the town orders came through that no one was to leave the train.

It was now fairly obvious that we were not going to be let loose in any populous area. We had learnt from previous halts that the routine was to have armed guards placed at all strategic exits before the train stopped. We also learnt from Canadian porters that the approach to the station was over a bridge prior to stopping, the perfect outlet for any determined train-jumper.

Five of us were all ready, wallets bursting with Canadian dollars and a dedication to beat authority. As the train slowed and began clanking over the bridge, underneath which traffic flowed through busy Calgary, we jumped to the trackside. From there it was a quick scramble down the bridge structure and, whacko, we were on the loose in Canada.

We created quite a stir in the local shops as we tried to buy stockings and other goodies, none of which we had ever tried to buy before. The Canadian girls looked extraordinarily beautiful to our eyes and they gave us a wonderful welcome. This was the greatest fun we'd had since our last leave in New Zealand.

Then the decision came that threw all our scheming awry, we opted to buy local beer to take back onto the train. Although not a great beer drinker myself it was obviously of great importance to my fellow pilots so off we went. This was where we started running into complications. Like New Zealand, Canada also had strangely quirky liquor laws. We found that while you could buy beer at practically any store you first had to get a licence from the Post Office. All this took time. Finally, happy with our purchases and loaded down with cartons of beer under each arm we arrived back on the station – just in time to see the back of the train disappear down the track.

The five of us stood there in a state of shock – no longer feeling quite as smart as a few minutes before. Hughie Dean, Bill Gray, Rex Garnham, George Lowson and I were gazing at the empty line that we knew stretched for thousands of miles across Canada. Somehow we had to get back on our train.

While we were still standing in a sort of bewildered trance a station guard came up to us and asked us to follow him. We obeyed as if mindless. Just where he was taking us we had no idea. He led us into a very large office in which was an equally large desk at which a smiling gentleman rose to greet us. With his pleasant Canadian accent he invited us to take a seat and told us he already knew of our problem.

Though we had no notion as to his executive position we later gathered he was the General Manager of the Canadian Pacific Railways. A most engaging man and a great human being, he told us that he had fought in the last war with New Zealand troops. Knowing that a train full of New Zealanders was passing through he had come to the station to wish us well, only to find that here were five of them very obviously in need.

He told us he would see what he could do and we sat mute and a little embarrassed as we listened to him working the phones, obviously trying to juggle the other scheduled trains so that we would finally catch up with our own troop train. This finally done he rose, went over to the wall, opened up a spacious bar and invited us to join him in a drink. We could hardly believe our luck.

Then, in what we saw as great style, he arranged refreshments for us, bade us farewell and wished us good fortune. Suddenly, thanks to this very kind and understanding gentleman (in every sense of the word), we were transformed from five very lonely sergeant pilots wondering what we were going to do next to an excited group all set for a wonderful trip across Canada with first-class tickets in our hands.

And there was more, an incredible bonus. On boarding our train, still hardly able to credit our happy chance, we found a girls' band on board. What a party that turned out to be, shared with this charming group of Canadian womanhood all the way to Montreal.

And that was where the music stopped, literally and metaphorically.

Naively, we had nursed the idea that we would not have been missed and would be able to rejoin our troop train unnoticed. What a shock it was to be greeted at each halt with variations on the refrain: "Oh, so you are the five pilots missing from the troop train."

Finally catching up with our train, we found it on a sideline at Fort William surrounded by knee-deep snow. As we approached a very irate squadron leader met us – I hesitate to use the word "greeted". After a verbal dressing-down we were taken to a camp at a place called Debert. The camp was appallingly cold, surrounded by ice and frozen mud. Accommodation was in large huts with tiered bunks heated by huge oversized burners in the centre.

It was a case of stay warm and gasp for air or turn down the heat and freeze. A small town called New Glasgow was the nearest place to try to have some fun but over-boisterous play was not very welcome in this rather conservative town. To be fair, the folk were pleasant and made us very welcome and we did have some high jinks there.

As a memento we removed the very large hotel sign, only to discover later that there was no place to hide it on board ship. We were glad in the end to simply abandon it.

In retrospect much of our behaviour during that period was little more than boyish pranks, some not too bright either. And they continued until we came face to face with the realities of war and the need for self-discipline, for the safety of others and our own survival. However, it seemed that until that time came we were just going to have one hell of a time and no amount of discipline was going to stop us.

At last we boarded our ship in Halifax, an unimpressive looking vessel called *Derbyshire* requisitioned from the Bibby Line. The port was a hive of activity, there seemed to be ships everywhere, intermixed with destroyers. With our kitbags over our shoulders we lined up and made our way on board together with what seemed like thousands of others including a large contingent of Canadian aircrew.

It was to be a nightmare journey across the Atlantic as far as Iceland. The ship was hopelessly overcrowded; there were queues for everything, showers, meals, toilets and even bunks and the odd bit of deck space.

Granted, the food queues grew noticeably shorter as the seas became bumpier and at time mountainous. But in all it was a dreadful trip, there were no bunks for most of us and we had to alternate with the crew as they went on shift. Incredibly this quite ancient ship was acting as one of the escorts for the entire convoy, which meant that we were constantly turning and sailing broadside on to the enormous and at times breaking seas.

The speed of passage was minimal as we were governed by the slowest ship in the convoy. Now and again there were sightings of wreckage from ships sunk out of the preceding convoy – an ominous reminder of the dangers we faced. My respect for the courage of our merchant seamen and our naval crews increased tenfold as I stared out at those heaving grey waters and their hidden menace and realised that while this was just one trip for us it was a continual ongoing nightmare for the sailors.

Many of the Canadians had never been to sea before, in fact had never seen the sea at all. Some were terribly seasick throughout the entire crossing, and sailing through the wreckage of the previous convoy did little to boost morale. Our armament consisted of a few very old-fashioned machine guns. Some of us were chosen to man these things and act as the ship's defence.

The huge and I mean very huge and breaking seas that we encountered were full of ice and intimidating in the extreme. We practised the abandon ship drill daily but even while going through the motions I wondered what chance of survival we could possibly have in such mean-looking waters. However, Lady Luck smiled at us on that trip and we finally arrived at the port of Reykjavik in Iceland.

Excitement grew as our ship slowly made its way to the wharf, the pent-up energy of hundreds of young men eager to get off this heaving tub, get ashore, mingle with the locals and see the sights. The daylight was a strange dull grey but that didn't stop us crowding the rails and bending over to shout friendly words of greeting to the locals helping with our docking or standing watching us.

It was then that we received a shock for which we were totally unprepared. They all stopped, looked up at us, then deliberately turned their backs. When we looked more closely at them we noticed they were all wearing black armbands in the centre of which were small Union Jacks. And when we drove through the city to our camp on the outskirts what few citizens we saw turned their backs or looked away. What a wonderful welcome that was.

We were told on arrival at camp that this was the anniversary of the day that Britain had taken them over as a defence precaution. German propaganda had made a meal of that one and had fairly well convinced most of the Icelanders that not only were they hard done by, but that we were bad news: news that was likely to become worse if Iceland became the focus of a major theatre of war.

We also wondered at the few signs of life in the streets but later learned it was 1 a.m. and the 'daylight' was as dark as it got even that close to midnight. It was truly one of the lands of the midnight sun. In fact, during our short stay in Iceland there was no darkness. We shuddered to think what it must be like in mid-winter.

The Icelanders had much to feel aggrieved about. Hostilities had stopped work on some of their major projects, including one to pipe hot water from the thermal area to the city. Another major irritant to the locals was that the British military immediately started driving on the left which was contrary to Icelandic practice.

Our camp was out in the country, a sprinkling of poorly insulated Nissen huts each kept warm with a centrally placed pot-bellied wood stove. The hot springs were nearby with a small settlement and restaurant which permitted some limited fraternising with the locals but they were nervous to be seen talking to us. However we still managed to get into a bit of very real trouble.

One of our number advised another who shall be nameless that if he wanted to have a prostitute there was a special house down at the village that would meet these needs. The nameless fellow went down to the house, knocked on the door and asked for service. That's when all hell broke loose. The address was the home of the local mayor.

Next morning all New Zealanders were lined up at an identification parade. Fortunately no one was recognised. Such minor pranks kept us sane in a dreadful camp that was run by a CO who was quite crazy. Perhaps it was the conditions which made him that way but we did notice throughout the war there were some pretty useless senior officers in out of the way places. Possibly it had much to do with the fact that they had seniority but no track record and Command placed them where they could do least harm.

At last we were to re-embark for the hazardous journey to Britain. This time it proved a complete contrast to our recent trip. We boarded a ship of the Ulster Line whose name I can't recall. She was a much smaller ship than the *Derbyshire* but faster. We set off for Greenock in Scotland at high speed and without any naval escort. We would have been a difficult target for a submarine and our only real hazard was air attack. We arrived without a single action station alarm and barely had we tied up at the wharf when we were hurried off the ship and on to a train.

Next stop was Uxbridge where we found ourselves in the heart of the giant RAF reception centre. We had finally arrived. As Des Scott in his delightful book *One More Hour* commented, Uxbridge was not so much the home of air crew as its Devil's Lottery for it was here that each of us would be allocated the role we were to play in the air war over Europe.

While some would be posted to Fighter Command, most would go to Bomber Command and there would be other postings to such work as Coastal Command. What we probably did not really appreciate until much later was that our destinies were being decided during our short stay at Uxbridge. If it was a lottery I have to say I felt I won it. To my delight nine of us, of which I was one, were posted to 53 OTU (Operations Training Unit) No. 4 Course, RAF Heston – my first step to Fighter Command.

First off, a brief leave loomed large. Money was burning holes in our pockets, substantial backpay for the period during which we'd travelled from New Zealand. We were also advised not to venture into London, and particularly the heavily bombed central areas, unless we knew our way around and were used to blackout conditions. Needless to say this advice was ignored. A group of us went, saw the sights, managed to get separated and completely lost, missed the last trains running that night and arrived back the next morning somewhat the wiser and with considerably less money than we had the day before.

That was the last crazy action we had together as a group, as friends who had shared great fellowship together, tested the tolerance and patience of our instructors, and had finally made it to Britain. Here there was a real war going on. Everywhere we looked we were confronted with the reality of the violence and terrible destruction that had been launched at England. British fortitude was evident. We knew without being lectured there was a huge task ahead and we were now part of that task.

IV

Reality Dawns

I doubt whether I could adequately convey the feeling of intense tingling excitement I felt, and I am sure my fellow NZ pilots also felt, when we arrived at Heston. We could hardly credit the sight of Spitfires taking off and landing, of others around the perimeter waiting for someone to fly them – could this really be happening to us? Would we actually soon be flying one of these incredible machines?

The atmosphere of the aerodrome was to us electrifying. Above us was the sound of Rolls-Royce engines purring, a sound we were to learn to love, and not far away the great barriers of barrage balloons over London. In the centre of the tarmac just in front of one large hangar were the remains of the wreckage caused by a massive land mine, dropped courtesy of the Luftwaffe two nights before.

We were taken for a general look-see and then driven to our various billets which were private homes bordering the airfield. Our hosts were ordinary Britons, wonderful, obliging people very conscious of the fact that we were all in the front line in this war. Some of us made friendships with our hosts that were to last for decades.

Training began immediately. One intriguing item that had all of us crowding as close as we could was a cut off section of a Spitfire – just the area of the cockpit erected on a stand. Later we would each have the opportunity to sit inside what looked to us a very tiny cockpit and familiarise ourselves with the layout, well aware we had to get it right first time – in this aircraft there was no such thing as dual flying before going solo.

Stores loaded us up with an incredible load of equipment: helmets with oxygen masks attached, microphones, and Mae Wests, which were an extremely efficient flotation device named after the well-known American actress of the period. They did indeed make the wearer look as if he owned the kind of large mammary glands for which Miss West was famous. Years later I read that she was delighted to hear the RAF had named their lifejackets after her.

Then came our parachutes, the harness so low slung that we could use it to sit on while in the cockpit. When it was my turn to actually sit in the mock-up Spitfire cockpit I found it incredibly crowded – there was so much gear around one's face there was only just enough room to peep over the oxygen mask. Looking down at the instruments required a physical effort. At the time it was a major shock to realise that we were expected not only to fly in these conditions but also to have the quick reactions necessary to fight. Perhaps because it was a case of needs must, we very quickly accustomed ourselves to having that clutter all over our faces and were soon fitting into those tiny cockpits like a familiar glove.

The instructors were a great bunch of ex-operational fighter pilots all walking around with their top button undone, the privilege adopted unofficially by those who had served in combat. I can assure you they had our deepest respect. However as instructors they seemed to pay little regard to our very limited experience. To them we were simply a very welcome group of young men who had the coveted Wings on our uniform, so we could fly aeroplanes

The fact that we had never flown an aircraft with a retractable undercarriage nor operated a variable pitch propeller and had last flown our delightful if antiquated Hawker Hinds back in February seemed of little matter to them. In fact it was on 6 June 1941 that I first took off with my instructor, Flying Officer Read, in a Miles Master trainer.

This aircraft had the familiar Rolls-Royce Kestrel engine. The conversion course consisted of a one hour forty minutes dual and three solos around the circuit – total 4 hours 35 minutes' flying time. This was to be followed by a 1 hour 20 minutes flight around the sector with the instructor and then a 45-minute test with the flight commander to get the OK for Spitfire solo.

Nine days later it was a case of, "Here is a Spitfire, Rae, take it away old chap." The last two duals plus my now to be epic flight all took place on one day, 11 June. I imagine that rookie pilots when faced with their first big solo act in many varied ways. I know when first seated in the cockpit of what was to me an extremely powerful aircraft – one I was about to take into the air alone behind those belching exhausts – that confidence wasn't exactly what I was feeling.

Taxiing was in itself quite difficult as the long nose and protruding exhaust outlets made forward visibility virtually nil. To offset this a pilot had to taxi with a zigzag movement and considerable caution. I had another problem with this particular Spitfire, as it was one of the older models with a pump handle on the right hand side. To select the wheels-up procedure it was a case of first select, take your left hand off the throttle, grab the joystick and then use your right hand to pump furiously to bring up the undercarriage.

Sounds simple enough but try to imagine yourself as that very tense pilot who had already had his first shock by opening up the throttle – witnessing the belching flames coming from the exhausts – holding the eager Spitfire straight, feeling it take off amazingly quickly and suddenly discovering how super-sensitive it was on the elevators.

I had been warned about those elevators but the reality of trying to control them with the unfamiliar left hand while madly pumping with the right was something else. The result was a most unprofessional undulating take-off until that stupid undercart was up. But what now? My first time to take a look out of the 'office' – where the hell was I?

The barrage of balloons looked damned close but where was the aerodrome? I was miles out of the usual circuit. Below me was nothing but masses of unfamiliar buildings, stretching to the horizon, strung with a tangle of roads. Oh what a difference from taking off at Ohakea and seeing the green fields and the few easily recognisable roads.

I finally got myself back into the circuit although still seemed to be travelling at an alarming speed. However, I was finally into the controlled cockpit-check, busily engaged in levelling flaps and pumping wheels down, watching my speed and fiddling with the unfamiliar microphone. So engrossed was I that I forgot to slide back the canopy. The result was that after 'flaring off' I went to poke my head out to take a peep at the runway from under the exhausts and bang, my head hit the perspex hard.

In my tense situation it was far too late to try raising my hands to open the thing so I decided, wrongly, to proceed with my landing and try to guess just where my height was in relation to the runway. I levelled off, held it steady, and began to think what an extremely smooth landing it was when I suddenly dropped in a dead stall – crashing onto the undercart and damaging it considerably.

That was my shocking first effort and, dare I boast, my last bad landing with those beautiful Spitfires. I was also rewarded with my one and only endorsement in the back of my logbook under the terse comment:

Crashed – inexperience.

All the rest of the NZ contingent consisting of Pilot Officer Reg Baker and Sergeant Pilots Ray Phillips, Jim McIvor, Hughie Dean, Ted Carpenter and Les Ford came through the OTU course unscathed and were posted to various squadrons throughout Fighter Command. One Canadian pilot was killed when he flew into a balloon cable.

Looking back at my record of training, preparation for possibly close combat against the enemy, it seems very sparse indeed, but it did not to any of us at that time. We were still endowed with the supreme confidence of youth and dangerously over-confident. My total flying time on a Spitfire was 15 hours 25 minutes. I had logged cloud flying (twice), formation flying (three times), low flying (once) and dog fight tactics (three times). All other flying activities once only and no chance at all to even test fire our guns.

We enjoyed every moment of the flying but the unspoken question in our minds was would squadron commanders enjoy having us as part of their squadron?

It was a great Operational Training Unit with some interesting characters within the staff. The most outstanding was our Commanding Officer, famous World War One fighter pilot Wing Commander (Taffy) Jones DSO, MC, DFC, MM. A Welshman, he was a vibrant controversial figure who always seemed to get into strife with Higher Command. There was also Wing Commander J.A. (Johnny) Kent DFC, AFC, a Canadian reputed to have received his AFC for testing balloon cables by flying into them in a Hurricane. I never managed to confirm this but, regardless, he was a very impressive man who gave us words of wisdom and a timely warning at a period in our flying career when it was urgently needed.

Using graphic descriptions of the grim realities of the air war we were now very close to joining, he left us with no illusions. Ahead was no "play way" and the price of a mistake could be terribly permanent.

I was the lucky one from our NZ group as I was posted to our own 485 Squadron stationed in 11 Group (the most active group that operated close to and south of London). Our station at Redhill, near Reigate, was part of the Kenley Wing.

V

First Operations

Redhill was a beautifully situated airfield nestled in the countryside of Surrey, south of London and not far from the town of Reigate. The surrounding countryside appeared charming and peaceful but the activities within the fighter squadron were at maximum tempo. When I arrived as a starry-eyed fledgling fighter pilot to join what was already a battle-hardened group of very busy operational pilots, I knew it was going to be a steep learning curve.

It was mid-July, 1941. The mid-summer weather was perfect, day after cloudless day. And the days were long, with good clear visibility until after 10 p.m. The squadron was operating an intense rate of flights against the enemy. It was not unusual for pilots to fly on three major operations in a day, and pilots were averaging at least two flights daily.

In spite of this obvious excessive pressure and the inevitable occasional losses of fellow pilots there was no sign of weariness – in fact there was a highly confident and relaxed attitude within the squadron. I had a co-joiner, Sergeant Porter, with me on arrival. We were advised that we were welcome but needed to pack in as much cockpit time as possible before there would be any likelihood of operational flying.

I recall these as heady days. The wonder of getting into a fully operational fighter aircraft, taking off and climbing up and up into the blue skies of a perfect English summer, chasing the clouds, climbing through them, aerobatics limited only by one's own endurance.

I found it at once both eerie and exhilarating, testing the limits of my aircraft and myself, climbing up just to see how high I could reach. Climbing until the controls began to feel sloppy and I had the feeling that any minute I might fall out of the sky in a flat spin.

At that height my aircraft wallowed and wallowed and I found myself so busy trying to keep my flying speed up and maintain even the slightest rate of climb that I forgot to check my ultimate height. So I am not certain whether that delightful old Spitfire II did make 40,000 feet or not. But she certainly demonstrated that she had exceeded her useful flying ceiling. It was a case of ease gently on the controls, very gently indeed, and finally take the road downwards.

What an enormous difference in performance there was in each mark of Spitfire as the war progressed. Little did I realise that one day not far distant I would be at the controls of a Spit that could climb to 25,000 feet in less than 5 minutes, make 40,000 feet seem like a breeze, and deliver speeds far, far beyond what we found so impressive in those early machines.

Just eleven days after arriving at Redhill, and with another valuable eleven hours and forty minutes of Spitfire flying showing in my log, came my first operation. This was Channel Cover Patrol – nothing spectacular but important to those below needing our protection. We logged several of these uneventful Channel Patrols and then, suddenly, we were off on a completely crazy offensive. To this day I have no idea why we went there and no one else that flew in our flight even when asked years later could provide an answer.

I was flying as number two with Hal Thomas. We were just off the coast of France in the quite stupid line astern formation, which those in command stubbornly adhered to regardless of constant complaints. Line astern meant just that; with four aircraft in each Flight the leader had his number two right behind followed by the next number one and behind him his poor number two or 'Tail End Charlie' – the most dangerous and dreaded position in which to fly. With three flights of four making up the squadron of twelve that meant three very lonely, very shot-at, and least experienced pilots bringing up the rear.

On this occasion I was Tail End Charlie behind Hal. All of a sudden our particular flight broke away from the squadron and dived straight at and into the guns of Calais. The gunfire hurled at us was a sight to behold. Hell, I thought, this isn't a very healthy place to play around in. We went down to almost ground level, shot over the top of massive gun emplacements glimpsing men running for their guns, did a tight turn within the harbour itself and saw tracer bullets cascading around us.

It was utter madness. There were no enemy aircraft anywhere to be seen, just four Spitfires in neat formation giving gunnery practice to the German defence. As Tail End Charlie I was being baptised with fire. It also meant I was the last to leave that most unfriendly place, flying within inches of the churned-up sea, with what seemed every damned tracer bullet focusing in on me.

I never fired a shot and none of us received the slightest damage. Why we did it and more importantly how the devil we got away with it is beyond logic. That was my first introduction to direct action against the enemy. We did hear some vague explanation that the operation was designed to test the defence of Calais. A load of bull? Yes, that's what I think also.

My previous comments about line astern formation were based on the fact that fighter pilots, and in particular the less experienced, faced huge difficulties in trying to watch the skies around them. Imagine having to scan the vast area above and in all directions in front, behind, each side and then the areas directly below – all done repeatedly, particularly the deadly area directly astern.

Achieving this process of keeping a careful sky watch had to be done with calmness and precision. If you spun your head around in a constant panic you would see little or nothing. In fact most pilots in their first few encounters in air combat returned home admitting they'd seen very little of what happened.

Line astern – an already archaic flying formation that the High Command of those days insisted we use – was soon to become my pet aversion. Apart from all the problems just mentioned each pilot was expected to maintain a constant formation, particularly the number two with his number one who was constantly on a weaving course.

At times I found this particularly difficult – in fact under some situations impossible – as I was to discover on occasions during which my number one was violently manoeuvring and we were also under attack. How the hell, I asked myself, can you watch your tail and at the same time fly formation with an aircraft in front of you.

There was one particular pilot who was pointed out to me as the supreme example of flying as a number two, keeping perfect formation at all times even during the most violent operations. As a result he was always chosen to fly behind the CO. Certainly better than flying Tail End Charlie. I just couldn't figure out how he was able to achieve this perfection and watch his tail, so I asked him to explain.

The explanation shocked me considerably. In fact I worried for some time after whether he was placing others at risk, or just himself. There had to be a loss of vigilance within the squadron. As a fellow pilot I liked him and, as 'new kid on the block', it certainly wasn't for me to say anything. However he survived throughout the war so it worked for him although I'm certain his CO would have hesitated to continue flying with him had he known.

His explanation: he tried never to look anywhere but kept a tight formation and prayed!

You may well be asking: who made those decisions? Who were these men at the top? From what we heard at that time, and with history to confirm it, our leaders were not idiots – far from it. Like all of us, however, they were feeling their way, rewriting the textbooks on the hoof yet restricted by an intransigent attitude towards the correct formation and tactics for aerial warfare. They did listen to the men who were fighting the air warfare but only slowly did our tactics change.

Strangely, all that they needed to do was copy the tactics of the enemy. The Germans had learned and accumulated vast experience from the air battles during the Spanish war. But fixed ideas take time to remove.

The commander of our No.11 Group was Air Marshal Sir William Sholto Douglas. His predecessor during the Battle of Britain was our own New Zealander, Air Vice-Marshal Keith Park (later to achieve a knighthood). Both these men had strong supporters and strong critics. Whatever else they did our leaders believed in taking the war to the enemy. To me this period of squadron operation was exciting, intoxicating and – with the staggering display of power the RAF attained so rapidly after the battering Britain had so recently endured – dramatically impressive.

Our day-to-day routine during the summer of 1941 invariably started with an announcement that pilots were to assemble in the briefing room. If we were at the main base then the Wing Commander Flying would be there usually together with the Station CO and of course all squadron pilots. On the wall would be a large detailed map, usually of northern France, marked with the target for the day and other details relating to that particular operation.

There were various positions squadrons had to fill on any given operation. Top Cover was the most advantageous for attacking as you would be flying very high – sometimes well above 30,000 feet. This allowed a less restrictive position when keeping a lookout for the enemy but being wary of the first few tempting 'lures'. Just below this position was the target support formation – also an aggressive group but committed to stay over the target area. Then next below was High Cover, equally aggressive but committed to stay closer to the bombers.

During the operation many of the formations described could be heavily involved in combat. The bombers still needed protection as they withdrew so the next line of defence was the Escort Cover group and below them again the Close Escort, the most flak intensive job.

All positions were important and all had their particular hazards. I doubt whether there was ever a pilot who didn't have some sort of nervous reaction immediately after briefing, knowing that soon he would be flying into danger – perhaps extreme danger. I never heard any comments from them except perhaps that they were off for a nervous pee – but a tense feeling was always there.

My personal reaction was always the same, regardless of how mean the forthcoming show might look or how relatively easy: immediately after the briefing the palms of my hands would sweat. I could wipe them and wipe them but those damned palms would still sweat. However, I knew that once we were on the way then it would stop.

At take-off time, with engines running, we'd be sitting in our aircraft watching the movements of Wing Leader. The roar of Spitfires lined up ready for take-off in formations of four made a steady drumming. Then the signal from Wing Leader and the first four would open their throttles to a thunderous crescendo and move off, gathering speed. Immediately they are airborne the next four line up, take off, and so on.

I never failed to be awed by the sight and sound of our Spitfires taking off, climbing in formation to pre-planned heights to rendezvous with other wings from 11 Group and our Bomber Force. All over the sky there would be the flashes of reflected light giving glimpses of the huge armada of attack aircraft we were aiming at the enemy. We were issuing a direct challenge time and time again and our pilots were gaining much needed experience to counter the battle-hardened Germans.

The RAF was taking the war to the enemy. I must admit that I felt damned proud to be part of this incredible show of resilience from Britain. We were only very small pawns in this great battle for supremacy and had very little real knowledge of the value of what we were doing. At times when escorting those poor slow Blenheims and watching them being blasted with flak, when as close escorts we were having real trouble trying to fly slowly enough to stay beside them, we ourselves felt uneasy and vulnerable.

Throughout the entire period of take-off, rendezvous, and the flight into enemy territory there was always a strict RT (radio transmission) silence. Sometimes this silence would remain until well on the way back. But when the enemy started to lurk around to pick off the poor Tail End Charlies, particularly if one drifted too far back, then there would be too many voices.

Very occasionally we would receive a concerted full attack. Such attacks had to be turned and met and then the RT would come alive with shouts of warning. And God help the poor devil being attacked if some yob was talking his head off on the RT and blocking transmission. That said, most of the voices heard were transmitting genuine and important information.

In our particular wing we had two other squadrons based at Kenley. One was 602 (City of Glasgow) and the other an Australian squadron, 452. You could always tell when our Aussie friends were having a hot time as the familiar Aussie twang split the airways above the fields of France. It is easy now with all the facts and figures available to examine operations more critically but at that time we felt that we were doing a pretty good and important job.

The main aim of the RAF in 1941 was to force the Germans into retaining their main force of aircraft in Europe and hinder their efforts in the East. We now know that this did not succeed and because of the difficulty of operating over enemy territory our loss of pilots tended to be greater than theirs. For example during July and early August our squadron lost seven pilots but shot down only five Germans.

We now know also that during the entire phase the Germans lost only 33 aircraft and did not need to bring replacements back from the Eastern Front, whereas in the same period Fighter Command lost 98 pilots. Fortunately we were not privy to such information in those days and continued to maintain the offensive.

VI

People, Pilots and Personalities

From the previous broad overview of our activities as a squadron it might seem we acted as one, and certainly that's what High Command hoped would be the case. However, as a group you would find it difficult to meet a more diverse assembly of young men. What struck me on first joining 485 Squadron was that there was no display of arrogance yet an air of confidence prevailed. Nor was there any obvious division between officers and us sergeants except in accommodation, but that was the way of British service life and not of their making. Having said that, I didn't hear any officers complaining.

I was delighted to find quite a few members of the squadron whom I had known back in New Zealand. They included Gary Francis who played rugby with me in the Grammar Old Boys Club. Also Bill Middleton – he and I were in the Auckland Grammar 2nd Fifteen – and Frank Brinsden who had been an outstanding athlete from Takapuna Grammar. I had known him since his athletic days. As time went on there would be many more to join the squadron, men from my generation and the same circle of pre-war activities.

When the weather packed up and flying was on hold we sometimes had a 48-hour leave. With London so close this meant hectic times in the 'Big Smoke'. Which reminds me, there was one more outstanding attribute that all members of our squadron seemed to have to a high degree and that was that they knew how to play. And what better place to do this than London, even in wartime or perhaps because of it. Many of the combat reports from these activities are strictly censored.

Among the outstanding personalities in this fun-loving and at times crazy group was our CO, Squadron Leader Marcus Knight. He had earned his way to the UK back in 1935 as a ship's writer, become an instructor in the RAF and had the flamboyant and outstanding New Zealand ace 'Cobber' Kain as one of his pupils. The CO was a brilliant pilot, his flying ability in our Tiger Moth trainer, and his incredible landing accuracy on the perimeter right outside the door of our dispersal hut was a sight to see. Usually accomplished with a flurry of 'fish-tail' actions with his rudder to slow his forward speed, he would then float gently to a stop in an immaculate three-point landing.

On one occasion the squadron was lent a 'display Spitfire' which had been stripped of all her armament, extra gear and camouflage, and repainted in glittering silver. Marcus flew it over our airstrip in one of the most impressive exhibitions of aerobatics that I have ever witnessed. It was a staggering display of the incredible abilities of that classic aircraft, climbing up in vertical slow rolls and then gently 'rolling off' the top. As an encore he then landed her in front of us with great aplomb.

I can't list all of our squadron members at this stage although they all deserve a mention for their many and varied peculiarities. Flight Commander 'Hawkeye' Wells definitely had his own quirks and, as his nickname implies, his acute sight at rifle shooting was an asset worth having as a fighter pilot – and hopefully at sighting the enemy first. He was a popular leader. At squadron reunions over the years some stories are told and retold of many of those real characters who enriched our ranks.

One who stands out in memory for his quiet dignified personality was Flight Lieutenant Jack Strang, lost so tragically. We were just approaching the French coast as High Cover when he started flying erratically, peeled over and dived from 25,000 feet straight down towards the sea.

Bill Crawford-Compton was on one side of him and I on the other but he took no notice of our frantic signals. Bill, in desperation, finally broke RT silence, screaming at him as we followed him down. He could be seen slumped forward in his cockpit, apparently unconscious from lack of oxygen. Whether it was a malfunction or he had forgotten to turn it on we will never know. Our own vertical speeds were reaching dangerous levels so we had to pull away, sadly rejoining our squadron positions to continue with the offensive.

We were hardened at losing our friends during operations but the loss of Jack Strang in this fashion affected us deeply for a long time.

Some of our delightful 'scallywags' seemed to have nine lives plus a few more. One case was Sergeant L.P. Griffith – Griff to everybody except Hawkeye on one occasion. There had been an epidemic of minor damage to aircraft during taxiing and a special appeal was given by Hawkeye to take particular care. Soon after this request – the same day in fact – there was the sound of crashing and a horrible noise of metal being minced up. Everyone rushed out of Dispersal and there was Griff with his Spitfire halfway up the rear of Hawkeye's Spit. Griff looked out from his cockpit at the chaos, nodded to Hawkeye, and said: "Gee, Boss, I just didn't see it."

Only Griff's personality saved him from an immediate posting.

While on the subject of this brash young man – barely 19 at the time – I recall flying with him on an operation as Close Escort to the squadron of Blenheims. It had been an operation with a fair share of difficulties firstly with enemy fighters and then some heavy concentrations of flak that exploded uncomfortably close to us as well as amongst the bombers.

Momentarily I glanced across at Griff flying in the flight next to me and

I saw a large and very ominous puff of smoke from a flak explosion right underneath him. For a short time all was quiet on the RT and then suddenly a most indignant, high-pitched voice that could only be Griff broke the silence.

"I've been hit!" Then after a short silence: "I've been hit and I think I will have to bale out!"

The words came across with excessive indignation. All this time we were nearing the French coast and the British Channel was approaching. Once again this voice of indignation informed us that he was losing power. We could see he was losing height. It was going to be touch and go whether he would get far enough away from France to bale out with some chance of rescue. This piece of drama was dominating our valuable radio waves when suddenly a loud and unmistakable Aussie accent came on the RT: "Make up your mind and jump, you stupid bugger!"

To be fair, Griff's situation wasn't pleasant as there was a high risk of enemy fighters being attracted to an easy kill while he tried to retain enough height for a safe bale-out. At the same time he was taking his aircraft as far out to sea as possible to give Air Sea Rescue service a better chance of reaching him. When he did finally jump a couple of us circled around him as long as fuel permitted and then other aircraft took over.

The only thanks I got from him was when he paid me back the one pound he owed me with the comment that that was the only reason I had stayed with him.

I have to admit that when he arrived back at the base he looked great wrapped up in jerseys and heavy clothing, still well primed on rum. Griff later told us he'd been plucked out of the sea in a high-speed operation while his air cover kept off the 'bandits'. He was then taken to naval sick quarters at Ramsgate, given a hot bath and breakfast, and returned to Redhill. Those Air Sea Rescue crews were many times over our Angels of Mercy.

To my regret I never kept a diary of those war years and my logbook is my only personal reference. However, it gives quite an accurate account of events even if a bit clinical. In the vernacular of the service it is RAF Form 540 and was kept recorded by the squadron adjutant.

One entry of 9 September, 1941, states:

> S/Ldr Knight. Circus Operation to Bethune, several e/a were engaged
> in the course of which one was damaged by Sgt. Rae. Sgt. Russell failed
> to return. Sgt. McNeil crashed landed on aerodrome owing to broken
> seat. Squadron returned 12.55 hrs.

This typical matter-of-fact entry tells in a few words the incredible amount of human drama, which took place that September day. The operation had been as much about survival as attack, we were heavily outnumbered and had very little time to survey any damage we might have done.

'Tusker' McNeil, a likeable strongly-built young man noted for being heavy handed with his flying, had managed to demonstrate the incredible strength of his Spitfire. During combat he had pulled out of a dive at such extreme high speed that his seat bolts were torn out of their mountings, causing his seat to slide forward and jam against the control column. Somehow he was able to get his aircraft back to fly almost straight and level – but not quite.

Though losing height steadily he was still about 12,000 feet up when he crossed the southern coast of England. Reasoning that he could fly the aircraft on a steadily descending course at his present angle, he decided to make for Redhill. Clearly there was no possibility of flying a fancy approach circuit. On arrival he needed to be at just the right height and flying in the right direction to make the runway. As he got closer he controlled his height loss by judicious use of his throttle. Redhill was put on full alert as he came in on final approach to the unsealed strip which had a wire mesh covering.

The Spit's wheels touched but with the aircraft at an alarming nose-down attitude. Then things happened with spectacular speed. The prop touched, disintegrated, the nose slid under the wire mesh and a major proportion of the Spitfire ended up enveloped in a wire cage – including our still very much alive Tusker.

In his efforts to pull out of his dive and then fly home, he had managed to bend the thick and very solid control column at least 15 degrees out of line. The aircraft wings had also been bent upwards at least 10 degrees. He did receive quite serious injuries to his back, which suspended his flying career.

That particular operation also provided me with my first claim for a damaged Me109F. Everything had happened so fast there had been absolutely no time to see any results – it was a case of survival, not stay and admire the view. Stopping to admire the view was definitely not part of my combat plan on another occasion, one which I was to keep very quiet about during my long period of operation with 485 Squadron.

My logbook states baldly:

August 9. High Cover to Gosnay – landed Maidstone 2.15 hrs.

Such were our fuel limitations that any show, which ran over two hours, was pretty close to being marginal. And if a large proportion of the flight was at full throttle, then fuel at show's end would be very low indeed.

On this particular day the action had been exceedingly hectic. We had been on a Circus operation to Gosnay led by Squadron Leader Marcus Knight, and were fighting our way back after protecting our bombers. I was in the lethal position of Tail End Charlie. As each attack developed we'd turn to meet them, fight them off and reform. After one such skirmish I found myself very much alone – it was a case of turn and fight, turn and fight and slowly work myself towards the English Channel.

This situation often happened, particularly after a series of combats. The

sky would suddenly empty of aircraft. The big snag with this show was that
the sky only emptied of friendly aircraft but there seemed to be damned
black crosses everywhere else. I finally reached that beautiful English coast
in a lather of sweat and with petrol gauges that said the tanks were on
empty. There was a fair amount of low cloud so I couldn't get height and
look for a landing field.

My knowledge of the south coast of England was still very limited. I had
courses that I knew would get me to our very useful railway line which ran
straight from Tunbridge Wells to Reigate and our home at Redhill. But my
fuel situation was at such danger levels that I called control and asked for a
vector to the nearest base. Visibility was poor with increasing low cloud but
I set off with great confidence looking urgently for this unknown base.
Suddenly, bursting through some cloud I saw a very welcome sight – an
airstrip right in front of me.

I called on the RT but did not receive any acknowledgement, thanked
control for their help, noted the direction of the windsock, lined up the field
and let down flaps and wheels. I could see aircraft on the ground but there
were none in the air. It was a grass airfield with no runways but plenty of
room. With my fuel situation it was a welcome sight.

Level off, touch down – hell, this is a bloody bumpy 'drome – turned to
taxi over to the control tower and then stopped in disbelief. Everything was
ominously still. There was no movement anywhere. Then, horror of
horrors, I realised that the aircraft were plywood fakes. The aerodrome like
many throughout the UK was there to encourage the enemy to waste his
bombs, not for dumb pilots to land on. I switched off, momentarily stunned.
What the hell do I do now? While I was sitting in a state of shock a man
who was probably the local farmer came up to me.

"Sir, you are not supposed to land here. You were lucky you didn't crash
into those iron gates we have over there to stop German gliders landing."
His speech had the pleasant brogue of the land, far removed from that of
RAF ground crew.

"Where is the nearest 'drome to here?" I asked him.

"Just over that there hill and a small way down the valley," he replied,
helpfully.

I pressed the buttons on my petrol gauges – the indicators barely
flickered. Dare I risk it? The squadron would rib the hell out of me if I had
to be re-fuelled and rescued from here. This is where I made one of those
very dumb, very stupid decisions, the kind where if you come unstuck the
consequences could be catastrophic. My Spit was one of those that still had
a Hoffman Starter which fired cartridges similar to those used in a shotgun.
I had one only left so I tried it and the engine fired.

The farmer showed me the only safe way out and, with fingers
metaphorically crossed, I opened the throttle and took off, half expecting
the motor to cut before I had got the wheels up. I flew "up and over the hill"
as my farmer friend had described, took the chance there would be no one
in the circuit and landed at Maidstone aerodrome. As I taxied up to the

control tower the motor stopped.

My recorded operation time – which excluded my unofficial landing – was 2 hours and 15 minutes. Nothing particularly dramatic in that, but as far as I was concerned it was a lifetime. This incident of risk-taking stupidity was never reported to anyone during my service career. I guess Lady Luck smiled kindly on me throughout those war years!

A few weeks later we had a very pleasant diversion at Redhill. Our first WAAF (Women's Auxiliary Air Force) member arrived at the station. Everyone was anxious to see and meet her. She was a very pleasant and attractive young lady and we pilots were very keen to make her acquaintance. An interesting sideline to this event was that the first to succeed, to our utter frustration, was a young Canadian pilot who had been staying with us off and on over the recent weeks. We had been too busy to take much notice of him except to talk with him over meal times. Anyway, despite our irritation, he was the triumphant first escort of this charming young woman.

Our irritation turned to shock when a few days later the police arrived to arrest our Canadian 'pilot' who turned out to be a young 17-year-old impostor whose home was in Croydon. Apparently he had performed the same stunt at other 'dromes. He had been so plausible we'd been completely taken in. I never did learn whether our new Waaf had been responsible for sorting him out but it was a warning to us as to just how easy it had been to infiltrate our so-called security.

VII

Redhill to Kenley

Referring to that reliable if unimaginative RAF Form 540 I find an account of an operation to St Omer. For the record, my logbook states:

> 27/8/41 Squadron led by Squadron Leader Knight took off 06.22 hrs. cover Wing Circus to St Omer. Escort failed to rendezvous. Carried out the operation without support. Strong enemy forces were encountered which attacked the Squadron, resulting in the loss of P.O. Middleton who failed to return. Eleven landed 07.50 hrs.

Another example of many – and plenty happened between these dates – is the report dated 21/9/41:

> 12 a/c led by F/Lt Wells (DFC) to take part in Circus 101 to Gosnay. Very large number of E/A were seen. The Squadron was heavily engaged and became split up. 3 E/A were destroyed, 2 by F/Lt Wells and one by P/O Francis and one probably destroyed by P/O Compton. P/O Knight failed to return and presumably landed in France. One a/c crash-landed in vicinity of Bagshot. Telegram from International Red Cross Society that Sgt Russell is a PoW and has had his arm amputated.

Those entries give some idea of the intensity and trauma that were part of the every day combat situation our squadron faced.

Turning to the differences in tactics and aircraft that existed between the enemy and us: we had a beautiful flying machine in our Spitfire, more so when we were equipped with the Mark VB with 20 mm cannons. That machine was slightly superior to the Me109E at top speed and could out-turn it.

The 109F posed a different problem. It had a rated altitude of 40,000 feet plus and could outperform us at any height above 30,000 feet. Though it was slightly faster it could not out-turn the Spitfire.

All German aircraft had the ability to dive vertically from straight and level, always their means of escape as our motors would cut if we tried to follow. This was due to their direct fuel injection system which at that time had not yet been fitted to the Spits.

Our major disadvantage lay in any combat over enemy territory, just as the Luftwaffe had when over Britain. The defender in most cases had the advantage of height and could engage from above with superior speed in the initial attack. In a typical operation over enemy territory we flew in mass formation, the fighters closely guarding the formations of bombers. When scanning the skies from Close Cover it was possible to spot far above the odd flashes of light from our Top Cover and faintly behind and above them the small flashes or tiny dots of the enemy.

At some critical moment a section of that distant enemy would dive down and through the Top Cover. Their speed by advantage of height would at first be superior to the Top Cover. Some of our fighters would follow to counter-attack but Top Cover had to be very careful as further enemy aircraft could be on top of them in seconds. Further down, Escort Cover and Close Cover would be hampered by the need to fly at the slower speeds of the bomber fleets.

But quite rapidly the whole combat picture could change. As Flight Commanders and COs turned to meet the attack – throttles wide open and in some cases in turns so tight that oxygen masks were dragged down faces – pilots desperately manoeuvred to get their sights on the enemy. Instant response was the name of the game as the enemy strategy was one of hit and run. Even when caught in the very deadly situation of being alone with two, three or usually four of them we found their tactic was still the same – hit and run.

As we had to get home sometime there was a limit as to how long we could play that game. Sometimes they made a mistake and then we had one less problem.

An amazing situation which seemed to happen often in aerial dogfighting was the empty sky phenomenon. One minute there were aircraft milling all around in intense combat and then all of a sudden as you turned to meet the next enemy the sky was empty, not an enemy in sight.

Worse still, no friends either. Finding yourself alone over enemy territory was not a nice feeling. You knew damned well it wouldn't be long before you had some unwelcome visitors on the long flight home, hence the importance of the number two.

When the weather closed in and the cloud levels were low all major operations stopped. If this lasted for a few days pilots sought the excitement of combat in a type of operation that certainly provided the adrenalin but really had a limited effect on the enemy.

We called it a Rhubarb (where that name came from is anybody's guess). Rhubarbs were usually a flight of four aircraft that on dull overcast days took off on pre-planned courses usually with some definite target in mind. A favourite seemed to be distilleries, no doubt to cut off the enemy's wine supply. Trains were also good sport for a time but then the enemy started placing heavy guns on the rear trucks and that made it very unpleasant.

The Rhubarb flight would cross the Channel at zero feet to avoid radar detection then suddenly scream up and over the coastal gun emplacements before they had a chance to fire at us, followed by hair-raising low flying over tree tops looking for targets. If we were lucky, a military camp partly hidden in the trees would appear and we would open fire, creating chaos, then scream over a small village and then a distillery where our shells could be seen crashing into the buildings.

A quick look around for some more useful targets, nip in for a quick burst, and it was time to get the hell out of there on the strong probability a squadron of 109s was already airborne and looking for us. So a quick turn for the coast, over the coastal guns again in a different place but this time they would be ready for us and we would have a hostile farewell. No great achievements and in hindsight really considerable risks and quite a few lives lost. At the time we just loved our Rhubarbs and only regretted we didn't have more of them. I think we felt we were in some way thumbing our noses at the Luftwaffe, which I guess we were.

We had many changes of pilots within our ranks. Some moved on for health reasons, others arrived to replace members we had lost. On 24 September Sergeant Frecklington (Freck to us) received his commission and, together with Hal Thomas who had also recently been commissioned, was posted to Aden. Two days later Pilot Officer Mick Shand and Sergeant Pilot Reg Grant were posted to our squadron from 145 Squadron which operated within the Tangmere Wing being led by Douglas Bader. On 28 September we were advised that Sergeant Goodwin was a PoW.

Final Form 540 entry, in which details of squadron activities were recorded, for our stay at Redhill:

> 21/10/41 11.0 hrs. Squadron led by Squadron Leader Knight took off from Redhill on Rodeo to St Omer. Many E/A encountered. One destroyed by Sgt. Kronfeld and one damaged by Sgt McNeil, the latter being wounded in the arm during combat. Sergeant Watts landed at Redhill with his machine badly damaged by E/A. All pilots landed at base at 12.35 approx. Squadron moved from Redhill to Kenley.

At Kenley we were at an established base operating in the same wing but with the feeling that we were now more in the centre of things. We were certainly much more aware of being in a British base with the Grenadier Guards, our defence for the 'drome, on parade every morning. They manned the gates and their sergeants shared a mess with us. I found it a stimulating 'drome from which to operate.

VIII

Kenley – Into the Thick of It

This was a time for reflection on the tumultuous five months I had shared with a great group of fellow pilots. It was a jolt to realise that the squadron I joined those few months back had changed considerably. Friends were no longer with us, some reported as prisoners, some missing presumed killed, some posted to other operations. There were now a number of new faces in the squadron.

What surprised me was how immune we had become to our losses. I guess it was a natural defence mechanism against the reality of warfare. It needed the change of our home base to make me realise just how much we ourselves had changed. I had by then flown 31 times on operations within enemy territory and had had my share of close calls and what we called those "dicey moments". Strangely, I never recall thinking about the person inside the aircraft I was attacking, perhaps even destroying. I suspect that my fellow pilots developed a similar immunity, something I have no memory of ever discussing with them.

At Kenley we were no longer operating from a small satellite 'drome. Redhill had been a delightful station with a strong and perhaps slightly casual New Zealand atmosphere even though we were part of the Kenley Wing. Now we were very much at the heart of RAF Kenley where I found it vibrant and exciting to be part of its striking force.

The Station CO when we first arrived was Group Captain C.E. Bouchier, a highly energetic and popular man. Soon afterwards he was to be replaced by Group Captain Victor Beamish, well known in Britain as a pre-war rugby player who needless to say had an immediate rapport with the New Zealand squadron and was very active in flying operations. Squadron Leader Knight was still our CO although he was shortly to be replaced by Hawkeye Wells.

We were now well into autumn weather and flying activities were greatly reduced with a corresponding increase in social activities. Not all that difficult considering that London was only a short train trip away, there was a local pub quite near and a large population of Waafs on station. We, the sergeant pilots, were billeted in a private house just outside the station right opposite the main gates. We called it the Red House and, yes, it was coloured red but there was no other reason for the name.

Tony Robson had a small car that started when pushed vigorously. I think there was a fair amount of No.8 wire holding it together. It was rumoured that it also had a very special illegal type of fuel running it. However, one thing that car could do was carry an incredible number of persons sitting on various parts including the bonnet and rear guards. No wonder it was our major transport when setting off for the rail station or down to the Tudor Rose pub.

Later on Doug Brown and I decided we would invest in a car of our own which we bought from Hawkeye and Vic Hall. It was quite an elegant Morris but rather vintage. This purchase also gave us some much needed and valuable petrol coupons. There was a certain amount of sleight of hand regarding initial payment but off we set in grand style.

It proved a great way to travel for the first night but on the second time out the drive shaft packed up and we had what seemed like half the squadron pushing us home up the long steep hill. That ended our investment with cars. Doug and I returned the still unpaid vehicle back to Hawkeye minus the petrol vouchers.

Those who joined our squadron at that period must have thought we were having a ball. But our reduced level of operational activity was due more to the need for re-equipment, the replacement of losses sustained over recent months and of course the weather than it was to any wind-down. The pattern of operations also changed somewhat. Hurricanes were now fitted with bombs (immediately dubbed Hurri-bombers) and we were given the task of escorting them in some of their attacks over enemy territory. Every now and then we reverted to our large mass attacks and, during dull periods, to our suicidal Rhubarbs.

During December we had snow and the country really moved into the grip of winter. Came January 1942 and very little change although some of the squadron had by now become very operational within the Soho nightclubs. One in particular was a mecca for our most adventurous, generating not a few scurrilous stories. Harry the proprietor was soon well known to many of us and became a great friend to members of the squadron.

A few of the ladies who attended this club were held in high regard, and a few others with great wariness. Those new arrivals in the squadron who had had little or no experience with the fair sex would soon find that the boys had 'organised things', sometimes unbeknown to them. Inevitably when the new boys returned to base a combat report was demanded – though not always obtained.

At one session in the Tartan Dive – a favourite downstairs bar hang-out of New Zealanders in London – the boys became convinced that for some damned reason the most attractive girls seemed to swoon towards the Polish pilots, leaving nothing for us. Bill Compton suddenly stood up, said "to hell with this", adopted a very heavy Polish accent and immediately whisked off the most attractive female in the room. Long afterwards he insisted that it worked for him many times over. How he managed to keep up the pretence we had no idea. We often wondered what the women thought of his shoulder flashes with the words "New Zealand" emblazoned for all the world to see. Perhaps they had their minds on things other than reading.

Throughout the years we were overseas we never lacked for news and mail from our loved ones at home. Food parcels were especially welcome. We had no complaint about the food provided to us on station, in fact we were the pampered ones of the armed forces and when we visited our various hosts it was great to be able to take some much needed supplies with us. At that stage of the war shortages were beginning to bite and rationing was a much-needed reality.

I used the word "pampered" to describe us. That really was the case. In fact I think we attained the ultimate heights of being the spoiled ones of the UK when Lord Nuffield, chairman of Morris Motors, provided us with ultra violet sun-tanning lamps to offset the effects of lack of sunshine. A special room was set up for us at which we duly arrived at scheduled times for our turn at sunbathing. Rather attractive Waafs supervised these sessions and we all enjoyed the luxury of a slightly golden tan.

With Europe and the UK wracked by a deep, cold winter the weather continued poor throughout December, January and well into February. One of the most popular places for a pilot in that weather was in front of the blazing hot pot-bellied stove in the pilots' Readiness Room, which is where I was when Reg Grant, my friend and Flight Commander, gave me the opportunity of a lifetime.

That's not quite how I saw it at the time, nor I think did Reg. He strode through the door, bringing with him a blast of icy air, looked around, spotted me, and said almost casually: "Oh Jack, you're scheduled for a dawn weather reconnaissance tomorrow morning."

"Hell, Reg, you must be joking. The conditions out there are impossible," I said, hardly able to believe what I was hearing. A glance out of the window was enough to see that the cloud cover was down almost on the deck. In fact at times we couldn't even see the end of the runway.

"Sorry, Jack, you've been selected," he replied. "It's vital that HQ have this report." I thought he was about to enlarge on that but he shrugged his shoulders and left. Reg was never one to over-dramatise or make a big production out of giving an order. He had a natural flair for command and did so in an easy and relaxed manner, never allowing his own stress to show.

After the initial surprise had worn off the realisation grew that this might be an interesting challenge. Mixed in with that thought was some personal pride in the idea that I had been selected on my flying skills for a job in less than optimal conditions. Obviously somebody thought I was good enough to make it there and back in spite of the weather. Little did I know that this was to be one of the most thrilling flights of my career, forever etched in my memory for the pure joy of flying.

Next morning the cold was intense. A light layer of snow blanketed the entire Kenley Fighter Base. I'd just had a hurried cup of tea and been driven around the 'drome perimeter to my aircraft. Ground staff were already there to ensure all was well and the powerful Rolls-Royce engine was running at operational temperature.

Other Spitfires in neighbouring pens were stark silhouettes in the light from our transport. It was almost dawn but visibility was limited by the low cloud level. Someone had thoughtfully driven over the perimeter and out to the runway leaving a black track in the snow to guide me into position for take-off.

I wasn't feeling all that motivated to fly off into the threatening murk. My main thought was that the flight was utterly hazardous, if not bordering on the suicidal. Weather reconnaissance provided vital information for decision-making by Fighter and Bomber Commands, in fact all the commands of the RAF. However my assessment of the situation was that I'd be fortunate, apart from the risk to myself, to even get this valuable Spitfire back safely let alone with some idea of weather trends.

A cockpit check in the dim light from the instruments ensured that the altimeter was correctly set. It would need to be extremely accurate when returning to base in this kind of soup. Setting the gyrocompass was also essential, as I wouldn't have much time for playing around with it once airborne.

Ice crunched under the wheels as the Spitfire taxied into position. The take-off was uneventful. A shower of ice chips and the Spit was airborne. I selected wheels up and immediately at 300 feet was flying by instruments in dense cloud.

There was no break in the clouds at 10,000 feet but there was increasing turbulence, tossing the Spit about not to mention the pilot. No change at 15,000 feet except for one small break then back into towering cumulus. At 20,000 feet still great masses of cloud. Finally, at 25,000 feet the Spit burst out and above into the wondrous sight of a golden dawn.

It was a sight I would always remember. I thought of the millions of people below still asleep or awakening to a dull bleak day. What certainly didn't occur to me at that moment but I realised later must have been happening was that I would have a companion in the sky. Probably not so very far from me, perhaps just across that English Channel.

With certainty a Luftwaffe pilot would also have been in the air that morning. The date was 10 February, 1942. There would have been feverish activity on his side of the Channel as the powerful *Scharnhorst* and *Gneisenau* battleship-cruisers readied for their dash through the Channel two days later. It would be a voyage that depended on the massive cloud cover to hide those giant warships of the German navy and handicap the striking power of the RAF.

Our squadron was to become heavily involved during that moment of history. And, yes, I did make it back to base without incident thanks to a very efficient air controller and massive amounts of luck. Not for the first time was it driven home to me that a Spitfire is not the most steady of platforms to control by instruments in exceptionally turbulent conditions. My first sighting on return was a mist-shrouded Reigate. I knew my way back from there, low and slow beneath the cloud cover which was down to 300 feet or lower.

That day has ever since been a special memory, a definitive moment in my flying career. Even now, years later, when I fly long distance as a passenger in a modern jet, I make sure I am always awake at dawn. At such times I feel compelled to slide open the window shade for a peek at the wonders of golden sunlight on cloud, to live again that first incredible moment when I first encountered such a sight.

Then I become uncomfortably aware that my fellow passengers don't appreciate the invasion of bright light into a darkened cabin, and guiltily close the shade again. But I never fail to sink back into the seat cushions with the thought that I am extremely lucky – I still have my memories.

On that day cloud blanketed England and all of northern France so there was little of note to report. Two days later, on 12 February, we were to be completely shaken out of our state of lethargy. On that day Group Captain Victor Beamish, together with his number two, was on one of his quite unofficial jaunts along the English Channel which usually took him dangerously close to the French coast. About 9 a.m. he saw a sight he could scarcely credit.

The great German battleships *Prinz Eugen*, *Scharnhorst* and *Gneisenau*, surrounded by a massive protective aircraft umbrella and well clear of the security of Brest harbour where they'd been skulking for months, were steaming at full speed in a north-easterly direction. The obvious intention was to sail directly through the Channel and break out into the North Sea – what an affront to the British navy.

Immediately after Beamish landed the news was spread throughout the station. We were placed on Full Readiness. This meant sitting in our aircraft in full flying gear, engines warmed up and ready for immediate take-off. At any moment all hell was going to break loose. There was no snow on the 'drome but the clouds were still very low. There was a ceiling of perhaps 600-700 feet with towering masses of cumulus threatening all flying above that: a hell of day to set forth on a major battle with the enemy.

The timing could not have been more perfect for the daring dash. The atrocious weather was ideally suited to the German navy's move and a frustration to us. We sat at Kenley for hours in our aircraft until told to return to our dispersal hut and wait there. Finally, we were briefed for Operation Fuller in which we would escort torpedo bombers to the attack.

Words cannot adequately describe the incredible chaos and sights of raw power, incredible bravery and sheer will to survival that we encountered. They are scenes which will live with me throughout my life. We never sighted the torpedo bombers we were supposed to escort, at least not as a formation. I did fancy that I caught sight of a Beaufighter though, being literally shot to pieces as it vainly tried to make an attack on the mighty *Scharnhorst*.

This was when we, I am sure by pure accident, dived through the broken low cloud and found ourselves in a very unhealthy position flying alongside a wall of fire-power from the belching guns of that battle-cruiser.

Our flight was led by Flight Lieutenant Gary Francis with Sergeant J. Liken. I was with Reg Grant. Hawkeye had led us through the initial break in the clouds but suddenly there were just the four of us surrounded by masses of the Luftwaffe who appeared to be even more confused than we were. In fact, the guns from the warships seemed to be just pouring metal at anyone silly enough to be there.

Reg and I got ourselves involved in a dogfight, resulting in Reg destroying an Me109 which spun into the sea. I didn't wait to see what happened to mine: I knew it had been considerably damaged. Even flying out of this mass of turning aircraft and into cloud knowing there were many others about was playing Russian roulette. All in all it was an unimaginable shambles in which we were among the survivors.

Sadly many of our RAF comrades were not. The German navy with the protection of Mother Nature won that round hands down. The British press next day was full of the achievements of our New Zealand squadron. Hawkeye's flight sank an E Boat – the Allied name for German motor torpedo boats – adding to our score for the day of four aircraft confirmed destroyed and several others damaged. Our successes were the only good news in a sorry picture. Sadly, Fighter Command could only claim 15 enemy aircraft down for the loss of 16 pilots of our own.

The nation was deeply upset by the spectacular success of the German naval breakout. However with hindsight, even with a highly organised onslaught against those ships, given the same atrocious weather and cloud cover I consider they would still have been extremely difficult to stop. And the loss of life and aircraft would still have been massive.

The sight of the firepower from such giant ships made me very thankful indeed that I was not the pilot of a torpedo bomber aircraft, or even worse one of those who flew the slow old Swordfish directly into that inferno. Such action required the ultimate in supreme heroism. Men were asked and they responded.

It reminded me of something a French general said of the massive frontal attacks directly into machine gun fire by British troops in the First World War. It was magnificent, he said, but it wasn't war.

For the rest of February flying was minimal, then in March things livened up somewhat with a few major attacks into enemy territory. Unfortunately not keeping that diary leaves me with some guesswork here but somewhere around this time my old friend Harvey Sweetman, companion in practically every operation including some very shaky do's, set off with me to support our troublesome Griffiths who was about to embark on the hazardous path of Holy Matrimony.

The wedding took place in a charming church in an outer London suburb where we met Mary, his attractive wife to be. Harvey was best man and I acted as an usher. The ceremony went without a hitch and Griff was all set to take off on his honeymoon but, alas, there was a problem – he had no cash. Typically Griff, he seemed completely unconcerned – so much so in fact we were sure that he expected us to set him up. What else could we do? After all it was his wedding day and Griff would always be Griff.

Meanwhile, back in the world of combat some ominous changes were taking place. We had heard reports that the Luftwaffe had a new fighter with a radial engine supposedly very fast and manoeuvrable. Hawkeye and his flight encountered some that gave them deep concern and afterwards felt lucky to get home unscathed.

He conveyed his concern back to High Command where his description of a high performance Focke Wulf 190 was doubted or at least received with some disbelief.

However we were very soon all going to experience the extraordinary capabilities of the new FW190s. The date was 28 March. We were on a sweep to Cap Gris Nez. Our wing, flying High Cover, was being led by Group Captain Beamish. Well below us we sighted a large force of 190s attacking some Spitfires and immediately dived on them.

With the considerable advantage of height and our added speed from the dive they should have been at a distinct disadvantage. But to our shock and surprise they immediately turned, gained height in what seemed a very short space of time and were attacking us. We had attacked them at what we later learned was their rated altitude of 12,500 ft. We could still out-turn them but found we had to be extremely careful.

I had a very quick deflection shot at one that peeled off and flew downwards in a cloud of smoke. My camera shot later showed that he was at extreme range although we later learned that the FW190 had a much smaller wing span than the Me109 so perhaps his range was closer than calculated at the time. It was written off as a 'probable'.

For us the most appalling part of this conflict was the fact that we lost our highly regarded Group Captain Beamish though no one actually witnessed him being shot down. I and my number two Marty Hume became involved in our own private battles as our particular part of airspace had become very unhealthy. We sought the cover of cloud, which was just below. Unfortunately this cloud proved deceptively thin and we found ourselves as two roving Spits, with very many Me109s cruising about just below the clouds probably waiting to pounce on odd men out such as we were.

They were very tempting targets for us but one of the blighters spotted me just when he was almost in range. It was a case of damned if you do and damned if you don't, so we had a running battle all the way to the coast. One of our attackers got involved with me in some tight turns at zero feet, stalled and crashed into the deck. At least it was a novel way of destroying an Me109. Back at base the feeling was that whatever results we might have had that day could never offset the loss of a man so deeply respected throughout Fighter Command.

Fighter Command at Uxbridge was so bent on getting to the bottom of his death that they decided to question all the pilots involved in that combat and arranged for us all to be transported to Uxbridge. I was in a cinema in Croydon when a sign was flashed onto the screen instructing me to report to my transport waiting outside – a case of the long arm of Fighter Command reaching out to pluck us from our pleasures.

I never did hear if any useful information came out of the inquiry, as my fighter pilot career was about to take a quantum leap into a vastly different combat area. My last flight for some time with Squadron 485 was 6 April. On my return Hawkeye told me he had received a posting for me. I was to report immediately to Wembley Grounds to be issued with tropical kit and receive further instructions. I had a sneaking suspicion as to where I might be going but, full of excitement and expectation, I had to wait for what seemed like ages before having it confirmed.

Then I was off on a train to Glasgow and then to Greenock, the very place where I had first arrived in this land. That had been less than twelve months before yet it felt like half a lifetime. From the rail station a van transported me to a well-guarded wharf where I had my first breathtaking sight of an aircraft carrier.

Towering above me, completely dwarfing everything including surrounding buildings, was the great blunt bow of a vessel I was later to learn was the USS *Wasp*. This massive ship was here courtesy of President Roosevelt, his answer to Winston Churchill's urgent plea for help with the transport of Spitfires so desperately needed for the defence of Malta.

Malta was to be my next challenge.

IX
Malta

Every pilot on arrival must have been stunned not only with the importance of what they were witnessing but also the magnitude of the undertaking in which we were about to be involved. Fronting us was a very real and spectacular statement of Anglo-American co-operation: Mark VC (four-cannon) Spitfires were being efficiently lifted by crane onto the carrier's flight deck while all around us a businesslike stream of state of the art war materiel flowed on board. The Spits were painted a pale blue camouflage slightly lighter in shade to that which we had been used to in the UK – a reminder we were going to a very different theatre of war.

My first experience on board was to be warmly welcomed with a real Southern accent and then passed on to an equally pronounced 'Nuu Yark' accent. I was carrying my sole possessions in a very light kitbag as we had been instructed that our maximum weight of personal items was not to exceed 10 lb. My Rolliflex camera weighed about 4 lb, so personal items were very limited indeed. After being shown to a quite comfortable-looking bunkroom and leaving my kit bag in a locker, a tour of the giant ship was offered which proved an expedition in itself.

The entire ship gave off an air of spick and span orderliness. Everything gleamed, lamp glasses glinted, all equipment stowed for instant use, the whole impression being one of maximum efficiency against a background buzz of constant activity. On the flight deck it was fascinating to watch the Spitfires being landed by crane, pushed onto a giant lift and then taken down to a large hangar deck already looking very crowded with Spits.

The Americans retained a minimum of their own fighter aircraft: nine Grumman Martlets of the US Navy's Fighting 71st Squadron stood on the after deck. There was not quite enough room for the 47 Spits in the hangar so a few were hoisted up on ropes and remained there suspended until ready for take-off. I was to learn later that one of those hanging in the air was to be mine.

Initially my own situation was not the easiest as I didn't know anyone from either of the two squadrons, 601 (County of London) or 603 (City of Edinburgh), nor had there been any official advice as to which I was to join.

No time was to be wasted by the USS *Wasp* and at 10 a.m.on 13 April she
left Greenock, slightly damaging a screw on a mud bank. At 6 a.m. next day
we were moving slowly down the Irish Sea escorted by the Royal Navy's
battle-cruiser HMS *Renown* and six British destroyers.

Most of us had fairly certain ideas that our destination was to be Malta
but now there was the sudden realisation that we would also be flying off
this carrier to get there. And to my horror I also discovered that with the
exception of a very few of my fellow pilots the rest of both squadrons had
little or no experience in combat. Virtually all the squadron flying time had
been non-operational. Their CO, Squadron Leader Lord David Douglas-
Hamilton, had considerable time as a flying instructor but not the type of
experience he and his men would sorely need in the very near future.

Both 603 and 601 Squadrons had proud records gained during the Battle
of Britain. It can only be assumed that these two famous squadrons had
been chosen on past reputations, without examination of their present
content, to join the battle for survival in the beleaguered island of Malta.

It was noted in the CO's diary the day before we sailed that nine of 603's
pilots, including one of the flight commanders, had never flown on
offensive sorties. There was a furious stir within the Air Ministry when this
news reached them but much too late for any serious corrective action.

It was just another of those bureaucratic shambles that seemed so much
an inevitable part of wartime. Those of us in the know fervently hoped the
enemy also had them.

I stood on the flight deck on 15 April watching the coast of Ireland
drifting slowly out of sight and wondering what was to be in store for us
all. We had just been to a briefing by Wing Commander J.S. McLean (a
New Zealander) who told us we would be taking off from the carrier at a
point in the Mediterranean just north of Algiers. There, out of range of the
Luftwaffe, we would fly in formation just off the African coast.

That information had barely registered before we also learned that we
would have 90-gallon auxiliary tanks under our fuselages to which we must
switch over immediately after take-off. If for some reason the switchover
failed we would have nowhere to go. Attempting a landing back on the
carrier was not recommended, as the Spits were not fitted with arrester gear
(the large tail hook which carrier-based aircraft use to pick up the arrester
cable and come to a very rapid stop before they run out of deck).

Assuming the fuel switchover worked as planned, we would have
enough fuel to get to Malta but with very little to spare. Because of weight
restrictions, required by the very short take-off space on the carrier flight
deck, our cannons could carry only a very limited amount of ammunition.
And if indeed any combat situation was encountered we would have to
jettison our spare tanks to gain speed and manoeuvrability – a kind of
frying pan into the fire choice.

We had plenty of time to think over these scary possibilities, not
improved by our appraisal of the length of the flight deck. As we gazed at
it day after day the length seemed to get shorter and shorter, while the

Spitfires with their four cannon, 90-gallon overload tanks and numerous spares got heavier and heavier. The problem wasn't helped by the rumours of the shortages of food, soap and cigarettes to be faced in Malta, leading to a frenzy of buying from the fabulous PX store on board this luxury ship and thus more weight for us to carry.

Strictly against orders, wing panels were unscrewed and many extras pushed into the spaces between. Pilots lay awake at night worrying about what they had added. Next morning, after another look at the flight deck, they would nervously remove items they thought might weigh too much. My extras were mainly cigarettes although the weight of the soap and canned food I included worried me somewhat.

Life on the ship was excellent and the food first class. Breakfast I learned could include two eggs 'over easy' or any other way plus maple syrup. As with all US Navy ships, the USS *Wasp* was 'dry'. There was no alcohol provided, not even for the officers. The ship's captain was a bright and breezy chap who constantly assured us that our take-off would be "a breeze". The ship, he told us, was capable of speeds in excess of 25 knots, and – as there would be an expected wind speed of at least 20 knots – we would be airborne well before we reached the bow. We sure hoped he would be proved right, though few of us were fully convinced.

There was some excitement on 16 April as we watched the destroyers manoeuvre in small circles dropping depth charges on a suspected U-boat. The next two days consisted of lifeboat drill. At 3 a.m. on Sunday, 19 April, the *Wasp* passed through the Straits of Gibraltar, meeting two more destroyers. This gave her the protection of a battle-cruiser, two other cruisers and eight destroyers. The Royal Navy was leaving nothing to chance.

As we were to learn in a very short time – while making ready for this epic flight – thousands of tons of bombs were falling on Malta. Field Marshall Kesselring, determined to take this island, which was such a thorn in the side of the Afrika Korp's North African campaign, had a strike force of 600 aircraft in Sicily.

Dawn on 20 April was our planned time for take-off. Twelve Spitfires had been moved up onto the flight deck. At 4.15 a.m. we were up and having breakfast aware there had been a major problem, which could have been very serious. Up until this moment the fuel tanks of the Spitfires had been kept empty for safety reasons. However, now that they were being filled some of the auxiliary tanks had shown leaks. In spite of the very real hazards crewmembers managed to repair them, which was a remarkable feat.

There was one sudden change that gave me a twinge of conscience at the time although I could do little about it. Squadron Leader David Douglas-Hamilton came up to me at the last moment to advise that as I had to lead a section my aircraft, which was still up on a sling, would have to be flown by a Canadian sergeant pilot and I was to take his plane. There would be no time to transfer our personal gear, which had to be left in the aircraft.

On inspecting what was now my aircraft I found this poor man's very carefully parcelled and obviously exact 10 lb of gear. Dare I tell him about those extras in the wings? I was now unable to remove them. He was a very nervous person so all I could say was that there was some extra weight in the plane and to give her all the power he could. That was a pretty stupid thing to say really because every one of us would be doing just that.

We boarded our aircraft in the hangar deck and one by one were pushed backwards onto the lift, then up onto the flight deck and moved off the lift for the next one. Aircraft engines then had to be started. We'd been warned that if an aircraft engine didn't start or showed any problem then it was likely the Spit would be pushed over the side, as time was critical. The *Wasp*'s own fighters had taken off and were circling above. The sooner we departed the ship, the safer this convoy would be.

I heard later that the Spit I should have been flying did have quite a struggle taking off and the poor Canadian flew for miles just above the sea. How about my own take-off? The engine started without a problem and minimum time was taken to bring the temperatures up to safety. Then a quick cockpit check – boy, it had to be quick – and I was guided into take-off position. True to his word, the captain had that ship at maximum knots into a very welcome head wind. Sitting there with brakes hard on, the rev-up signal was given and I opened the throttle steadily until I felt the tailplane trying to rise. The aircraft was straining to go. We all knew the drill by heart: snap off brakes, move forward gaining speed rapidly, the amount of deck in front disappearing, then airborne long before reaching the bow.

The skipper had been quite right; I had plenty of deck and to spare although it no doubt helped having only the Canadian's correctly weighted personal baggage. Once aloft, came the anxious moment of switching to the auxiliary tanks. None of us had any problems so off we set in various formations for the long flight to Malta. The crew of the *Wasp* operated with maximum efficiency that day and had the 47 of us airborne in 20 minutes.

The squadrons separated into two loose groups as keeping close formation would use up too much fuel. Our key leader was Squadron Leader Jumbo Gracie, a great man with an outstanding personality. Jumbo had been sent to London under instructions from the Malta Air Officer Commanding, Air Vice-Marshal Sir Hugh Pughe Lloyd, another great airman whose attributes will be told later in this story. Jumbo had gone to the UK to convey personally to the top brass the exceedingly desperate situation in Malta and how vital it was that the embattled little island receive the help of a considerable boost to its air defence.

His plea for more Spitfires was heeded and we were the major reply. A small number had already arrived a few weeks back via the British carrier *Eagle*. Jumbo Gracie came back on the carrier with us and during the trip briefed us on the conditions we would encounter. He pulled no punches. I can still visualise him standing with a cigarette holder clamped between his teeth (I don't recall ever seeing him smoke) telling us of the brutal air battles we would soon be meeting, of the massive odds against us, of the day and night bombing we would be facing. He really laid it on although we were to learn he was not exaggerating.

Those happy promises of what was awaiting us gave me cause to ponder just what was in the mind of each pilot as we flew sedately on this historic flight with low revs and a speed of about 200 mph to conserve fuel. The weather was perfect. As the sun rose the sea changed from a dull grey to a beautiful deep blue, a colour I had read about so often. The coast of North Africa was on our right as we flew towards Tunis.

As to what other pilots might be thinking, we later learned there was one who had very different thoughts to the rest of us. An American pilot who had only been in the squadron a month, must have decided Malta was not the place for him. Possibly the thought that death might be awaiting him motivated his subsequent behaviour.

Immediately after taking off from the *Wasp* he flew in the opposite direction to us, heading for Algeria. He belly-landed his Spitfire on the south side of the Atlas Mountains and went to the nearest American Consul, claiming to be a lost civil aviation pilot. We could only speculate that his fear of the unknown made him choose to desert in the face of the enemy.

We had been given an official flight path, which took us just outside of Tunis, at that time still neutral French territory. However, this change of course would have caused considerably more usage of fuel so we were unofficially advised that it might be prudent to fly directly over Tunis. Needless to say we did just that. It was fascinating to look down on this attractive harbour and watch a squadron of French bi-planes climbing up to intercept us.

For a short moment it looked as though this could be interesting but it was not to be. When still a few thousand feet below they all levelled off and dived back to ground level again. Obviously they didn't like what they saw when up close, or perhaps they were just wishing us well. The next concern that we had was an island called Pantelleria. This was a Luftwaffe fighter base so we gave it a wide berth.

We knew when we were nearing the historic island of Malta without having to check our flight plans – it was the delightful booming, resonate voice of Group Captain A.B. Woodhall (Woody), Bader's former flight controller. His was the voice we would quickly learn to live by and love over the skies of Malta. At that time he was just an interesting controller directing aircraft in what sounded like a raid of enemy fighters. Apparently there were a few Me109s about but we didn't see them.

At last, three and a half hours after leaving the *Wasp* we were over Malta, auxiliary tanks jettisoned. Jumbo Gracie's squadron flew into Luqa 'drome. As we flew over to land at Takali, Squadron Leader Douglas-Hamilton then took a risk he was soon to discover was a major no-no at this stage of the war in Malta. He led his flight of four in to land in formation, as was the drill back in UK.

He certainly didn't look at the 'drome very hard. The devastation that greeted us was almost beyond description. The 'drome itself looked of reasonable size but there were bomb craters all over the place. Buildings that might have been dispersal huts were just shells and the windsocks, riddled with holes, hung limply on their poles, useless for indicating wind direction.

Into this chaos Squadron Leader Douglas-Hamilton led his formation and by some enormous stroke of luck the four landed without mishap although there were a couple of very dicey last minute swerves around some bomb holes. We settled for landing in pairs after seeing that performance, not without anxious moments for some of us.

On that particular day we flew into a moment of history without realising the enormity of the struggle of which we had suddenly become a part. All around us was a war-ruined landscape while incongruously the blue Mediterranean gently lapped on the shores of this jewel of an island.

I have read the comments of some pilots who, struck by the beauty of the land, enthused about the rocky coastline, the tiny green fields with their white stone walls, white stone buildings, the grandeur of the Mosta Dome, Grand Harbour, Gozo Island nestled close to the main island, and Sicily with towering Mount Etna only 50 miles or so to the north. It is now more than half a century since that day and I can't recall having had any of those poetic thoughts.

Maybe they were there then but now all that remains is the memory of appalling destruction, of a feeling of immense determination that somehow we would help stop this brutality, and a great sense of urgency to get ourselves better organised. Foremost in our minds was to meet those pilots who had been bearing the brunt of the onslaught, learn everything we could of tactics and problems, and join with them to defeat the blasted enemy.

At that moment of arrival on 20 April, 1942, it was a case of climbing wearily from the cockpit, feeling the blast of heat from the dusty land on which we stood and being greeted by a Maltese with a type of wheeled cart who offered to carry any gear including parachutes and the special 10 lb of personal gear that belonged to my Canadian friend. This reminded me to look around and see if I could see his, or should I say my, aircraft anywhere about.

With surprise I spotted it quite near as it was being pushed into a meagre aircraft bay. I went over to him together with my new found Maltese friend, climbed aboard and with a pocket screwdriver removed some of the wing panels. Out came carton after carton of cigarettes, packets of soap and some tins of Spam (sadly I had chickened out and removed some of the Spam back on the carrier).

The quite shocked young Canadian gazed in amazement at the extras that he had managed to lift off the carrier – and only just off the sea – while the Maltese kindly loaded this pile of goodies onto a waiting transport.

The very nervous but likeable Canadian made no comment and I did share some of the spoils with him. Did I feel conscience-stricken? Well, I rationalised to myself, the situation had been completely out of my control and after all I did pass over to him his neatly parcelled 10 lb. He responded by handing over my camera and some odd personal items.

By the way, the particular aircraft, which the Canadian flew to Malta for me, was a burning heap less than an hour later when the 'drome was fiercely attacked. Only a few aircraft had been refuelled and armed ready for take-off. The 'drome didn't have the luxury of petrol bowsers for re-fuelling, they had all been destroyed in previous raids, and four-gallon tins were a laborious substitute.

Many of the Spits we brought to Malta also carried much needed extra parts and extra radio equipment, hence the strict control on weight. Getting the new Spits ready for combat took precious time and the raid taught us a bitter lesson. From now on we knew we had to have a much better plan in place when next we received further deliveries of these vitally needed aircraft.

Far too many were destroyed on the ground by a sequence of continuous bombing raids, which went on right throughout the night and the next day. Many aircraft that did survive sustained serious damage from flying shrapnel. We were now in the front line and the enemy was not going to allow us to forget it.

That first night we were shown to our sleeping quarters which for the sergeants were in part of a private home, a typical Mediterranean dwelling built with a centre courtyard in which there was a shady garden. In some houses the garden also had a fountain. Our rooms were sparse of furniture with bare walls, floors bare of carpet but a reasonably comfortable bed.

Apart from sleeping there we spent very little time in our quarters. In fact, within the first week of our arrival we had a 250 lb bomb crash through the roof and partly through the floor to remain lodged there. By some miracle it didn't explode. Needless to say we all made a hasty exit, ending up sleeping on the floor of a nearby church until the tricky object was removed and our roof and floor repaired.

Normally we stayed in our beds during air raids, as we desperately needed our sleep. If we'd opted to run in and out of air raid shelters we'd have had no rest at all. We sorted that one out pretty quickly but in a few weeks other problems presented themselves, one of the worst being Malta Dog or in plain language diarrhoea. This was a very debilitating condition, which took some time to develop as we were still in a fairly healthy state from the good food we'd been fortunate enough to enjoy previously.

Now that we were in this land of extreme rationing it was a different story. We did have a few contacts in the black market, a means of illegal trading that flourished wherever food or any commodity was rationed. However I heard it said, and could not help but agree, that if it weren't for black-market food we probably wouldn't have been able to keep flying. It was only on rare occasions that we went to the hush-hush spots to eat. Most times I'm sure we were eating horsemeat but as we were paying heavily for the privilege we didn't ask.

In between it was the normal routine of bully beef in very small portions morning, noon and night, and a continuous plague of dysentery. When flying it was noticeable that 'blacking out' was more prevalent; but we adjusted to that. It rankled to know that our enemies the Germans and Italians were living in luxury in nearby Sicily, doubtless with wine, women and song added. Perhaps that luxury would soften them!

But I've jumped ahead of myself. On our first evening in Malta we all assembled in the officers' mess and were welcomed by the Air Officer Commanding, Air Vice-Marshal Hugh Pughe Lloyd. As I've said earlier, this man was an exceptional leader who played a vital part in our ultimate victory – probably much greater than has ever been acknowledged. He never claimed to have any idea of the operations relating to fighter aircraft and relied heavily on those who did, such as Woody, Gracie and others. A master strategist, he had a complete faith that we would win and manipulated his limited resources of aircraft to continually launch attacks on the shipping which was Rommel's lifeline.

At his disposal he had two outstanding photo-reconnaissance Spitfires (better known as PRU Spits) that could operate well above 40,000 feet. They carried no armament, depending on their height and speed to evade the enemy. These aircraft flew regularly over the ports of southern Italy, Sicily, and southern Yugoslavia to bring back the vital pictures that served to pinpoint our targets. With this information he played his operations like a game of chess – waiting until the convoys were almost fully loaded before sending in his squadrons to blitz them while still in harbour. Flight Lieutenant Harry Colbeck (a New Zealander) was one of those hard working PRU pilots, deeply respected for the important and dangerous work they tirelessly continued to do.

When the convoys moved out onto the open seas the RAF in Cairo was alerted to keep them constantly on the run. In this way Lloyd managed to starve Rommel of his supplies. Malta really was a huge thorn in the side of the Afrika Korps and for that reason the enemy was desperate to neutralise us.

The other side of our Air Vice-Marshal was his wonderful optimism and morale-boosting presence. While we were all crowded into the officers' mess for his official welcome the air raid sirens wailed and soon after the guns of Takali just below us started firing. The cacophony was deafening. Then the bombs could be heard whistling down (we were assured that as long as you could hear them whistling you were safe!).

Most of the pilots in that room were not convinced and had dived to get under the billiard table. Air Vice-Marshal Lloyd, standing with his drink still in his hand, said above the noise: "Listen!" We could hear the sound of machine guns firing.

"Hear that gentlemen? Those are our guns, from a Beaufighter. We've got them on the run!"

We weren't too sure whether we really had yet but he was genuinely convinced that with our arrival the tide was about to turn. He was also known to stand on our 'dromes during raids refusing to take shelter. Later, when the battle for Malta had really been won, he was replaced by our own New Zealander Sir Keith Park.

Sir Keith was undoubtedly also a great man and the world owes him much as the commander of the Battle of Britain. However we in Malta at that time felt that the replacement was more of a political stunt than anything else. The great service to the world given by Air Vice-Marshal Hugh Pughe Lloyd was largely overlooked although not forgotten by those of us who once dived for the billiard table while he stood erect.

The next day, apart from all the bombing, was full of interest. We met during a spell in the raids to be sorted out and advised on when we would be in operation. I can still see us as a group of eager young pilots just waiting to get into action, not unmixed with a sense of apprehension after witnessing the incredible odds we were going to face.

Squadron Leaders Stan Grant and David Douglas-Hamilton were sitting at an improvised table out on a grass verge examining their lists of pilots. It was easy to see there was considerable concern between them and also discussion with Wing Commander Jumbo Gracie. What they were trying to decide was how to gain some form of balance between those known to have experience over the skies of Malta, those who had operational experience in the UK and those who really should never have been sent here at all.

There was an obvious disparity between the newly arrived 603 Squadron and the squadron of veterans in 249 Squadron so they decided to do some juggling between pilots. We were a long way from the 'bull's wool' of Fighter Command in Britain – here decisions were made on the spot and the forms filled in later (sometimes). All this juggling of names – and a request from New Zealander Ray Hesslyn and Australian Paul Brennan on my behalf – led to my finishing up with them in the crack 249 Squadron. I could hardly conceal my delight.

X

Into the Cauldron

One piece of information that emerged from our talks with the veteran pilots (who, in our book, was anyone who had been operating in Malta for more than a few weeks) was that common sense dictated battle tactics. That meant we flew line abreast, not line astern. On Malta the obsolete and dangerous line astern formation had long been consigned to the Dark Ages of aerial combat. The new tactic had been honed in the hellfire of battle. Quite simply, the line abreast formation gave pilots that slight edge which could make the difference between the quick and the dead.

Line abreast, or its Malta equivalent which was the 'finger four' configuration was an attacking formation in which each pilot covered his partner's outside part of the sky, in particular the rear area. The formation also allowed pilots to maintain greater combat speed. There was nothing particularly brilliant or innovative about this decision. Our enemy had been flying this way throughout the war years and we were simply copying a sensible battle tactic. At least in Malta we were away from the red tape and the controversy, and allowed to make up our own minds.

We also learnt of a major and very worrying problem the Malta squadrons had been facing, and that was the severe restrictions of trying to operate a fighting force with only a small number of serviceable aircraft. The air controller was daily forced to watch his radar screens show large bomber forces building up over Sicily while unable to scramble defensive fighters until the main force was almost at Malta and the numerous enemy fighters already over the island.

It was a guessing game. The controller had to judge the size of the force and decide whether it was the real thing or only the beginning of an even bigger wave following. If he scrambled his fighters too soon they would later have to face swarms of enemy fighters sent over specifically after the main raid to attack them as they tried to land with little fuel left and no ammunition to fight back. If he scrambled them too late the bombers would already be raining down their loads of death.

This was sobering information, making us realise just how vital were the aircraft we had just delivered. To give some idea of the fury of the bombing raids, by next morning after our arrival, 39 out of the 47 Spitfires we'd brought in were either totally destroyed or inoperative. Surveying the wreckage, the unspoken question in our minds was how many would still be operative tomorrow? That night the raids were heavy and furious and the damage again extremely serious.

On 22 April, two days after flying off the deck of the USS *Wasp*, I was on readiness at Takali, aircraft checked and re-checked, waiting for my first scramble from Malta. The sun had risen above the surrounding buildings and it wasn't long before the heat began to beat down on that war-torn aerodrome. Already my Mae West had boosted my body temperature. Soon the straps would be a clammy irritation around my shoulders.

Then the phone rang. The airman of the watch grabbed the receiver. We all started to run before he had time to grab the Very pistol and fire off a red flare for immediate scramble. Sometimes the call meant we were placed on standby to sit sweating in our planes ready for the signal to scramble but this time it was an immediate take-off.

I started the motor, taxied into position, and took off. Wheels up – no green light? Switched on the radio to hear the controller's instructions – no sound. My radio was dead and I was faced with the chilling fact that all of my aircraft's electrical systems were unserviceable.

What to do now? My first operational take-off on Malta and I was of absolutely no use to the flight, in fact more likely to be a danger to them. I flew alongside my number one, indicated with hand signs that I was without radio and broke away from the formation, peeling off without the slightest idea as to what I was going to do. Would I have time to get back to base? Very doubtful; with that urgent scramble the raid was probably damned close. It would sure have helped if I could have known what was going on but my lot was a very silent world.

With absolutely no idea of the local topography I decided to fly south and climb as rapidly as possible. The dazzling blue above appeared empty but I knew this could change at any moment. If my climb was sustained for too long and headed in the wrong direction I could find myself meeting the attacking force with no forward speed. Worse still, I would be all alone and just asking to be surrounded.

So instead I decided to gain just a moderate height, enough to give me some attacking speed, watch my tail like hell and wait for the action. The wait was a very short one, as all of a sudden the guns of Malta exploded, especially over our home 'drome. Moments earlier I had thought about getting back to base but the quiet skies over Takali had become a cauldron of ack-ack fire. The defenders' multi-barrelled pom-poms sliced their lethal streams through the attacking Ju88s whose bombs in turn were exploding on the aerodrome. Not at all an inviting place to land.

Diving on to Takali were at least 20 Ju88s with a fighter escort above of about 30 Me109s. There was only one thing to do and that was to meet them head on. With my present speed I would never be able to catch them by trying to follow. It was a case of here goes, head on it's got to be.

Our own pom-poms and Bofors guns were filling the sky with hot metal but those 88s looked oblivious. The German pilots were damned courageous, diving through the barrage without wavering and when challenged by my Spit they just kept on coming. Each attack flashed by in split seconds. My cannon shells I'm certain were smashing into them. Some crashed according to later reports but I didn't see them, nor try to claim them.

It was just a moment and they were all past but now there were those most unfriendly Me109s to contend with. To be alone in this situation, constantly turning and meeting first one and then the other of them and with no speed advantage, was not a situation of choice. They made very few mistakes. My shots at them probably damaged one or two but these pilots were like my old adversaries in northern France, dangerous and very experienced. When on your own, outnumbered and with limited ammunition, you have major problems. It's a case of surviving the best way you know how. Maximum vigilance was the key – a gut-wrenchingly constant turning and straining to watch behind, above and below.

The only answer was to get down low. We had faced similar situations over France and the English Channel but here I had the additional problem that we had to land sometime while these blighters were still making passes at me. I knew the 109s wouldn't follow me into a low-level scream around the houses and streets of Malta. They knew that – aircraft on aircraft – their chances of matching turn for tight turn with a Spit without spinning out into the deck were poor.

Once out of that mess it was back to see what more damage if any could be achieved. Without a radio there was no way of telling whether the raid was over or not, and there was no sign of my flight though fighting was probably still going on to the north.

The situation was critical, petrol getting fairly low, not much ammunition left and not a clue as to what was happening. Thankfully I spotted some Spits returning and approaching Takali so flew to join them. But the saga hadn't quite run its course. As we circled the 'drome, down came a swarm of Me109s and attempted to attack the Spits as they levelled off to land. The aerodrome guns, especially the repeat-firing Bofors, opened up a massive barrage but those very determined 109s still strafed the Spits even after they had landed between the huge bomb craters.

My turn came and I received a similar treatment. By this time it was a case of having to get down somehow. Without instrument lights there was no way of knowing whether the undercarriage was down and with the ground crew sheltering from the 109s' cannon shells it was unlikely anyone would be in a position to fire a Very signal at me if it wasn't. Suddenly I could feel the thrum of the wheels spinning below me. Moments later came the relief of touchdown.

That was my first combat flight on Malta and what an initiation it was. It was wonderful to climb out of my aircraft in a complete lather of sweat, find a shady spot, lie back and just relax with a cigarette. The flight time in my logbook read 1 hour 25 minutes, longer than average for a Malta dogfight and to me a very long time. I should add here that with the atrocious conditions under which our hard-pressed ground crew were operating we had to expect the occasional maintenance problem. It was just the luck of the draw that my first operation met such a major problem.

Without doubt the ground crews of Malta were a superbly courageous group of men who worked tirelessly day and night. Many times it was only to see their work blown to pieces and having to start again. All this while the aerodrome was under attack with only the minimal shelter of makeshift holes in the ground or slit trenches.

One incident illustrates the enormous tension under which our ground crews were forced to operate. There had been a large air raid, the bombing had been intense and the men were crowded together in a shelter, which had a sheet of iron as the roof. As the "all clear" sounded one unthinking wag went out and got hold of a large boulder then, whistling loudly in imitation of a falling bomb, threw it onto the roof. The stampede from those inside was so panic stricken that one of them was trampled to death. Most of those men had never seen a Spitfire before and yet they were the ones we depended on to keep us in the air.

Our shortage of aircraft, when compared with the Luftwaffe, was pitiful. We new arrivals were to discover that although every combat started off in company with at least one other Spit ultimately the sheer numbers of the attackers forced a separation. The result was that during the return to base stage with ammunition spent it was inevitably a period of fighting for survival. When serviceable, those great but now ageing Hurricanes operating from Hal Far, on the east side of Malta, would try to give us some cover when landing. They did a sterling job against enormous odds and we sure appreciated the help they were able to give.

XI
The Island Battle

It didn't take pilots long to realise that the four cannons on our new Spitfires were more of a liability than a help. The cannon-laden Spits were heavier on the controls and, as two cannon could do all the damage needed, the extra two had to go. We felt it was more important to retain the aircraft's superb high manoeuvrability rather than increase the firepower. Without fuss the changes were made, doubtless without filling in the umpteen unnecessary forms required by regulations. After all, as we told ourselves, there was a war on in Malta.

May 1st proved to be a day in which things went badly wrong for me and provided a success for Hitler and Co. It was an operation that exposed the great weakness of having inexperienced pilots trying to learn in a highly dangerous combat area. A fellow New Zealander Bert Mitchell, like myself, had gained a reasonable amount of experience in the UK and was aware of the wiles of our enemy. Together we were instructed to fly with two senior officers. It was fortunate that they both ultimately proved to be excellent and courageous leaders but unfortunate for me as they both had to learn and I unwittingly became their first object lesson in just what not to do.

The four of us had taken off with Bert flying as the number two and myself as the number four. The idea was for them to get used to flying in the line abreast formation and to practise the necessary 'cross-over' turns that this formation required. The cardinal basic rule of covering each other at all times was well and truly understood by both of them. Woody had warned us that there were a few "little jobs"(109s) about and to watch out for them. We had climbed up to about 25,000 feet and practice turns had been operated smoothly.

Suddenly I spotted a familiar yellow-nosed Me109 at 6 o'clock. It was approaching unusually slowly. I was straining to see if his number two was following as I knew that there would be at least one other 109 somewhere nearby and if we waited we might get a shot at them. What I didn't know was that when I reported this 109 all three turned to look at it and then continued to do so, forgetting about my now completely unprotected tail.

Suddenly I heard a scream over the radio from Mitch: "Break left, Jack!

Break, break, break, Jack!"

With that first yell I began to turn immediately. That's what saved me from being blown to pieces as the 109 had come up under me and fired at short range. But for Mitch's warning it would have been a direct hit. As it was my control column was blasted out of its base, cannon shells exploded into my flying boot, most of the instruments were shattered and to add to the problems my instinctive action when breaking into the turn had been to give full throttle. The throttle was now hanging useless and the aircraft was in a spiralling power dive.

I was thrown to the floor of the cockpit with the G force and for what seemed an eternity lay pinned there by the force of gravity. Clawing my way up the side proved impossible then all of a sudden the stricken aircraft gave a sudden jolt and I was hurled right out of the cockpit. It was indeed fortunate for me that many of us had on the advice of the old hands left our sliding hoods open just in case. It was wiser to put up with the cold and the wind noise in favour of a quick exit. The temperatures in Malta were not too bad until you got up very high.

Anyway it was a lucky day for me that my hood was open and I was thrown out.

Another problem then arose. I wasn't my coolest and calmest person at that moment as I started to grope feverishly for the handle of the ripcord. To my horror I just couldn't feel it around anywhere! Where the hell was it? My almost panic groping continued while I dropped like a stone. One thing that was noticeable was the soft cushioning effect from the rushing air. Then quite amazingly I remembered the emphatic words from an instructor way back:

"If you can't find the ripcord just look for it."

How about that? And how stupidly simple; on looking down there it was dangling out in the wind, partly pulled out in my fast exit from the aircraft. How lucky can you be? One pull and bingo suddenly all was quiet and peaceful. A quick assessment of the situation showed I was drifting down well out to sea. I calculated the odds. There had been reports of pilots on rare occasions being shot up in their parachutes. There was also the possibility that any rescue craft, which tried to reach me, would be attacked. I still had what looked like about 15,000 feet of height so my only chance of reaching land was to try and side-slip the parachute.

Well, here goes, I thought. I grabbed some of the cords and pulled. At first this seemed to be working just great. Part of the canopy collapsed and there was a noticeable drift towards the island. A second tug produced another sideways movement but at the same time I developed an alarming swing as if on the end of a giant pendulum. For a frightening time it wouldn't stop and for a very scary moment it looked as though I could quite easily fall into the canopy, which at one time was partly below me. This stopped my little game of side-slipping except for very timorous tugs producing a very gentle sideways movement.

However the important result was obtained probably more by the wind blowing in the right direction than any ham-fisted help from me. What my constant swinging did do was make me feel quite nauseous. At last the rocky countryside started to approach rapidly. It was a case of trying to dodge the menacing rock walls and avoiding the more rugged terrain. I was also worried about my ability to land with one injured leg. I had no idea how bad the injury was but I could feel the squelch of blood in my flying boot.

The landing was far from a textbook example of how to do it but it was wonderful to be back on mother earth. I was grateful to be able to just lie there next to a stone wall and wait for help. So much for my fond expectations. Instead of help a shotgun appeared over the stone wall followed by a very excited and hostile Maltese. He approached me muttering in Maltese with his finger white on the trigger.

He either did not speak English or did not want to understand me and his excitement was increasing. Then the most wonderful sight of all appeared, a group of British army boys from the 4th Buffs.

One lesson all fighter pilots in Malta learned from my confrontation with that Maltese. We stopped recording our victories with swastikas painted on our Mae Wests. That was where my problem arose. The swastikas had acted like a red rag to a bull. In the future, large roundels of red, white and blue appeared as added insurance.

What happened to me some 25,000 feet above Malta that day was what I suspected: I had been set up by a simple ruse. Some two months later I had it confirmed when I spoke to the Luftwaffe pilot who shot me down. We met in hospital. He told me he was a Sudeten Czech, Lieutenant Herbert Soukup.

His combat strategy would never have worked with an experienced group but served him well on that occasion. He had sent in his number two to approach slowly from behind, hoping that when he was spotted all eyes would be on that aircraft while he attacked the nearest Spitfire without being seen. His simple plan worked like a charm.

In fact he thought it was a great joke. Strangely or perhaps not so strangely, I did not share his pleasure but had to admit to our stupidity. I was his thirteenth victim and his last as he was shot down soon after. I still have a small snapshot photo of him and once wrote to him at the PoW address given to me but never heard back.

It was not unusual to meet some of our enemies after they'd been shot down and when you think back it was not really surprising to find that with odd exceptions they were very similar to us. Just young men who by chance of birth happened to be on the other side, each as convinced as the other that he was fighting for the rights of his people and homeland – or Fatherland. Not an easy concept to argue against. We did meet the odd arrogant Nazi and they were a pain.

But back to personal problems: first it was a case of being transported to the hospital. One of my beautiful New Zealand-made flying boots had been cut off my foot. Not that it was worth keeping as it was peppered with bits of metal and cannon shell. It was interesting to discover that the leather and wool combination of our boots was a very effective bullet-proofing as most of the debris did not penetrate.

I was sorry to lose those boots. They were later replaced with UK-made boots which were acceptable but not as good.

The damage to my leg was not great, one fairly large hole through the base of the main lower leg muscle. This was encased in plaster so that I could walk about with the aid of a crutch.

I also had some small metal bits in the forehead, which were removed and stitched up, and bingo it was a case of almost new and able to hitch a ride to the nearest village for some local fun. At least that was what I had in mind but the powers that be in our military hospital thought otherwise. In the main that was our tyrant of a nursing sister.

In the same breath I should add that the nursing sisters and staff of the hospitals of Malta did a wonderful job often under stressful conditions while contending with shortages of many medical supplies. Mtarfa Hospital where I found myself was quite close to Mdina, which was referred to over the German radio by Lord Haw Haw as the Holy City of Malta in which the fighter pilots skulked and hid.

It was where our billets were and also the officers' quarters and we must admit that we did not mind skulking. It was an interesting twist to the Nazis that with all their cruelties they did try and avoid bombing hospitals and such places as Mdina. This is not to say that many stray bombs didn't find their way there. The island after all was not that big and the flight path of the bombers when attacking Takali aerodrome was usually over the hospital or Mdina.

After a couple of days of standing to attention for morning inspection and then trying to get back into a bed that had the sheets drawn as tight as armour-plating it was time to say enough was enough. The surgeon who had performed my minor operations was also the senior officer, fortunately a very likeable Canadian, with the rank of lieutenant colonel. The tyrannical sister had become a challenge to Paul Brennan, my Australian friend, and myself so we decided to do a bunk and clear out for the day.

We knew where our clothes had been stored and with the help of two lovely and helpful nurses we got out of the ward, hired a horse and small carriage and set off with all the pleasure associated with that of defying authority and in particular bucking an over-riding authoritarian female. The day out was not a great success. The local wine – all that we could find – tasted terrible. And, as we discovered, it didn't mix very well with antibiotics. However we did have a lot of fun and laughs with some of the friendly locals.

Suddenly, in front of the small shop in which we sat, a fully armed platoon of army men appeared. A sergeant marched in saying he was here to arrest us. That really made our day.

The army NCOs always had difficulty with us as we were by now either flight sergeants or warrant officers and a little bit of pulling rank on them always threw them into confusion. We learnt they had been searching for us for hours over a considerable area of Mtarfa and Mdina. We listened politely, thanked them for providing an escort, requested they find us a transport to get us back and away we went surrounded by the military.

With Malta in the throes of a life and death struggle this idiotic situation was like something out of *Alice in Wonderland*. The farce continued. On return we were formally charged with escaping from a military hospital and brought before our Canadian CO. He pronounced a formal reprimand for the ears of the attending army sergeants, dismissed them and then invited us into his office for a pleasant chat. During the course of our conversation he apologised for the "over the top" discipline and arranged a transfer to a much more peaceful ward with a less stringent sister.

However we should be tolerant and admit that perhaps the actions taken were with concern for our health and in no way a personal vendetta. Life for us became much more tolerable, although the desire to get out and back into the air was a constant urge. The bombing raids were continuing with massive intensity and the conditions on the island were becoming very grim indeed.

XII

Operation Hercules

Malta was badly hammered by a massive tonnage of bombs during the early months of 1942. The Luftwaffe launched 4,900 aerial sorties in March followed by an incredible 9,600 in April. In two months this amazing little island withstood twice the tonnage of bombs that fell on London during the worst 12 months of the Blitz.

In the six weeks to mid-April 6,700 tons were dropped on Malta's Grand Harbour. The women and children of Valetta and those who lived in the areas around our three aerodromes showed immense fortitude. Right across the island the entire population suffered continuous bombardment.

Whenever we walked down to Takali carrying our flying gear (there was little or no transport serviceable) it was a tonic to meet rows of small children standing along the side of the road waiting to give us small religious tokens to carry with us when flying. Their actions were very important to them and they believed fervently that their prayers would help and guide us. There is no doubt that the Church provided an enormous strength and sustenance to the population of Malta.

Fortunately for our military strategy, Britain had earlier broken the highly secret German High Command communications code and was able to obtain vital information on German military strategy and the movement of supplies by convoy. However, this was a Catch 22 situation as Allied Command had to be very careful not to display such pre-knowledge by taking precipitate action. To do so would have been to disclose their hand, so elaborate precautions were taken. For example, if a large convoy was known to be on the move it had to be 'discovered' by a reconnaissance Spit or other aircraft before attacking.

From intercepted communications the Allies learned of a major plan or operation codenamed Hercules. The plan, adopted by the German High Command after an urgent meeting between Hitler and his top generals, aimed at the invasion of Malta. Put forward by Field Marshal Kesselring it involved input from Goering, Mussolini, Admiral Raeder (Germany's Invasion Commander-in-Chief), General Rommel and the Italian High Command.

At the meeting it was made clear to Hitler that to achieve the Afrika Korps' objectives in North Africa, Malta would first have to be neutralised and eventually occupied. Operation Hercules would ensure the achievement of this objective but Hitler had reservations as he felt it would place heavy demands on German resources. However Kesselring urged Hitler and Goering to attack and take Malta.

"Keep your shirt on, Field Marshal Kesselring," Hitler is reported to have said, grasping Kesselring's arm after tempers had run high. "I am going to do it," Hitler added.

Our PRU Spits were reporting considerable work being done to Catanian airfields that looked like preparation for gliders. Daily we stood on the bastions of Mdina overlooking Takali and watched as more of our aircraft were bombed and sent up in smoke. Though we still had a few Spits operating to stem the daily assaults, clearly a showdown was imminent.

In late April news came through that we were about to receive another delivery of vital aircraft. The date, we were told, was 9 May. However there was to be an enormous difference in the reception of this intake compared to that experienced by our group when we flew our 47 Spits into Malta on 20 April.

The main reason – or at least the excuse given to us – for the lack of organisation planned for our arrival was that it was to maintain secrecy. Apparently too much preparation would have advertised our coming. This time it was a case of to hell with secrecy we are going to be highly organised in all respects. To do this the army, marooned merchant seamen without their ships and indeed everyone available including pilots, were called in to help, plus of course our always available and willing ground crew.

Thousands of bags were filled with sand to create new pens for the expected aircraft. Pens were built at Luqa, Takali and Hal Far (the Fleet Air Arm base). It was tiresome, energy-sapping work in the heat of mid-summer Malta. Much of the organisation behind this was due to the driving force of Jumbo Gracie. To dramatise the situation he had erected a gallows at Takali with instructions that the first man found dodging or thieving would be hanged. (Naturally I have never seen this ever officially recorded.)

As the planned delivery date drew near aircraft fuel in four-gallon tins was stored in each aircraft pen together with ammunition ready for arming the cannon. Pilots were briefed and allocated to a numbered pen. Each arriving aircraft, pre-allocated a number, was to be taxied to its matching numbered pen where the waiting pilot, in full flying gear, would be ready to take over. The incoming pilot was to be given an information leaflet on where to find accommodation and other details.

The army boys were mobilised to help in the servicing of aircraft, mainly handling the four-gallon petrol tins for the re-fuelling. Full turn around was expected within 20 to 30 minutes with all aircraft fully serviced and ready for take-off. Meanwhile our few remaining Spitfires would be patrolling the air space above each aerodrome.

Crunch time was coming and we were ready. My own personal involvement in all this was damned frustrating as my leg just refused to heal. I was in and out of hospital with my leg in plaster and still needing crutches. I doubt if I was much use in the overall scheme of things. The only consolation was that our squadron, owing to the shortage of aircraft, was doing very little flying.

In fact some pilots were fighting a wonderful misinformation war by going down to the operations centre and with Woody's help broadcasting cross-conversations as if they were in the air. This did cause some confusion to the enemy who scrambled intercepting aircraft to find them. It was surprising how often they reported Spitfires shot down when there were none in the air at the time.

But what preoccupied us night and day were the massive preparations to save Malta. Woody called our five key 249 Squadron leaders together in secrecy. The five, CO Stan Grant, Flight Commanders Laddie Lucas and Buck McNair, Ronnie West and Raoul Daddo-Langlois, met in the Valetta Intelligence Room at 9 a.m. After settling with a drink Woody took them to the end of the room and went over the main points of the delivery strategy.

In spite of the disastrous outcome of the delivery of the 47 Spits in April an arrangement had been made at the highest level to allow the huge American aircraft carrier USS *Wasp* to make a second run with another 47 Spitfires. The ship was at that time back in Greenock waiting for the new aircraft to be loaded and would sail as soon as she was ready. The delivery was codenamed Operation Bowery.

The plan was that as she passed through the Straits of Gibraltar she would join the British aircraft carrier HMS *Eagle* with its complement of 16 Spitfires. A battleship, a cruiser and numerous destroyers of the Royal and US Navies would escort the two carriers. The flotilla would sail through the night to the usual fly-off point just north of Algiers.

The 63 aircraft would take off early in the morning and land in Malta within three and a half hours. The five pilots selected by Woody from our 249 Squadron would lead them, using their local knowledge of conditions on Malta to minimise any likely problems. *Eagle* was then to return to Gibraltar for a further 16 Spits. In this way some 80 aircraft could be expected on Malta within the next two or three weeks. The five pilots were told they would be leaving for Gibraltar the next day together with Wing Commander McLean.

This was a time of severe shortages on Malta. Everything, ammunition, food, fuel, armament was in seriously short supply. Even our anti-aircraft guns were rationed to a very restricted supply of shells. Medical supplies were also a worry and fuel was so low that it was well nigh impractical to support other aircraft on shipping strikes. In the face of all this we had to obtain and hold full air supremacy over the island.

Throughout this time of shortages and disasters, continuous bombing and mounting military and civil casualties, there still remained an amazing attitude of complete confidence and optimism. Despite the fact that the tide of battle was clearly running against us, civilians and military alike seemed imbued with an indomitable spirit.

The tide turned on 9 May 1942. On that historic day 64 Spitfires took off from the two carriers near Algiers. Of these 60 made it all the way to Malta. One failed to gain enough power at take-off, crashed into the water and went under the carrier. The assumption was that the pilot mistakenly tried to take off with his propeller running in coarse pitch. Another crash-landed in Algiers, a third was shot down on our circuit at Hal Far by a 109.

The fourth pilot, Jerry Smith – a Canadian – had a charmed life. He achieved what all of us had at times thought the impossible. When he took off he accidentally jettisoned his 90-gallon overload tank and, with nowhere to go, elected to try to land back on the carrier. He succeeded on his second attempt. The story goes that the strictly dry ship provided a round of drinks and presented Jerry with US Navy wings.

For him to have succeeded without a landing hook on his aircraft was considered to be an extreme fluke. As soon as his aircraft came to a stop he wanted to fit on another tank immediately and take off again for Malta but the top brass decreed otherwise. Instead he was flown to Malta from Gibraltar. Sadly, he was later killed on the island.

Back on Malta the excitement among us at the sight of so many of our fighters arriving safely hit fever pitch. The long hours of back-breaking preparation were well rewarded as the Spitfires – with fresh pilots, fully armed, fuelled and ready for battle – were back in the air again in short order, most of them in about 15 minutes or less.

As expected the Luftwaffe came over in force. This time they received a real hammering. By the next morning, 10 May, 46 Axis aircraft had been destroyed and a further 20 damaged. While all this was going on another matter of great importance happened almost unnoticed. HMS *Welshman*, a Royal Navy fast minelaying cruiser (she could travel at over 40 knots) had slipped into Grand Harbour during the night with life saving cargo, berthing at 6 a.m. on 10 May.

The ship was a major target for any marauding Luftwaffe attack so the army moved smartly, unloading the precious stores within 14 hours. This enabled her to leave again with minimal fuel on the hazardous return journey, camouflaged as a French destroyer and flying the French colours. The *Welshman*'s cargo included powdered milk, canned meat, dehydrated foodstuffs, ammunition, aero-engines and parts. Thanks to this wonderful ship and crew, together with the Royal Navy's submarine *Upholder*, Malta was kept just breathing.

Meanwhile other momentous decisions were being made. On the same day as the *Welshman* arrived in Malta, Winston Churchill signalled General Sir Claude Auchinleck, Commander-in-Chief Middle East, as follows:

> The Chiefs of Staff, the Defence Committee and the War Cabinet have again considered the whole position. We are determined that Malta

shall not be allowed to fall without a battle being fought by your whole army for its retention. The starving out of this fortress would involve the surrender of over 30,000 men, Army and Air Force…. Its possession would give the enemy a clear and sure bridge to Africa.

On 15 June the Allies launched Operation Harpoon, a desperate and ambitious plan to break the siege of Malta. Two large convoys started for Malta, one from Gibraltar and the other from Alexandria. The Alexandria convoy had to sail close to highly militarised zones and received such a battering from air attacks they were forced to retreat. The convoy that set off from Gibraltar consisted of six merchant ships, one battleship, two carriers, and four cruisers, one minelayer, and 17 destroyers. When it arrived within range of our fighter defence, only two of the six cargo ships remained afloat. The battle for Malta, we realised, still had a long way to go.

The air wars were far from over. In fact, as the month of June progressed the attacks increased in ferocity with the Italian Air Force (Regia Aeronautica) now joining the fray. At long last I was permitted to fly again, although my leg continued to give trouble. It was still in plaster but I could now walk without crutches, or at least hobble to my aircraft when scrambled. It was great to be back and again be a part of this seemingly endless air war. The first entry in my logbook since being shot down on 1 May was dated 5 June 1942:

Scramble Defence of Malta. 0.50 min. Nothing seen.

Sometimes now when I read short unemotional entries such as the above and remember what actually happened during that flight I realise how important a diary would have been. Raoul Daddo-Langlois was flight leader that day. His number two was one of our new arrivals from the last delivery of Spits. I was flying number three and my number two was also a new boy. There were quite a number of Me109s flying over the island. The idea of this flight was to familiarise newcomers with the formations and possibly give them some combat experience.

We four were flying along straight and level, tensely watching the skies and ready for action. Suddenly Raoul's number two winged hard over. In the flying atmosphere in which we lived that sudden action meant 'break hard, being attacked'. Raoul and myself were half way round before we noticed that this oaf was just playing around doing a full roll.

"Gosh, it was getting boring. I could see the enemy fighters but they were a long way from us, so I thought it would be fun to do some aerobatics," he said later. Raoul was absolutely furious and gave the pilot a severe dressing down after we landed.

"I never want to fly with that fool again," he told us.

The pilot was Sergeant Beurling, a Canadian. Later because he was always referring to just about everyone and everything as a "screwball" we nicknamed him Screwball Beurling. He was a strange, intense young man who loved his flying. But he worried those of us whom he regarded as old hands by asking question after question. He had far above average long distance sight. Sometimes when air raids were sounded and we were not flying we used to stand on the Bastion of Mdina, straining to see the enemy formations approaching and count the number in the attack.

We were always amazed at the far-sightedness of some of the Maltese who would start getting excited and counting aircraft while we were still gazing at an apparently empty sky, unable to see a thing. We soon discovered that Screwball had even better sight, beginning to count long before the Maltese had made their first spotting and giving the direction in which the enemy aircraft were heading.

Later I was to experience this incredible ability when flying with him over Malta. On one occasion when I was leading a flight, Woody had warned us of a very large formation above at 10 o'clock and that there were others approaching. Suddenly I spotted them without the usual Canadian drawl from Screwball beating me to it. Just as I smugly reported them over the R/T came Screwball's easy drawl.

"Sure, Red 1, but there are another lot of the screwballs attacking us at 7 o'clock."

Once again his eyesight was superb, the aircraft were only just coming into view seconds after he spoke. He went on to become the most successful fighter pilot in Malta. His flying was excellent and his deflection shooting as a result was incredibly accurate. Strangely he did not like to lead and preferred others to obtain tactical positions. His final score at Malta was 28 confirmed destroyed.

With the increased participation of the Italians the opposition was more varied and combat operations more hectic for some of us during July. We found that in general they didn't press home their attacks with any ferocity and appeared to operate with a certain amount of timidity. For that reason we tended not to treat them with the same respect as we did the Germans.

Over the RT we referred to them as the "Ice Creams", knowing the German controllers listened into our RT natter (as we did with theirs). We used to tell our controller something like 'those Ice Creams have flown off again and left the bombers unprotected' or 'the Ice Creams wouldn't stay and fight'. We believe this was a basis for many heated arguments between our Axis antagonists when they returned to their bases in Sicily.

Listening to the enemy's conversations in combat was an extremely important part of our controller's tactics as the immediate translation was often a life-saving warning to us. This was referred to as the Y Service. Ironically, the attitude we developed towards the Italians proved dangerous at times as their fighters, although not as fast as the 109s, were much more able to turn and manoeuvre in a dog fight situation. Also among them were some very experienced prewar aerobatic pilots.

On one operation after attacking numerous formations of Italian

Re2001s involving multiple combats the sky, as so often happened, was suddenly empty. Well, almost empty. Still with me was one of the best number twos I ever had the pleasure of flying with – an Australian named Alan Yates. Alan was a great person to have with me in the chaotic flying that confronted us every time we entered combat and we shared many battles together.

There was one other aircraft with us in that piece of sky, a lonely Italian Re2001 completely at our mercy. I attacked him immediately and found myself involved in some incredibly complex combat manoeuvres that gave me extreme difficulty in obtaining anything like a direct shot. I could only see minor damage inflicted. To add to my problem I ran out of cannon shells. Finally it was a case of calling Alan in as he still had some ammunition.

Alan then tried, again and again, nearly getting himself into trouble with this difficult customer. We were getting nearer and nearer to Sicily and fuel levels were running low. I called Alan to break off the attack, as we had to return to base. The Italian was smoking badly and probably would not be able to get back so we turned and left him, setting off back to Malta.

To our surprise (and admiration) he turned back and chased us as a gesture of his defiance. If he ever did get back to his base, and both of us secretly hoped he would, I'll bet he had a wonderful story to tell.

One other operation etched forever in my memory also relates to combat against the Italians. Every now and then they would send over three giant three-engined Cant 1007 bombers in close formation, at considerable height and escorted with a massive protection force of close escort Re2001s and with both high escort and roaming escort of large numbers of 109s. The amount of bombs they delivered did minimal damage but each bomber had maximum protection using the cross fire from numerous rear guns.

We knew these arrogant flights over the island annoyed the Maltese very much and frustrated the hell out of us as they were there just as a bait with 109s just waiting for us to attack them. However we all hoped that some day the opportunity would come.

My logbook records that flight as 4 July. It was one of those rare days when everything goes right. We were scrambled relatively early, as the raid had not yet reached the island. Our flight was flying as three separate sections of two, climbing rapidly to gain maximum height. Woody was advising a very big "party" coming in with major formations of fighters and that there were also some "large jobs" there for us.

Woody's vectors proved to be immaculate. Alan Yates was again with me. As we levelled off at about 28,000 ft. there below were swarms of enemy fighters. The 109s were sweeping over the huge gaggle and below them was formation after formation of Re2001s. Underneath all this mass were three large Cant 1007s flying towards Grand Harbour.

The three pairs of Spits reformed at our agreed ceiling height. Laddie Lucas was our new squadron leader, and so the decision was his. What we were seeing was an obvious bait with all those fighters just waiting to carve us up. It looked like sheer suicide to dive in there, and yet…? It was so unusual not to be hassled by fighters at this moment, to be able to observe and have time to formulate strategy. Those heavily protected bombers looked so tempting. Then, crisply over the RT, came Laddie's decision.

"I'll go down and take the left bomber. Raoul you take the right. Jack, you cover us and if OK then take the centre one."

As the last to dive I expected to have a great mass of fighters who would be attacking the first two pairs, but the speed of the attack caught them completely unprepared. Instead of having to defend the others there was my huge Cant looming up to be destroyed.

The result of this attack was a morale boosting for the island. The Maltese were delighted to see those arrogant bombers eliminated. There were never any repeats. I can still recall thinking, "This is bloody madness" as we dived through the armada. I guess that's why we got away with it.

Speaking of madness recalls the courage and incredible luck displayed in a very short and colourful combat career. This involved a likeable and cheerful but inexperienced New Zealand pilot who arrived with the large contingent of Spits and flew with a squadron from Luqa. Almost immediately he was involved in an attack on some Ju87 dive-bombers attacking Grand Harbour. He dived after the Ju87 right through the massive Malta flak, was hit and had to bale out.

A couple of days later he was up again and once more attacking a Ju87 but to his misfortune this time he achieved the rare distinction of being shot down by the rear gunner. Once again he baled out and survived. Not long after this we were standing outside the remains of our dispersal hut and listening to the roar of aircraft engines high above us. We knew that it was an enemy fighter sweep being engaged by some of our Spits.

Suddenly we heard gunfire. It was the recognisable sound of 109 cannon fire, not ours, and then out of the blue haze above came a Spitfire obviously in very bad shape. We could see that a large piece of his tail unit was in tatters and would be extremely difficult to control.

We watched anxiously, expecting the pilot to jump at any minute. In fact we were all trying to will him to jump. It was plain to see he would never be able to land and could lose control at any minute.

"Jump damn you, jump while you have enough height," was the unspoken thought of all of us. But no, on he came making a slow skidding highly unstable turn. Then unbelievably he put his wheels down and headed for our aerodrome, losing height rapidly. He tried to turn into wind but had no control, went sideways over our flight-path and crashed into the rocky bank on the other side.

A large plume of smoke and dust billowed up as we watched in horror, convinced the pilot had been killed. There was a rush to the crash site. To the utter amazement of everyone, from underneath the smouldering wreckage came a voice:

"Get me out of here."

Incredibly he was in remarkably good shape although his back was injured and he subsequently returned to New Zealand. When asked why he didn't bale out instead of taking such a dreadful risk his reply was that he was sick of baling out. Someone must have been looking after him, for when his parachute was examined it was found to be full of shrapnel and pieces of cannon shells and would never have opened.

XIII

Hercules Abandoned

Flying was gradually becoming more orderly to operate, there were more aircraft serviceable and although we were still feeling the effects of a poor diet and continual Malta Dog which weakened us physically we were definitely gaining the ascendancy in the air. We could now send some aircraft up early so that we could gain tactical height and then send others off later that would have sufficient fuel to cover us when we needed to land. The fighter defence was no longer on its knees and could meet the enemy even before they reached the island. They didn't like this change and fought back with mounting ferocity during the month of July with wave upon wave of attacks but now they were paying a much heavier price.

At the same time my own problems were not improving. Owing to poor diet and avoidance of medication while flying, my leg became quite badly infected. Though unaware at the time, I flew my last operation with that wonderful 249 Squadron on 30 July 1942. My logbook entry states:

Scramble to cover flying boat 30 minutes.

After that operation I was forced back to what seemed the inevitable confrontation with the hospital authorities as I was returned there for urgent treatment. Some of those characters seemed to delight in forcing their authority on any poor soul who arrived sick and defenceless into their little domain.

One of the rules that I detested and opposed was the handing over of all personal clothing and being issued with a drab garb very similar to prison clothes (stripes and all). I was also told to hand over all personal valuables including my Rolliflex camera. I refused point blank. I had just taken some medication, which was making me feel quite ill and groggy. Fortunately I had one temporary advantage over the ward sister, in this case a sergeant very much the parade type with a voice to match. My rank now was flight sergeant (one rank above his) so the battle of wills set in.

I knew that ultimately with my state of health the result was a foregone conclusion. It is hard to convey the atmosphere in that ward but it was certainly tense and electric. Most of the beds were full of Maltese, all sitting up with mouths agape at seeing this unpleasant sergeant being challenged. He then informed me that he had sent for the matron and the colonel and would have me arrested. To maintain this confrontation I had tried to remain standing but found my legs were getting wobbly.

Suddenly another sergeant marched into the ward followed by about half a dozen soldiers. What the hell was going on now, I wondered. To my utter astonishment he stopped at the end of my bed, did a sharp left turn to face me, stood at attention and saluted.

"Excuse me sir," he said, staring straight ahead. "Advice has been received from headquarters. Your commission has come through. Congratulations from our Commanding Officer and we have been instructed to move you to the officers' quarters."

With that, the soldiers carried me on a stretcher out of the ward. What an incredible piece of timing.

The comparison in treatment was unbelievable. I found myself in a spacious private room with a view from the window towards the sea. There was a small fridge and inside were two bottles of beer, a jug of ice water and some odd biscuits. After being made comfortable in bed, first the matron paid me a visit and then the colonel. For some time I just lay and revelled in the luxury.

While aware that in any military machine there has to be discipline and structure, and part of that structure is a hierarchy of rank, I sometimes had a small niggle of resentment against the excessive line of distinction in the British service between officers and NCOs. Within the squadrons it was barely noticeable and between pilots in Malta there was virtually no difference. But in other parts of the services and within the social structure of Britain the differences sometimes bordered on the unjust.

I occasionally had to remind myself to be careful otherwise I'd develop a chip on my shoulder. I decided that now I was an officer I would enjoy it. Well the chip nearly came back the next day when I met the German pilot whom I mentioned previously. A soldier came into my room, saluted, and asked if I would like to meet a German prisoner under guard in the next room who had asked to see me. Curious, I agreed.

The German was duly marched in, sporting one arm in a sling. His grasp of English was remarkable since he had only been a prisoner for about six weeks and had known very little of the language previously. After discussion with him (and confirmed by records since the war) I realised he was the blighter who had shot me down that day back on May 1st.

Conversations with him were interesting although he was inclined to be arrogant and not very likeable. According to him I was his 13th victim (and his last). I nearly got that chip back on my shoulder on discovering that he had been living in this state of luxury while for weeks back I'd had to fight it out in vastly inferior conditions.

My resentment soon abated as I continued to enjoy at an even greater level the wonderful service of the RAF and to revel in the anticipation of again flying our superb aircraft. Another surprising news of immense honour was to learn that I had been awarded the DFC. Wow! What a wonderful parcel of news coming my way. I was also advised that I would be flown out in a Hudson to Gibraltar and on to the UK soonest available, subject to health.

Thinking back over that period I realise how strange the cessation of our operations really was. There were no celebrations or get-togethers, no speeches, no special farewells. Various members of our squadrons at Takali (and the other squadrons at Luqa) quietly embarked at night as their turn came to fly back to the UK for a well-earned rest. The battles in the air continued overhead but it now felt something like a relay race in which we had handed over the batons for someone else to carry on.

When at last discharged from hospital I met up with Ray Hesslyn and we stayed at a hotel in Sliema where we bathed in the warm waters off the rocky foreshore. Although it was awkward having to wrap up my plaster cast each time I went into the water the relaxing effect of the sea bathing was superb. During our flying none of us had touched much alcohol as with our poor diet and low state of health it would have been courting disaster. In any case neither Ray nor I was what could be described as a heavy drinker. The 'hard stuff' was definitely not part of our diet.

However, here we were with time on our hands so we decided one afternoon to try a drink, which had always been regarded as an absolute no-no for pilots during flying periods. I've forgotten its Maltese name but it was a drink similar to anisette. We bought a bottle each and sat in the lounge of the hotel to see what this 'stuff' was all about. It was a clear liquid, which turned cloudy white when water was added. The taste was a very mild aniseed, which to us seemed more like a soft drink.

We sat quietly drinking throughout the afternoon, feeling more and more that it was a bit of a damp squib as there were no apparent effects. The hotel, an elegant structure with very high ceilings and curved marble staircases, was largely occupied by rather stuffy and slightly elderly ex-navy wives who had been marooned there. Ray and I were just beginning to feel somewhat relaxed and feeling perhaps a little bit mischievous when the gong sounded for dinner.

So up we got and strolled fairly carefully into the dining room to find we were the only males, the rest of the tables being taken up with our sedate ladies. The service proved to be rather slow and my bladder told me that I had better find a place to go. Saying cheerio to Ray, I set off out of the dining room trying to walk steadily. This was not the easiest thing to do with my plastercast even when sober. In my present state it proved to be extremely difficult.

Once out of the dining room I stood bewildered, as I could not remember any toilets on the ground floor. Looming in front of me was this beautiful curved marble staircase. Oh well, what the hell, in my happy state it was a matter of up you go or else. So I clambered and clumped my way up, found the necessary toilet and was then faced with the task of making my return.

I can recall standing at the top of that long staircase and thinking how dumb to suffer the strain of trying to walk down there. Why, all I had to do was slide down that lovely wide banister. With that I launched myself off. I think my balance was lacking a few controls as the last thing I remember was seeing the marble floor coming up to meet me.

I came to with Ray kneeling beside me surrounded by a large group of very concerned ladies. I heard one of the ladies saying, "I cannot understand how this could have happened. If he had been drinking I could have understood."

"We must get him to a doctor," said another, but Ray Hesslyn chipped in with "He doesn't need a doctor," got his arms under mine, hoisted me on to my feet and off we staggered. Next day I had a very sore head and a stiff neck but on seeing where I crashed there was no doubt that Lady Luck was still looking after me.

We quietly flew out of Malta that night in a Lockheed Hudson. It was 17 August, 1942. Seven hours and 15 minutes later we landed at Gibraltar. Transport planes during war years didn't offer luxury travel but we were grateful to sit back in the austere seating and hope that there were no wandering Ju88s patrolling our air space.

Neither of us spoke very much on that trip and I am sure that Ray's thoughts would have been similar to my own. Many men we had fought side by side with in Malta and had learned to respect would never be flying back to Britain as we were now doing. I felt an immense sense of relief mixed with a great appreciation at having been given the privilege of taking part, albeit such a very small part, in one of the most critical battles of this crazy war.

Mixed up with these thoughts were visions of meeting up with some of our squadron friends back in London. Quite a few of our 249 boys were due on leave soon, including Canadian Willie the Kid, my Australian friend Alan Yates, Screwball Beurling, and New Zealander Gray Stenborg, to name a few.

But there was one final cruel twist of fate still hovering over some of our outstanding pilots. On their way back to Britain their heavily laden aircraft overshot during the landing at the difficult Gibraltar aerodrome. The pilot delayed his decision to go round again just a shade too long and as a result stalled and crashed into the sea. George Beurling escaped and also Alan Yates, but other pilots including Willie the Kid and civilians, among them a mother and child, died.

Now that those dangerous and momentous days are part of history the following few statistics covering the battle of Malta may be of interest.

The Final Sum

Axis aircraft destroyed	1,252
Axis sorties against Malta	26,000
Civilians killed	1,540
RAF aircraft lost in combat	547

RAF aircraft damaged	504
RAF aircraft destroyed on the ground	160
Total RAF operational flying hours	112,247

(Source: National War Museum)

Ray and I had a great time in Gibraltar. We hadn't seen so many luxury items for sale in shops for a long time. But first there was one interesting lesson we had to learn from our drinking episode, and this was that the warning against drinks such as anisette when flying had considerable merit. We both found our thinking and vision still fuzzy. All we needed was a drink of water to feel quite woozy again. This lasted for two or three days which perhaps accounts for some of the strange purchases I made.

That said, I can add with feeling that I have never ever made such purchases for myself again. What made me do it? Was it the months of living a life of dusty austerity? I'm damned if I know but anyway what I did proved many months later to be incredibly clever. Meantime here is my confession: I went on a spending spree of buying silk socks, silk underpants, silk singlets and silk pyjamas. Not just one of each but three or four. And even in Gibraltar they were not exactly cheap.

Five days after arriving on 22 August we heard that we were to be flown back to Britain in a Sunderland. We found it a unique experience. By the time Ray and I boarded the flying boat from a small launch we had accumulated quite an expanded baggage including many items we knew were scarce in Britain. Unsure whether or not our extra baggage would be welcome on board we consulted the skipper who gave us a cheery "no problem" but advised us to keep some of the items away from the customs inspectors back in Plymouth.

As a precaution we were advised to pass the restricted items such as liquors and exclusive cosmetics up to the aircrew to be stowed in 'the Bridge'. This we discovered was a cavernous space in the wing roots on each side of the instrument panels. We were shocked to see the amount of heavy items stowed away, our baggage looked minute in comparison.

Together with a couple of other passengers we prepared for take-off – not without a certain amount of apprehension after noticing some holes in the fuselage not far from where we would be seated. On asking our cheery pilot he offhandedly told us they were cannon shell holes from an attack by Ju88s on their last trip. He wasn't fooling – that is just what they were.

All four engines were started and mooring cast away. This was fun, more like setting off in a boat. He explained to us that his engines did not like taxiing for too long so he might need to stop and cool them before reaching take-off position. Our take-off was going to be towards Gibraltar so we set off out into the Mediterranean. After a while we began to wonder if we were going to taxi all the way to the African coast. Gibraltar and the shipping between us and the 'Rock' seemed to be getting a long long way away from us. Twice he had had to stop and cool his engines.

The exciting moment finally arrived. This was sure different to taking off in a Spitfire. The pilot gave his engines full throttle and we slowly – very slowly – gathered speed. The ships, which looked so small when we first started, were now growing larger. The pilot heaved back on his control column. We lifted slowly into the air and then plonk, dropped down into the clinging sea again. The pilot reached above him to wind a handle, which probably extended his flaps. Again he heaved on his control column and again we rose into the air and again plonked back into the sea.

The ships were now getting very close and Gibraltar itself not far away when the pilot gave another heave and suddenly we were airborne. We flew within a few hundred feet of the moored ships and crossed fairly close to the circuit of the aerodrome before setting our course for England. This would take us under cover of darkness outside the coast of Spain and Portugal, over the grey Atlantic and well away from the coast of France.

Experienced Sunderland aircrews will probably be highly amused at this description of our take-off and think it just the perception of a nervous single-engine pilot. Or would they? Rightly or wrongly we felt that the aircraft was severely overloaded. Being used to flying at great heights it was also a shock to learn that we would be flying over the Bay of Biscay – in fact all the way to Britain – at a height most of the time of less than 1,000 ft.

It was a bitterly cold cabin of unlined metal but each of us was grateful to be returning to Britain. Eleven hours later we arrived at Plymouth and the skipper proved correct; the bridge of the ship was not examined. When the customs officers left the aircraft we set to and unloaded our various spoils. What we had stowed away was really quite modest, the odd one or two bottles of top quality whisky.

Having done that we were staggered to see case after case of the most expensive whiskys and liqueurs – probably destined for fancy hotels in London – being removed from those vast wing-roots.

For us, another phase of service with the RAF had been completed. What did the future have in store? At the moment we really didn't care. It was great to be back in a land where some relative calm existed even though still engaged in a bitter war. The date was 22 August, 1942. Our only thought: London here we come.

XIV
Back to Red Tape Basics

A train journey and we were back in London, to me always an exciting vibrant city, impressive with its efficient electric underground train services. I loved its spacious parks, its pubs and clubs and theatres, and New Zealand House – a place to meet friends and collect mail. Belongings left behind before I went to Malta were stored there for me.

In London Ray Hesslyn met up with Paul Brennan. Both became friendly with Australian war correspondent Henry Bateson who persuaded them to jointly write a book on their Malta experiences. My days were occupied in arranging new uniforms, a bank account and reporting for instructions as to my next posting.

Most of us returning from Malta were advised we would have to do a period of instructing before returning to combat operations. I can't say that any of us looked forward to becoming instructors, preferring instead to continue on operations. However our Command knew better. We were well aware that we all badly needed a rest but would not admit it. I guess we were so 'psyched up' that we just didn't want to stop. We had lived for so long in the heat and dust of Malta and the interminable sound of air raid sirens day and night. Now here we were back in London on a rather cool damp day I suddenly realised that I did not remember ever seeing rain throughout those five hot summer months. Perhaps it did rain but I can't recall it. Now I was feeling rather cold in my tropical kit and thankful that soon I'd be issued with my warmer uniform.

It didn't take long to catch up on news of my old NZ Squadron after meeting John Pattison at the Regent Palace (there has been quite a story told over the years about that night and the adventures that resulted between us but they are completely censored from these memoirs). I learned that 485 Squadron was stationed at Coltishall in No.12 Group. Reg Grant was their current CO and from what I could gather they were having a ball in the sense that operational flying was at a minimum and everything else at maximum tempo. That decided me to pay a visit to the squadron over the last few days of my leave in preference to the bright lights of London.

On arrival I was told they were all away at the river swimming. Someone kindly drove me over and sure enough there they all were either lying on the grassy bank or skylarking in the sparkling water of a fairly fast running stream. While sitting with them, now wearing borrowed swimming togs, there was a sudden yell from the stream. Someone was in trouble and had disappeared under the water. We dashed into the stream, found the victim and pulled him to the riverbank.

He was damned heavy and lifting him up out of the river meant handling him in far from the correct procedure for a partially drowned man. When we finally laid him on the grass I immediately used what was then the accepted Schafer method of resuscitation, learned during my surf lifesaving days. He soon recovered and we wrapped him up and drove him back to the officers' mess.

That night after dinner he came up to me – he was not a pilot but from the station administration section – I expected that he probably wanted to say thanks. But no, he complained quite aggressively that he now had very sore ribs from my actions.

Apart from that incident, and a few repercussions throughout the squadron over my censored encounter with John Pattison back in the Regent Palace in London, there was nothing to say about the visit except that the squadron with Reg Grant at the helm was in wonderful spirit and obviously still very much a strong fighting unit.

Early in September 1942 I arrived at 57 OTU (Ops Training Unit) Hawarden, situated near to the delightful town of Chester, close to the Welsh border. The officers' sleeping quarters were in what had been Gladstone's home, a beautiful old building with gracious furniture. The aerodrome itself was a busy one; the instructors all ex-operational and an interesting mixture of nationalities.

My old friend Gary Francis was there and well established as a flight commander. It was surprising how often we had met up since our time in Auckland in the same Grammar Old Boys 2nd fifteen, then squadron days back in 11 Group and here we were meeting again – a long way from training under lights in the cold winter nights on the lower rugby ground of Auckland Grammar.

I was soon to discover the station was not all milk and honey. The quarters were superb, the instructors a great bunch, the pupils from all over the globe keen and willing to learn but there was one snag. It didn't take long to find it, all wrapped up in one wing commander. He had various nicknames so, while avoiding naming him because he may have (although most unlikely) someone who adores him, I can tell you that tacked in front of his name was either Wing Commander 'Flossy' or 'Fanny'.

My first encounter with him was at the formal interview when he summoned me to his office and instructed me to bring my logbook. I was left to stand at attention while he casually thumbed through part of my logbook. Then he closed it, looked up and in an affected voice said "quite impressive" and then "dismiss".

It most certainly wasn't a pleasant friendly welcome chat but it was a salutary reminder that I was now a long way from the fighting front and back in Training Command.

The next shock came within just a few moments. I was strolling away from the Wing Commander's office block when there was a sudden scream from his window. I looked up, startled. He was shouting like a man in a frenzy. An inattentive LAC airman had walked past me in the opposite direction without saluting. I was deep in my own thoughts and hadn't noticed him and of course I had equally erred by not calling him back and severely reprimanding him. The Wing Commander ordered him to go back and walk past me again and this time salute, and of course for me to acknowledge. It felt somewhat like a comic opera performance. However it reinforced strongly that I was back in a well ordered and disciplined military organisation. Thank goodness I saw very little of this over-zealous senior officer as I settled into my new role.

We had some extremely interesting fellow instructors from Poland, Czechoslovakia, South Africa, Rhodesia, Canada, Australia, and New Zealand. And our pupils came from an even wider area of the world including France, Belgium, Norway and the USA. We had one Czech instructor who was a brilliant pilot. He had a favourite stunt that he delighted in performing every now and then. Fellow instructors had the horrors whenever he did it but somehow he got away with it.

The stunt was one hell of an example to give our pupils. It was to bring his Spit to about 1,000 ft above the final approach of the runway, close his throttle and with a kick on his rudder coax his Spitfire into a 'flat spin'. When dangerously low he would open his throttle wide, stop the spin and gently land on the edge of the landing strip with barely any forward run. I never saw him do it myself, but have been assured he did.

One day he performed this horrifying-to-watch stunt when a senior officer from Headquarters happened to be visiting the station. He was grounded immediately. I never did learn of his fate but he was too good a pilot to discard.

One of the other Czech pilots, called Ruby because his real name was too difficult to pronounce, was also a delightful chap and an outstanding pilot . I am going to digress here and tell a story about Ruby that happened later during the war. He always spoke with great excitement and vivid description, and used two favourite swear words as part of his normal speech. One he continually used was the well known "f--- me", the other which I guess can be tolerated in print was "bugger me" so you can imagine the former in place of the "bugger me".

His story, told to a large group of pilots, referred to the problems that Fighter Command was having when the FW190s started their hit and run raids against the towns and villages along the southern coast of England. The 190s came in low and fast, and by the time our fighters had scrambled they were usually already back home in France. At low level the only aircraft that had a chance to catch them were the Typhoons. The patrolling

VB Spitfires were ineffective unless they had height and were already on the spot.

Ruby was one of those patrolling Spitfires when he saw a flight of FW190s attacking the coast and gave chase; but his gain on them was painfully slow. Then he looked back and saw some Typhoons behind him so he called out excitedly over the RT.

"Bugger me the Typhoons. Come on, the Typhoons! I look back. They are catching up. I say bugger me, come on the Typhoons. They are now very close to me, I turn again and bugger me they are not Typhoons. They are more FWs. I loop the loop and I bugger off."

That is a true story.

I was just beginning to settle in and get used to the change of life in the RAF, enjoying the reduction in tension. Occasionally we would relax in the fascinating town of Chester. As long as you didn't forget and cross into Wales on a Sunday when all the pubs were closed there were many delightful small villages and pubs to discover.

I said just beginning to settle and that was all it was before it was crunch time again. Never a dull moment from the day I joined the air force in what now seemed like centuries ago way back in New Zealand. My logbook records:

> September 27th from Hawarden to Ashton Down and return with Pilot
> Officer Sergeant. After returning from that flight, notified to report to
> number 24 (3) Flying Instructors Course (FIS) at Hullavington.

This was a shock. I was about to be plunged into the very heart of Training Command for the RAF, centre of correct procedure for everything, the place that required immaculate flying with every i dotted and every t crossed. I found my way there and to my delight who should be on the railway station also looking for transport to Hullavington but none other than Ray Hesslyn. My depression vanished and I now felt that together perhaps we just might have some fun on this dreaded course.

The two of us arrived at the hallowed officers' mess at Hullavington. There certainly was an absence of any welcoming committee so we strolled into the magnificent building. The lounge faced the runways with a sweeping view of aircraft landing and taking off.

Ray and I stood admiring the view and the surroundings when we were approached by a rather concerned looking airman. We told him that we had been posted to report here and asked if he could give us any information. By this time we had relaxed in two of the extremely sumptuous leather chairs.

"I am sorry, Sirs, but this mess is only for squadron leaders and above," he said with obvious agitation. "There is a separate building nearby but I am sure that you are not meant to be here – I will check for you," he added, his concern growing. Clearly he was worried that such a break with tradition as this might shatter the very foundations of RAF Training Command.

Off he trotted while we continued to lounge in luxury. Back he came with a relieved look and advised there had been an error in the posting instructions. We were to report to a satellite station called Castle Coombe where accommodation would be arranged.

Ray and I were happy to learn this. As two very recently commissioned pilot officers, we had in a very short time found the atmosphere far from a welcoming one. The fact that Ray was proudly wearing a DFM and Bar – quite a rare combination – meant absolutely nothing in this part of the RAF world. We were after all only two very junior officers.

Well, I guess that I had to get that really unimportant grouch off my chest. There was still a war on and, reflecting back with hindsight, the Training Commands of each of our countries in the Empire had performed the miracle of training thousands of pilots. Grudgingly one has to admit that if they had to be damned stuffy then so be it. That said, I feel sure that not all stations would have reached the heights of stuffiness portrayed at Hullavington on that particular day.

From that moment on we decided we'd have fun during the course and in so doing show 'em our extreme lack of desire ever to become permanent instructors.

We learnt that we'd be flying Master IIIs with radial Wasp engines and were assured they were a totally different aircraft to the original Masters fitted with Rolls-Royce Kestrel engines that we'd flown back in our OTU days. We knew them as a very basic wooden aircraft that needed a modification to the tail unit to minimise a very dangerous tendency to spin. Those we had flown were also sluggish and not the kind of aircraft one would choose for aerobatic frolics.

Well, they said, we were about to completely change our minds and would soon be throwing them all over the skies. We still remained unconvinced. Also any idea that Ray and I might have gained from our visit to Hullavington that this part of Training Command was a sleepy hollow was soon to be shattered. The OC of the FIS advised us we would be flying 50 hours of dual and solo and should complete the course between three and four weeks. This seemed optimistic to us as the October days were shortening and the weather suspect.

Another ex-Malta pilot and a special friend, Gray Stenborg of New Zealand, joined us, as did a Flight Lieutenant Polawski of Poland. We three New Zealanders agreed in short order that we were determined to return to combat operations as soon as possible. If this required being negative on the course it would be worth trying. Looking back now I can see that we had developed a rather arrogant and over-confident attitude. Maybe we felt that we would be able to serve much more effectively back in the war theatre and possibly we were right.

But in reaching that view the piece of the picture we ignored was that many hundreds of new and inexperienced pilots were about to enter a life and death struggle. To give them some chance of survival they needed the help of pilots like us to prepare them for combat. That was why we had been drafted into the role of becoming instructors and yes perhaps we had become just a little bit jumpy and in need of a rest from combat.

Our instructors were long suffering but not easily fooled. We soon developed a respect for them and even reluctantly began to enjoy learning to give the 'instruction patter' while in the middle of slow rolls, rolls off the top and other manoeuvres. It helped that the radial engine Masters proved frisky and lively, a delight to fly.

There was one pilot, however, who refused to be drawn and remained adamant he would get himself off the course and back on operations. This resulted in an open feud with his ever patient instructor. His first stunt, which certainly didn't help to make friends, was to wait until the instructor had gone through the format for a forced landing, had lost a safe height and was about to climb back for the pilot to take over. At that point the pilot turned off the switches and stopped the motor. I should explain the master switches were in our cockpit, as our instructors always took the place of being the pupils.

This action completely threw the instructor who made a complete hash of his approach and, at the last moment when disaster loomed, the pilot turned on the switches again and took over the recovery. The next day things between them went from bad to worse. As the instructor always flew from the front cockpit he had to climb up the starboard side of the wing holding on to the fuselage, carrying his parachute and helmet plus a clipboard. It was a relatively steep short climb.

On this day the pilot, waiting with the motor quietly ticking over, allowed him to reach the halfway point then opened the throttle. The blast of wind from the prop blew the instructor backwards; he lost his footing and fell to the ground.

When he got up he was absolutely furious and bashed the pilot over the head with his helmet and clipboard. The pilot then committed the ultimate sin. He again opened the throttle, but this time wide open. The aircraft jumped the chocks, ground staff scattered, the instructor was again blown off, and the pilot taxied out then took off solo on an unauthorised flight.

The pilot was normally a delightful, easy-going man whom everyone liked. Unless he planned this action deliberately it seemed so completely out of character. However he proved his point. He certainly did succeed in getting off the course but I believe he spent many hours of towing target drogues for gunners to practise on. And I'm not sure whether he got back on operations before us, but think that he may have.

At long last the Flying Instructors School course was completed. It had been a tiring pressurised time and every night we collapsed into bed desiring only sleep. A considerable amount of rough edges had been removed from our flying and some of our acquired bad habits hopefully removed. We had started on 1 October and finished on 24 October. Within that period we had flown 16 hours dual and 35 hours as pilot in command, including 3 hours and 45 minutes at night. Actual flying days were only $16\frac{1}{2}$.

It was now back to our various OTUs. Sadly 57 OTU was on the move and about to leave Hawarden. I arrived back just in time to find myself helping in this major location shift. We were leaving our cosy well-established station and moving to a newly built aerodrome up in the bitter cold of Northumberland, just in time for the forthcoming winter.

XV

On Operations Again

From the air our new home of Eshott looked absolutely devoid of any redeeming feature unless the lack of trees could perhaps be said to be a safety factor for the approaches. The aerodrome looked precisely what it was, a huge clay scar carved out from the surrounding green fields. The runways appeared adequate both in length and width but alongside each was very unforgiving deep mud. All buildings, even the central administration block, were constructed on the Nissen hut pattern of half circles of corrugated iron.

This fast-tracked, strictly business-like aerodrome was situated about 20 miles north of Newcastle and a few miles north of the township of Morpeth. We were not far from the coast. In fact our take-off towards the east took us over a beautiful beach near Newbiggin. In the days that followed, we used to look at this sandy jewel as we flew over it wondering what it would be like in summer.

On 6 and 7 November the entries in my logbook were slightly different to the usual list of ops. I delivered a Spitfire to Eshott from Hawarden each day and was then flown back as a passenger with other pilots in an old Harrow aircraft. My contribution to the shuttle service was then over and our new intake of pilots under training were arriving. A considerable number of the staff from Hawarden also came with us although there were many new faces as well.

We still had our older styled Masters with the Rolls-Royce Kestrel engines for dual instructing, at least a couple of which were still without the modified tail units. The weather had been threatening and very cold. Meantime, though the mud had dried most of it remained as large lumps of clay, leaving no room for error. Everyone was cautioned to keep to the hard surfaces whether landing or taxiing. We still had the snow and ice to look forward to as winter was rapidly approaching.

There was one major difference with this OTU – and as far as we were concerned it was superb. We could not have wished for a better Wing Commander Flying. The comparison with the one we'd left behind at Hawarden was chalk and cheese. This man was the perfect choice. His presence made it a pleasure to be involved in the constructive help we aimed to give those pilots here for the 'fine tuning' they needed before facing the enemy in combat. He was a man who stood no nonsense and led by example. We knew that with him in command of flying operations this was going to be a great period of service in the RAF.

He was none other than Wing Commander Jumbo Gracie, who had shared so much with us back in Malta and was to a large degree responsible for the critical fast turn-around achieved with the second major delivery of Spitfires there. We knew he was determined to deliver real achievers from this station with the skills needed for combat.

Involvement with our new intake soon filled our days, firstly with dual flying in our Master aircraft. We understood the intense pressure these pilots were experiencing, their glances at those sleek Spitfires dispersed around our 'drome, the feeling as they climbed for the first time into the mock up Spitfire cockpit just as we had once done in what now seemed many moons ago.

There was one difference. This bunch was considerably more able in the mechanics of flying than we had been at the same period when we arrived at OTU early in 1941. Their flying was more polished, they climbed to exactly 500 feet as instructed, executed a perfect 90-degree turn, climbed a further 500 feet then turned again.

Wheels were brought up at the correct time; speeds were perfect as per the book. Most of their rate one (and above) turns were also perfect. In fact we could see that as future fighter pilots they would probably be dead on their first operation unless they stopped looking into their cockpits, stopped worrying about perfect turns and started to fly with their head outside their cockpits, ready to sometimes slam into tight steep turns just for the hell of it. They were mostly a great bunch to fly with and very soon got into the spirit of flying with great enjoyment.

I was pleasantly surprised at the very marginal weather in which we were given the "all clear" to continue flying. Quite often we had weather with very low cloud base and marginal visibility in which the selection of pilots to send flying under such conditions was left to us. It was quite rare to close down all flying. Our particular flight was commanded by a South African, Lieutenant Keith Kulman, a very pleasant man with whom to operate which made it a very happy flight.

On one occasion we did have a sad accident despite all our attempts to head it off. We heard through the grapevine that some of our students were planning to low fly under a bridge at a nearby river. They were a damned good group of pilots who had been doing very well with their training and were almost due to complete the course. A highly competitive group they included Poles, French, Belgians, New Zealanders and Australians.

Just before he went on leave, Keith called the group together for a strong pep talk on the extreme danger of bridge under-flying and in particular the one that was rumoured as the current challenge. He reminded them they still had a lot to learn about flying Spits. He then went on leave and left me in charge. The very next day the tragedy occurred.

Our delightful outstanding Belgian pilot, one of the best on the course, was killed trying to fly under the very bridge he had been warned never to attempt.

With our flight commander away I had the stressful duty of officiating on his behalf at a very lonely and sad funeral. Many years later I was driven past the place where our Eshott aerodrome had once thrived and aircraft roared overhead. The land had long been returned to farm paddocks and it was hard to see any indication that the aerodrome had ever been there. I have often wondered since if that small cemetery was still there and whether his Belgian relations ever found his place of rest. How strange that with all the deaths we witnessed and were closely associated with over the war years it was those stupid needless ones that affected us the most.

When each of our courses neared completion it was customary for the student pilots to challenge their instructors to a dogfight. The high calibre of some of those pilots, in particular the Poles and the Czechs, ensured that we were often faced with some very formidable aerobatics. Many had accumulated considerable hours of glider flying back in their home countries pre-war. In addition some had chalked up many powered flying hours and were skilful pilots eager to have a go.

The aerial combats were fun and usually the final advantage was with the instructors, as we knew intimately the limits and tricks that could be coaxed out of our beloved Spits even if they were of the older vintage. That said, we were often pushed to the extreme limits of our flying skills but it was good to know that the fighting capabilities of our graduates was so high.

A considerable amount of time was spent fine-tuning their formation flying, such an essential part of operating as a fighter pilot. From take-off to landing, whether climbing or descending, in cloud or clear, close formation was a must.

Every now and then we would strike a pilot competent in every way but for his inability to maintain formation. The instructor would coax him closer and closer and then suddenly he would almost reflexively veer away. We never failed with any of our students on that score but it got very close at times.

Apart from Wing Commander Gracie I had one other ex-Malta pilot with me at Eshott, Flying Officer McElroy, a Canadian. Between us we spread the gospel of line abreast operational formation flying, giving the students ample practice and tactical lectures. At that time there was no official acceptance of this formation in the UK and line astern was still being practised. However we, who had been through the combat furnace, were confident that the days of old school insistence on this dangerous type of formation were numbered. They just had to be!

The cold of a Northumberland winter with ice and snow struck us severely during December. Temporary thaws brought a sea of mud making it a most unpleasant station from which to operate. Social life wasn't too bad; we had some hilarious unofficial mess parties with the usual competitions for placing one's footprints on the ceiling. On occasion we organised transport into Newcastle where there were some very good places for fun dancing and dining. Having to remember that it was a long way to get back if you missed the transport was the only snag to some great nights out.

There were one or two instructors who had their own cars but petrol had to be carefully managed. The nearby township of Morpeth offered no special nightlife though in that respect I was lucky. Laddie Lucas, my ex-CO of 249 Squadron in Malta, had a married sister living in Morpeth. She and her husband, a Dr Stenhouse, made me wonderfully welcome. Being so far away from our own homes it meant a lot to us to be invited into someone else's home.

Gwen was a very warm person with a bright mind and ready sense of humour. Her husband was an ardent trout fisherman with an enormous collection of flies and other equipment necessary for the sport he so obviously loved. He spoke of two- and three-pound trout with pride. I'm not sure whether he really believed my own (perfectly true) reports of the huge New Zealand trout, two or three times bigger. In fact I felt a little embarrassed to state them as it sounded as though I was boasting. It was a problem I had struck before in the UK so I usually avoided the subject. Anyway I am sure that he already knew.

It was a happy home with the sound of laughter from happy young children. Strange how some magic moments can be created that stay with you for a lifetime. On one such occasion when I was staying with this very special family I was luxuriating in a hot bath in their home – in itself a privilege, as hot water was a severely rationed commodity. While lying there I heard the laughter and giggling of two of the Stenhouse children. They were just outside the door and the thought of a stranger in their bathroom seemed to give them immense amusement, so I called out to them telling them that I was in trouble and could not get out of the bath because my big toe was caught in the plughole.

This caused incredible excitement, agitation and much laughter and I could hear them scamper off yelling excitedly, "Mummy, Mummy, the man in the bath has got his big toe caught," then the sound of feet running back to the door to see if I was still in trouble. The reliving of that moment came many years later when I had the honour of being invited to England by Thames television for the *This Is Your Life* programme that featured Wing Commander Laddie Lucas.

There for the occasion were two of Gwen's now very much grown up children, a tall Robin and his now beautiful sister Barbara, and to my surprise they still remembered me as the man who'd had his big toe caught in their bath plughole. Gwen Stenhouse was also there and it was a wonderful reunion.

January 1943 brought increased activity in short bursts as the weather permitted. It was also an opportunity to flight-test our various aircraft. However it was generally a period of inactivity in which we were continually snowbound. Came February and at last it was back into operational instructing. We were also asked to do some unusual flights. On one occasion our station hosted members of the National Fire Service from Newcastle. They arrived in their formal uniforms and part of the hospitality was to take them flying – in particular over 'their territory'.

My passenger seemed very keen but nervous. I tucked him in and asked him if he wanted any aerobatics but shook his head vigorously with a vehement "No thanks". We took off and I flew him down over his territory near Newcastle. There was a fair amount of turbulence but reasonably mild. He was sitting in the front cockpit and seemed to be fine. I told him I would dive down close to his home base which I did and gave him a close view more or less at roof top height, calling out to him to see if he wanted to see anything else.

My only reply was a mumble. I could see him shaking his head so guessed he was not feeling so good. When I landed back it was to help out of the cockpit a very sick individual. He had made a terrible mess in the cockpit. I was quite embarrassed, having believed I was giving him a special treat while all the while he was in pure misery. I think that some of the others survived all right but not because of my flying.

The business of taking passengers on special flights added quite a pleasant diversion to our usual duties. However when the weather improved instructional flying became quite busy again and there was little spare time for jaunting about over the countryside. For a reason that I never did figure out the station 'Queen Bee' (our terminology for Waaf Senior Officer in charge) asked me if I would take her as a passenger on a special flight, assuring me she had cleared it with the Wing Commander Flying. I explained – reluctantly I might add – that I just didn't have the time available for some days and suggested someone else. She was not to be put off and said that she was prepared to wait, as I was to be the pilot. I was flattered no end but puzzled as to why she was so insistent.

A few days later the opportunity for the flight came and we took off in our only spare Master. Our destination according to my logbook was to Bulmar and return. I have no memory of the place whatsoever but I surely have vivid memories of our flight. Flying Officer Jackson was a very pleasant lady and an absolute flying enthusiast particularly for aerobatics. She confessed that it was for this reason she wanted to fly with me. A very flattering situation indeed even though entirely unjustified but she would not know that. So with my large inflated ego in control I was easily persuaded to take her through the usual basic manoeuvres of barrel rolls, slow rolls etc.

But I was doing them with deliberate care because I was acutely aware that this particular Master was without the tail modification and might develop an unpleasant spin if stalled. The pleasure and enthusiasm of this charming passenger was infectious. She kept on begging me to put the aircraft into a spin, saying she had never been in one. "Oh please go into a spin," she begged. Ego then took over and the responsibility of the pilot in command was forgotten.

I recalled pilots saying you could come out of a spin provided there was plenty of height and at the critical moment you opened your throttle wide and blasted air over your rudder to regain rudder control. The aircraft should then respond very slowly.

So height was the critical factor.

The countryside over which we were flying was bleak and very hilly. I warned my enthusiastic passenger to belt up tight, climbed to about 13,000 feet, lifted the nose, closed the throttle and waited for the inevitable juddering and the initial sinking feeling. Suddenly the aircraft dropped and violently whipped into an erratic yawing spin. Alarmingly, although the speed of the spinning action increased, the nose did not seem to want to drop which meant I couldn't get an airflow over the rudder.

My foot had been instinctively pressing hard on the rudder bar in opposition to the turning motion but so far without effect. We were losing height at an alarming rate. Opening the throttle initially didn't produce an immediate response from the engine apart from some spluttering and smoking. Finally the motor responded and I opened the throttle wide in short bursts. The vibration felt terrible but there was now a very slight feel of response from the rudder with massive vibration and a slight decrease in our violent spinning action. Slowly the nose dropped and at last the spinning felt more under control.

However, the rugged terrain below was approaching at an alarming rate. Fortunately, in fact very fortunately, we were heading down a valley and this gave just enough room to very delicately apply pressure to the elevators and she slowly responded. The aircraft still felt unstable and required very gentle handling to bring it back to normal flying attitude. Yes, the unmodified Masters can be brought out of a spin but, hell, never ever again for me.

It was a case of a very stupid pilot making the wrong decision, risking another life apart from his own, and this time getting away with it but only just. I knew that when we got back to base this aircraft had to be immediately listed as unserviceable until the airframe had been completely checked. After the beating it had just endured there was a strong possibility of structural damage.

There were bound to be questions asked as to why all the fuss but the requirements of operational safety left no choice. I also resolved to persuade the administration to have all Masters that needed the tail modification be given priority to action.

By the way, my charming passenger was thrilled and excited with her trip, especially her first experience of being in a spin. What a damned fool I had been. It would be funny if by some chance she were to read this part of my memoirs. What would her thoughts be now, I wonder.

During April the weather became noticeably warmer. Flying settled into a very busy routine. Even the North Sea was developing an attractive sparkle. Our lovely beach that we so regularly flew over was looking more inviting every day. There was talk amongst us that we should organise some transport, take our swimsuits and pay a visit. Unbeknownst to us, while we were still only talking about it, a group of Australians and New Zealanders had already set off for the 'great beach adventure'.

On arrival at that beautiful golden sandy beach the four stripped and, tense with excitement, raced each other to be the first to dive in, shouting with glee. Their exodus was even faster. They declared that the only thing which held them back from exiting faster still was their inability to walk on water.

The water was barely above freezing level or, as one put it, brass monkey temperature. Even after the first shock they had difficulty believing the experience and went back to dip toes in just to make sure they hadn't imagined it. They hadn't!

After such a negative report I never did venture onto that beach. Regardless, it really was a beautiful coast and we often flew over it with enjoyment. In particular the famous Farne Islands which brought back stories of heroine Grace Darling. This particular area was included as part of our low flying zone.

The advance of summer also meant a considerable increase in offensives by the RAF Fighter and Bomber Commands. Some of our longer serving instructors were receiving postings back to operational squadrons and I began to hope that perhaps my turn would come soon.

One morning nearing the end of April I received instructions to report to Jumbo Gracie. Great! This might be the news that I was waiting for, I thought. I knocked on his office door and entered. He greeted me with his usual friendly welcome, opened a very official looking form in front of him, cleared his throat and said:

"Congratulations! You have been posted to Canada as an instructor. The indication is for promotion and the posting is to take place immediately."

I stood in front of him completely stunned, almost too shocked to reply.

"Is this official? Do I have to go? Can I refuse and request a different posting?" I said at last. He sat quietly looking at me with his inevitable cigarette holder clamped in his teeth – as usual with no cigarette in it.

"Yes," he said. "This is an order from Training Command. You know full well the formal procedure and the consequence of refusing. I will ask you to leave this room and when I call you back I will again restate this order. If you refuse I will have no alternative but to place you under arrest."

The twinkle in his eyes belied the seriousness of his words.

"You had better think very carefully before I recall you," he added. "I suggest that before you return with your answer it may be a wise move for you to take a few days' leave. A Spitfire could be made available for your use should you need it. I'm sure you could benefit by contacting or visiting your friends in the New Zealand Squadron at present stationed at Westhampnett near Tangmere."

Immediately after this shock interview I contacted my friend Reg Grant who was the current CO of 485 NZ Squadron, only to learn he was about to leave the squadron to commence a tour of Canada and the USA. However he said to leave the matter with him and he would see what could be done. A few days later I was again summoned to the Jumbo's office. After entering and duly saluting he invited me to take a seat. I did so, expecting the worst.

"Quite extraordinary," he said, smiling broadly. "I have just received an alternate posting for you. There has been a recent change of command in the New Zealand Squadron and you have been requested to rejoin them. However, meantime you are to report to 118 Squadron at Coltishall in No. 12 Group. Your other posting for Canada still remains with me, but not surprisingly I have a Canadian volunteer who will qualify for that immediate posting."

How he managed the change for me I will never know. As I left his office his last words to me were: "Good luck, Rae – but I'll bet you I'll be back on ops before you."

It was a bet I would have lost. Yes, he was back on operations before me. He managed to get himself posted to a Mosquito squadron operating over Berlin and tragically he was killed on one of those hazardous trips. The RAF lost a wonderful and brave man in Wing Commander Jumbo Gracie.

My service as instructor at Operations Training Unit Eshott was completed on 28 April. On 3 May I was flying with 118 Squadron from Coltishall.

Top: Members of Course 5C, Ohakea, 31 January 1941. From left to right, back row: Carpenter, McHardy, Rae, Coakley, Hamlin, Reid, Crowhurst, Lowson; middle: Duff, Page, Boucher, McIvor, Farrow, Blewett, White, Holding, Sutherland; front: Gray, Phillips, Whittacker, Grumberly, Hesketh, Lange, Garnham, Barry, Dean and Taylor. Over one third pictured would not survive the war years.

Middle: September 1940. Flight B Course 5C, New Plymouth. Ready to begin flying those frisky Tiger Moths. Author pictured centre.

Left: Crossing the Atlantic in the *Derbyshire*. Jack used this seaman's bunk when he was on duty.

No. 4. COURSE
R.A.F., Heston   May 28th, 1941

Back Row: Sgt. Collinson, Sgt. Batchlor, Sgt. Barbour, Sgt. Baz, Sgt. Clazton, Sgt. Evans, Sgt. Campbell, Sgt. Bremner, Sgt. Phillips, Sgt. McDonald, Sgt. Cameron, Sgt. McIvor, Sgt. Rouleau, Sgt. Dean,
Middle Row: Sgt. Fish, Sgt. Carpenter, Sgt. Ford, Sgt. Spenge, Sgt. Preece, Sgt. Ames, Sgt. McCloud, Sgt. Hood, Sgt. Rae, Sgt. Gordeau, Sgt. MacAdam, Sgt. Crist, Sgt. Rickman.
Front Row: P./O. Busbridge, P./O. Crakanthorp, 2nd/Lt. Mitchell, 2nd/Lt. Booth F./Lt. Jaffrey, W./C. Kent, D.F.C., A.F.C., G./Capt. Jones, D.S.O., M.C., D.F.C., M.M., S./Ldr. Llewellin, 2nd/Lt. Montgomery, 2nd/Lt. Gross, P./O. Baker, F./O. Cookson.

Top: No. 4 Course, RAF Heston, May 28, 1941. The course that introduced the pilots to Spitfires.

Bottom: Officers' Mess Dinner at Eshott

OTU. Jumbo Gracie is on 'top table' extreme right and the author is sitting just in front of him with back to camera.

Top: At Redhill. On the wing is Sgt Harvey Sweetman. In the cockpit is the author indulging in some modest boasting. Standing looking doubtful are P/O Crawford-Compton, P/O Francis, Sgt Cochrane, P/O Clouston and Sgt Kronfeld.

Bottom: Pilots at Redhill. On the plane,

from left to right: F/Lt Strang, Sgts McNeil, Frecklington, P/O Francis, Sgt Krebs; standing: P/O Macleod, Sgts Cochrane, Griffith, P/O Crawford-Compton, Sqn Ldr Knight, Sgt Kronfeld, P/O Clouston; sitting: Sgt Rae, P/O Barrett, Sgt Sweetman.

Top: Sergeant Pilots 485 (Redhill). From left: Russell, Sweetman, Thomas, Maney, Goodwin, Porter. Front: Rae and Ralph.

Bottom: The author with 'Griff' Griffith and Harvey Sweetman outside 'Fieldways', the NCOs' sleeping quarters at Redhill.

Top: Squadron members at Kenley. On wings, from left to right: P/O Clouston, Sgt Liken, Flt Sgt Goodlet, P/O Palmer; on nacelle: Sgt Robson, P/O Gaskin; standing: Sgt Shaw, P/O Mackie, Sgt McNeil, P/Os Crawford-Compton, Hume, Pattison, Sgt Rae, P/O Killian, Adjutant, Sqn Ldr Wells, P/O Gibbs, Sgt Russell, P/O Shand; kneeling: Sgt D. Brown, P/O Checketts, Sgt S. Browne, Sgt Leckie.

Bottom left and right: The squadron crests dear to the author's heart, 249 and 485. The 485 motto says 'We Fight on Forever.'

Top: A Spitfire being hoisted on board USS *Wasp*, on the way to Malta.

(US National Archives)

Bottom left: A Spitfire taking off from USS *Wasp* on 20 April 1942, prior to the 4 hour

10 minute flight to Malta, 667 miles away.

(US National Archives)

Bottom right: Stan Grant DFC watches 109s above the airfield. *(Lucas collection)*

Top: Watching the action from the mess quarters at Xara Palace, Mdina. Left to right: Pete Rathie, Raoul Daddo-Langlois, Ozzie Linton and Buck McNair.

(Lucas collection)

Middle and bottom left: Air Vice-Marshal Hugh Lloyd and Group Captain Woodhall. *(Lucas collection)*

Middle right: Paul Brennan, Jumbo Gracie and Ray Hesslyn on Malta. A great trio. *(Lucas collection)*

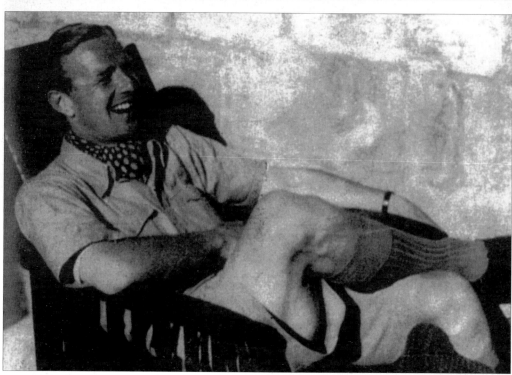

Top: Ozzie Linton (left) and Les Watts of 249 Squadron.
(Lucas collection)

Bottom: Sqn Ldr Laddie Lucas, the new CO of 249 Squadron.
(Lucas collection)

Top left: S/Ldr Lord David Douglas-Hamilton (CO 603 Squadron).

Top right: 249 get another 'confirmed'. The wreckage of a Ju 88 on Malta.

Middle: 'Defender of Malta'. Another Chrisp painting records the heroics.

Left: ' "Boss", he said, preserving at least some reverence for his commanding officer, "I couldn't fault that one." It was the ultimate accolade.' Sgt George Beurling (centre), S/Ldr Laddie Lucas on the right with 249, August 1942.

Bread	11	ozs
Biscuits	1	"
Flour	1	"
Tinned meat	4	"
M. & V.	1	"
Steak & Kidney (tinned)	1	"
Bacon (tinned)	-	
Cheese (tinned)	-	
Chocolate	-	
Milk (tinned)	1	"
Sugar	1½	"
Tea	½	"
Salt	¼	"
Sardines	-	
Salmon	-	
Herrings	-	
Pilchards	-	
Potatoes (tinned)	1	"
Onions	-	
Vegetables (tinned)	2	"
Vegetables (fresh)	2	"
Tomatoes	-	
Peas (processed)	1	"
Peas (dried)	-	
Marmite	-	
Cooking fat	-	
Jam	½	"
Fruit (tinned)	-	
Fruit (fresh)	1	"
Meat and fish paste	-	
Margarine	1	"
Cigarettes	40 per week	
Tobacco	2 ozs per week	
Matches	1 box per week	

(Reproduced from the **Official History of the Second World War, Army Medical Services, Campaigns in General History,** *pages 623-4.)*

Top left: Takali aerodrome, base to 249, under attack.

Top right: Soukup. The Sudeten Czech

Me 109 pilot who shot the author down.

Bottom: Daily rations on Malta, Spring to Autumn 1942.

Top: The adversaries. FW 190 (left) and Me 109F (right).

Middle: August 1943. Six Me 109s were destroyed by these four pilots on one operation: Sqn Ldr Johnnie Checketts (3 destroyed), P/O Bruce Gibbs (1), F/O Jack Rae (1) and P/O 'Tommy' Tucker (1) are congratulated by 'Bill' Jordan, the New Zealand High Commissioner.

Left: F/O Gray Stenborg and P/O Jack Rae just back in London from Malta wearing Maltese crosses. Soon afterwards the wearing of these crosses was banned.

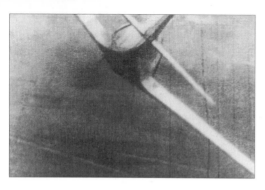

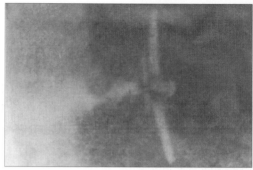

Top left and right: July 15, 1943. Author's combat film showing one FW 190 destroyed (top) and one probable (below).

Middle left: The progression of desires as a POW? This is the interpretation of one of the author's fellow inmates.

Middle right: The lament of aircrew prisoners of war, copied from a fellow POW.

Above left: The Polish banknote so carefully treasured by a female 'forced labourer', given to the author as a way of saying thanks.

Right: A rest in the blizzard. Some of the 10,000 Allied Air Force POWs from Stalag Luft III sink exhausted in the snow. This 95-kilometre forced march in January 1945 was perhaps the worst episode of their captivity.

XVI
Biggin Hill

It was an exhilarating feeling that stayed with me as I packed my meagre belongings and said farewells to my many Eshott friends. Soon I would be back into front-line operations. In anticipation, the adrenalin was already flowing in my veins. Soon I would be flying with guns that had been armed; soon I would again be part of a team standing listening to a briefing on the next foray into enemy territory, gazing at the large map showing the operational area.

The briefings were designed to cover all the details we needed including the height of our operation and any possible dangers we could expect. I also knew that again the palms of my hands would be breaking out in that uncontrollable sweat prior to taking off, though once flying it would be completely gone. There was also the comradeship, the indefinable bond that develops within an operational squadron, whether in the air or at play in the local pub or Soho clubs. That's why I was so thrilled as I set off for Coltishall in No.12 Group, the first step back to No.11 Group and my old NZ Squadron.

Hey there, Jack, did you really have all those exciting thoughts and immense pleasure of going back onto operations? Hell no – of course I didn't. All that self-analysis is the result of years of hindsight after the event, trying to give some form of logic to the actions and motivations of youth. We were then young men engulfed in an overwhelming sense of adventure and challenge, serving in the magnificent RAF against a ruthless enemy who had to be stopped and would be defeated. With that picture in our heads we did not need any other reason.

On arrival the procedure was to meet the CO and squadron members. My stay with them was going to be short but at the time I was unaware of this and looked forward to getting to know everyone. The next day it was the usual and necessary flight.

My logbook entry records it as a Sector Recco, a means of familiarising oneself with the locality. In the first week with them I was surprised that twice on one day there were scrambles as bandits came into our area though no contact was made.

After a couple of weeks with the squadron I was placed on a 'Dawn Readiness'. This usually meant only the minor inconvenience of having to get up in the dark and cold, get into your flying gear, stumble into a waiting transport, drive down to the aerodrome, check that your parachute, maps, etc., were all ready and by the aircraft, say a sleepy good morning to the ground crew, note that the engine had been warmed up for take-off and then after putting on your Mae West crawl under a blanket and go back to sleep.

Anyway, I thought as I prepared for dreamland, this was sleepy 12 Group. Nothing much is likely to happen here. My companion pilot, a friendly fellow who was new to operations, seemed nervous. However he followed my example and also curled up for some sleep. We had hardly had time to close our eyes when there was a jangle on the 'phone and the buzzer went for an immediate scramble.

This was incredible – like old times. It was still partially dark and take-off was up into a grey sky. There was no wind and no time wasted taxiing onto a runway. Once clear of the dispersal area we opened throttle and took off across the runway: there was plenty of room on this huge aerodrome. My number two was following but a long way back and this was not a time for waiting.

Control was already directing and advising there were two bandits at 25,000 feet heading towards our area of Norfolk. Previous experience with this type of scramble did not fill me with anticipation that we would find our quarry but it was a necessary warning to our enemy to keep away.

The Spit VB performed well at climbing up to the 20,000 feet height but would slow up somewhat above that. We were still climbing at full throttle, my number two drifting back slightly. Just as we reached the 20,000 feet mark the controller started getting very excited.

"Can't you see them? You are almost next to them. You must be able to see them!"

My head was spinning around like a top. Just above, there were some thin stratus clouds but nothing in sight. And then, damn it, there was one FW190 glistening in the sunshine streaming through the cloud. He was at least 1500 feet directly above me, flying fast in a nose down configuration and outside my range.

If I fired at him it would only be a wild gesture. It would also mean a 90-degree deflection and an immediate stall of my own aircraft which was now in an almost vertical climb and would have to be brought slightly over the vertical before firing.

A few split seconds of indecision and he was well past me, then suddenly the second FW190 appeared but even further away. My number two was still struggling up behind and arrived as I reluctantly turned and looked at two diminishing dots disappearing over the North Sea and back to their base. If we had been flying Spit IX Bs we could have chased and caught them. Oh well, I thought, we can now talk about the ones that got away and enjoy a good breakfast.

The controller had made one of those rare successful interceptions. Well almost: it was not the most gratifying feeling to suddenly find yourself 1500 feet or more beneath the enemy and on the verge of a stalled condition. Just another few minutes of climbing and the story might have been vastly different. Although I experienced many other close encounters over the combat years for some reason that single split second indecision has always left me wondering and of course now I will never know.

Maybe I should have fired. I would certainly have stalled and gone into a spin, that's for sure, and then my number two might have been at the mercy of two FW190s. Again I might just have fluked a hit; perhaps, perhaps.

I did very little further flying with 118 Squadron. My last operation with them was as escort for a flight of Beauforts attacking E-boats. My stay with 118 had been from 3 May 1943, until 17 May, just 14 days. The request made when back in Eshott to re-join my old 485 NZ Squadron had finally borne fruit and although quite happy serving with 118 Squadron I was delighted to return.

The 485 (New Zealand) Squadron was at that time stationed at Merston which was a satellite of Tangmere from which 486 (New Zealand) Typhoon Squadron was also operating. Des Scott was their CO and Reg Baker the CO of 485. Our Flight Commanders were John Pattison and Marty Hume. The officers' living quarters were at a gracious large home and Chichester was the nearest town.

The squadron was equipped with Spitfire VBs, the clipped wing version. This modification took away some of the Spitfire's beauty of line that we had grown to love but results as far as performance was concerned were quite remarkable. They had a fast rate of climb up to 6,000 ft and at lower levels a considerable increase in speed.

A point worth noting here is the incredibly conservative approach that Rolls-Royce had towards giving pilots the full potential power of those beautiful engines. In all the earlier Spitfires we used to gaze at that sealed 'gate' on the throttle with a certain amount of awe, aware that if we were ever desperate enough to crash through the gate we could only sustain that extra awesome power for a limit of five minutes. Whenever the seal was broken explanations were required.

Now all of a sudden it was a case of let's live recklessly, with full maximum power on call at will. The super-charger fan blades had been shortened, releasing a greater amount of power for low-level use but sacrificing performance at higher levels. And while at low level we were now quite a potent force, coming into production as the perfect answer to the FW190s, at the higher levels the spectacular Spitfire IXB was master.

The air war tactics were now gradually changing in our favour. In the earlier period of the war we had been forced to operate with a compromise aircraft that could perform reasonably well at all heights. The Germans on the other hand came out with their 109Fs, superb aircraft that could fly higher and outperform us at those altitudes. Later the FW190s came into production. This was an extremely high performance aircraft, which for some time gave us major problems.

However, it was not all doom and gloom. We simply had to operate against them with great care. We still had faith in the Spitfire and the backroom boys who kept continually modifying this amazing aircraft. They seemed always able to provide answers, though my enthusiasm for the clipped-wing Spit VB and its lively low level performance on one occasion got a few of us into a certain amount of hot water with the top brass.

At that stage line astern formation was still the norm throughout 11 Group Fighter Command. When would they ever learn, I often wondered? I preached the line abreast gospel wherever and whenever I could, explaining at length its advantages to the fellows in 485 and also to Des Scott. What was needed was some hands-on work so I persuaded Marty Hume to let me take him with his flight for some practice line abreast flying. After a few hours of flying they became quite proficient.

About this time Des Scott happened to pay us another visit in which he told us the Typhoons had the speed and firepower on the cross-Channel attacks to inflict a fair amount of damage. The problem was that the defending Luftwaffe then came up in force and the Typhoons had to fly hell for leather home lacking the manoeuvrability to turn and fight while the Germans nibbled at them.

We got around to discussing the potential of our clipped winged Spits at the low level that the Typhoons were operating. With these Spits flying line-abreast and arriving just as the Typhoons were on the way back, we could with a little luck have quite a party with the marauding Luftwaffe. It was all covertly arranged; we would have a flight of four VBs ready to join the Typhoons on their next show.

We didn't have long to wait. Des phoned to say there was a dawn show the next morning so three of Marty's flight together with myself had our aircraft serviced and ready, and were just about going to bed for the dawn operation when Des phoned again. It was all off. The show was cancelled and there was hell to pay at Group. The heavy hand of discipline never reached down to me or to Marty but Des Scott stopped a rocket, as did Squadron Leader Reg Baker. The reason given for all the administrative fury was breach of security. Fortunately Des Scott had shoulders broad enough to weather the storm.

We were involved in some various Escort Covers during May and June with no particularly hectic combat with the enemy. Then we became immersed in a concentrated exercise of mock deck landings. An area the size of a carrier flight deck was painted onto a section of a runway at Tangmere and we were given a naval 'batman' to guide and control our 'deck landings'. It required a slow approach, virtually hanging on our props.

The difficulty was that the long nose of the Spitfire made visibility extremely limited and complete trust had to be given to the batman. We also didn't like the feel of flying a Spitfire virtually sagging slowly down in a partially stalled condition. Surprising ourselves, we soon became quite adept at it, gaining complete confidence in our batman who was a very competent and patient operator.

After some seven practice flights we flew to Ayr in Scotland on 16 June. On 23 June we boarded the carrier HMS *Argus* where we had our first look at a couple of modified Spitfires with landing hooks. They certainly couldn't be regarded as navy frontline Seafires: in fact they looked very grubby and uncared for with the engine covers rattling. The only difference was that hook under the belly.

I have wondered since if perhaps it was only nerves that made us look at those aircraft with suspicion and distrust. The HMS *Argus* was an old ship that had been part of the Italian navy in World War I. She had been converted to an aircraft carrier with a very short flight deck. And that wasn't the only problem we discovered. The Fleet Air Arm CO, a very helpful, cheery chap and an excellent host, explained to us as tactfully as possible that the Old Man – in other words the Captain of this obsolete ship of the Royal Navy – did not particularly like any flying personnel, be they navy or air force, and had no faith in their effectiveness.

He had advised 'Wings,' our Lieutenant Commander (Flying), that he would not sail the *Argus* above 10 knots regardless of how much wind there might or might not be over the deck. That certainly didn't make us feel very welcome. We also infuriated him by not standing to attention as we sailed past more senior ships. In fact I did hear that he just about had a fit when he saw one of the boys having a nervous pee over the side before his turn to fly. We sailed out into the Firth of Clyde past numerous ships including giant battleships and cruisers of the Royal Navy and then set a steady course sailing past the beautiful island of Arran.

The seas were calm which was fine for us but there was only a slight wind which meant that with the ship stooging along at 10 knots we would need a lot of this limited deck to get down. Those hooks had better hold! As it happened, there were one or two nail-biting moments but we all did our required four landings and take-offs without incident. I still have the signed statement in my logbook from the Lieutenant Commander (Flying), which states: "Passed Initial Deck Landing Training – 4 Landings HMS *Argus* 23rd June, 1943."

We wondered just what the reason was behind this very special exercise. Some thought that a possible landing in Norway was anticipated. If so, I think we were fortunate it didn't take place. Whatever it might have been it would almost certainly have been a shaky do. Just as well we never found out.

We returned to the aerodrome at Ayr and next day flew back to Tangmere where two interesting events were happening which concerned me personally. The first was to learn on arrival that a certain New Zealand flight sergeant was giving a lot of trouble to the station warrant officer – in fact he was detained in the guard house.

The troublesome sergeant turned out to be my friend William (Bill) Harcourt-Jones. I should have guessed before I was given his name. Bill meant trouble wherever he was but he was still one hell of a great guy. He'd become rather stroppy after a harrowing night crash in a burning Hurricane. However on our request the station warrant officer relented and let him loose so that we could celebrate together.

The other major news on the station was that fellow New Zealander Jim Gunn (he and I had been on 5 Course back in NZ) had just had a pretty hectic wedding on the station and left on his honeymoon only the day before. I was to meet him in London the very next week, a meeting that would prove to be of some importance and embarrassment in my later service career.

Things were moving rapidly for us. We had just returned from our trip to Scotland sailing with the Royal Navy to learn we would be moving immediately to Biggin Hill and given the latest Spitfire IXBs to fly. We were electrified by the news. The station commander at Biggin was the renowned South African Squadron Leader 'Sailor' Malan, our top-scoring pilot until Johnnie Johnson overtook him in 1944. Our Wing Commander Flying was to be fellow New Zealander Alan Deere and Johnny Checketts was our new CO. No time was wasted. By 1 July 1943 we had moved to our new base and a day later we were flying the new IXBs.

XVII

Permanently Grounded

There was something magical to me and I suspect to everyone in our squadron in our arrival at Biggin Hill. There are many other Fighter Command stations in Britain with equally proud records of achievement, from some of which we had already operated. However there was still something very special in looking around what was to be our base and seeing our future IXB Spitfires standing in front of Dispersal headquarters just waiting for us to fly them.

And if you believe that you'll believe anything. What I have just described is so much pie in the sky. Many years have elapsed since that day and memories have clouded with imagined ideas of what we probably should have appreciated about our transfer to Biggin. In fact I don't think there were any special thoughts at all or comments from anyone apart from a general pragmatic observation that it was great to get our hands on a damned good aircraft.

The first day included a meeting in the briefing room with Group Captain Sailor Malan and Wing Commander Alan Deere to update us on tactics and other matters of procedure. And then the greatest news of all was given to us as though it was a brand new discovery, given with the ingenuous reason that it was to help us adapt to our much faster new aircraft. Yes, at last Fighter Command had relented and we were now going to fly line abreast – or a very close relative referred to as Finger Four. At long last we were to operate as a potent fully aggressive force.

The next day we were up and flying the new Spits. The difference in performance was dramatic. There was no doubt that our brilliant British engineers had struck gold this time. Up to this period of the war they had done wonders in constantly improving our Spitfire but this time it was a giant leap forward.

There was a noticeable extra surge of power from the moment of take-off. The 700 hp Merlin gave us a climbing rate of 5,000 feet a minute allowing us to reach 25,000 feet in five minutes with a ceiling of about 44,000 feet. When we approached 12,500 feet there was a jump in power as extra blowers in the supercharger came into play.

At full throttle there was a noticeable whip in the front section of the engine cowling. This was something I never felt at ease with and preferred to switch off that function until after climbing past the 12,500 feet, then close the throttle before switching on to the 'monster'. The cherry on the top of all this was that our top speed was well in excess of 400 mph straight and level.

And while still ecstatic with the performance of the IXBs we found we had been given another wonder, one which would at last eliminate a major drawback that had plagued us in all our contacts with the Luftwaffe. This was direct fuel injection or the Bedix Stromberg system. Incorporation of this system of fuel supply into our engines meant that we could push the control stick directly forward (applying anti-G force) and dive without the engine cutting. Our enemy had always been able to do this and the quick dive had always been their standard form of evading us. We on the other hand had to bank before diving thus losing precious response time. Clearly the forthcoming air wars were going to be vastly different for us, at least until our wily enemy found counters to our changes in tactics.

Firstly a short picture of the situation at Biggin: we had replaced 611 Squadron (West Lancashire Squadron) who together with the Free French 'Alsace Squadron,' led by Commandant René Mouchotte, had not long before our arrival shared the honour of shooting down the 1,000th confirmed enemy aircraft for Biggin Hill.

Each squadron had shot one down during the same operation but as to which shot the 1,000th was ignored and the honour shared. Biggin Hill pilots of both squadrons enjoyed a massive party held at the Dorchester in London.

The French had the ability to organise the most superb wines for any party, as we were to find out later. We would now share Biggin Hill and all our operations with our Free French comrades. Our officers' mess was superbly situated with large windows looking out onto a long inviting swimming pool while beyond and below stretched a tree-enshrouded landscape in a most beautiful part of England.

Our sleeping quarters were adequate and ideal and situated quite close to the mess. The nearest very popular pub was known as the 'Jail'. A quick trip to the suburb of Bromley enabled us to catch an electric train, which took us to the centre of London in a very short time. Croydon and Purley were also favourite playgrounds, in particular the Purley Ice Rinks.

We were also fortunate to have two American pilots, Major Jim Haun and Captain (Pappy) Walker. Sadly Pappy was killed on 14 July after which Lieutenant Travis joined us. These men had been sent to join our squadron to gain experience. We thought ourselves very fortunate to have them because they brought with them a Jeep with an apparently endless supply of petrol, which provided a useful means of transport for all sorts of non-military operations. Lieutenant Travis flew with me as my number two on a few occasions, and in American parlance was a great wingman. I recall that one operation of ours was extremely exciting and successful.

I was also struck by the professional look of the Intelligence and Briefing

Rooms. Elsewhere these were often corners of some draughty Nissen hut. At Biggin they were impressive. The Intelligence Room was covered with maps, easy chairs technical papers, confidential Air Ministry publications and photos.

This room gave access to the Briefing Room which sported a huge map of the target area, completely covering the wall behind the briefing platform. This map included the south-east of England, London, the Thames, the Channel, the North Sea, Holland, Belgium and France as far west as Cherbourg. On the map a red ribbon joined Biggin Hill to the targets we were to be attacking for that particular day.

Call signs for the day were arranged. Our wing leader would have one name, and each of our squadron leaders their own call signs. Times would be set and watches synchronised. Sometimes the 'show' would follow soon after the briefing but with others there would be time to stroll back to the mess and relax, or try to. Some might have a beer, the French more likely to have some of their Algerian wine. In fact they seemed able to drink this potent wine, as we would water. We found that when we had lunch with them a glass of this wine was invariably placed in front us. This was fine if there was no flying to follow. But we found the wine made us sleepy so on days with operations following lunch we avoided the offer with a "thanks but no thanks".

In general I found the French friendly though we didn't personally socialise with them other than at meal times and briefings. I guess we both tended to stay within our own groups. There were some damned fine pilots amongst them and my previous mistaken idea that most Frenchmen were physically small and generally excitable was completely nullified by this group. They came in all sizes and types just like any of us. Amongst them was one superb pilot with an outstanding personality who took as his name a well known French brandy. We understood that many of them had false names just in case they were shot down and captured which could then endanger their families in France. He was a six foot plus Frenchman who would operate with us as a fighter pilot and then disappear every now and then, be dropped into France on some highly secret mission, and then return to his flying.

He must have been someone of immense courage. Sadly he finally failed to return from one of these missions. I can only make these comments from hearsay, as what we gleaned about this French officer was never confirmed. Probably we should not have even been told the little we did know of such activities.

In early July there was little activity except to gain experience with our new aircraft, put in some cine-gun shooting practice, formation flying and air-to-ground firing practice. On 13 July we took part in a Rodeo to the Abbeville area. There were reports of a large concentration of enemy fighters but we didn't make contact with them, leaving our test of strength with the new IXBs still to come.

On 16 July we escorted United States Marauders to Abbeville. This was a very different situation in which the FW190s came at us in droves. We met them head on and dived after those trying to break through our defence to the bombers. In spite of their initial height advantage, which previously meant it was almost impossible to catch them, this was suddenly becoming a very different ball game.

We caught up to them rapidly. As we closed most of them lifted the noses of their aircraft, expecting to climb away from us. But oh no, we found ourselves flying at our own perfect altitude range, something that had once been just for them. Our rapid rate of climb must have been a nightmare for them – this was where they expected to have room to re-position and come down on us again. And when caught on a level plain their usual response was simply to zap away from us with just a push forward on the nose and a quick dive. This was their response on this occasion. Not any more my nasty Nazis, I thought.

We pushed our sticks forward and followed them down with ease in a vertical dive. Not being used to that manoeuvre and the anti-G forces, this action to us was initially disconcerting but here we were doing it and going like crazy and gaining. Then this particular Jerry nearly caught me out. He suddenly levelled out and while I was setting my sights on him to fire and clearing my head from the G forces he must have completely closed his throttle.

I came in dangerously close and at that range the scattered shells hit him from the engine area to the cockpit. There were some very uneasy moments of my own. I almost shot in front of him and, if he was still alert and he probably was, I might have bought it. I guess it was his last desperate effort before he ran out of evasive tactics. My cine-gun pictures taken at that instant showed his fuselage looming large and very close. On the same operation I was fortunate enough to compete with another FW190 with a similar result but in a much shorter time.

Throughout these memoirs I have always tried to avoid too much detail and blow-by-blow descriptions of combats. Those were violent times in the air wars and fighter pilots were renowned for regaling their unfortunate listeners with vivid descriptions such as, "There I was upside down in cloud with nothing on the clock surrounded by enemy fighters." That sort of talk was in most cases reserved for internal conversations. Remember we were very much hyped-up young men talking tactics amongst ourselves and often using this as a way of relieving stress.

We rarely thought of the person in those enemy planes but only of the plane itself. However now I find after all these years that when I get caught up in re-living a particular combat such as the one just described I cannot help but be acutely aware there was a person involved. Well, after having that little bit of morbid philosophy, let's get back to the events of those days.

These were eventful in the extreme both with our intense combat flying and our fabulous fun on and off the station. I recall a wonderful party at the sergeants' mess. It was incredible how many beautiful Waafs appeared as if by magic when such an event occurred. These incredibly hard-working women were employed either on the station or the nearby Operations Quarters where the positions of all our aircraft were plotted and also those of the enemy, and where instructions and warnings were relayed back to us within the combat zones. Those working in our Operations Quarters were a vital part of all our operations. In fact all the Waafs wherever found throughout the RAF proved to be highly dedicated and invaluable beyond measure.

Then the French squadron decided it would be a good idea to organise one of their famous parties at the Dorchester. There was no particular reason but it was one extraordinary party. I even got involved again with a motorbike. I've forgotten the horsepower but it was a BSA down in the 'gutless' classifications (2 hp or thereabouts) bought off Johnnie Houlton for a few pounds. It went well most of the time but just occasionally it would refuse to start.

One evening on the way back from Bromley railway station it just stopped. Doug Brown was with me and we were both very happy with the effects of earlier imbibing in the clubs of London. Doug must have been particularly so, as he pushed me for miles while I sat on the bike fiddling with the controls. Incredibly he made no complaints, in fact seemed to be having an hilarious time. His stamina on that night was quite amazing but finally the obstinate motor started and we were back at Biggin again. Doug, as I remember, never again accepted a ride.

The squadron also possessed a very large six-cylinder motorcar. The make, I think, was a Wolseley. I say the squadron but it really belonged to a syndicate of members and was acquired during the days at Merston when Reg Grant was the CO. Gary Barnett seemed to be a prime shareholder. It had one sole purpose and that was for any member of the squadron to borrow when there were occasions for intimate, very personal meetings with the fair sex when privacy was a prime requirement. It was understood that the user or users had to replace the petrol swallowed by this enormous gas-guzzler.

Known as the "Silent Six," it had been in operation some time before I rejoined the squadron so I'm not familiar with the original history. However there were plenty of stories, probably better censored, floating around about the exploits in that ancient car. Among all these activities there was now talk of renewing our famed visits to Oxted where our incredible New Zealand World War I veteran, John Ferguson ('Fergie'), would challenge various wealthy members of his community to open their homes and host us en masse. A rough diamond, he'd been wounded at Ypres in 1917, married his nurse, and settled at Oxted nine miles away. Having adopted our squadron, he would also persuade nurses from the local hospital to join in the parties. He only made one request to those hosting: that parties were not for officers only, but should include NCOs. Local residents had the greatest respect for him, and so did we.

Yes, there was still a war going on in case the wrong impression is gained from that preamble. In fact the air war was intensifying at a dramatic rate.

Logbook entries for the balance of 25 July onward list some nine major offensives in five days. Some of these far into enemy territory with names that today sound romantic or fascinating. Each day and twice a day that imposing red ribbon would stretch across the map from Biggin Hill to places such as Ghent, Armentières, Zeebrugge, Triqueville, Amsterdam, Fairville.

Each of those attacks brought up the enemy in strength but they were now operating with more caution and certainly far less arrogance. However we knew that our tenacious enemy would have been doing some deep thinking and we had best be careful.

One high level combat during that period is perhaps worth recounting. On 28 July we were operating as High Cover to Triqueville with Tommy Tucker as my number two. There had been a noticeable change as enemy attacks were now made in greater numbers and only with considerable initial height advantage in order to enable them to close at greater speed. In most cases if they did not succeed with their first attack they just kept on going away as fast as possible. However on this occasion as we were operating as High Cover we had the time to chase and catch up with some of them.

The first swarm of enemy aircraft were FW190s. With our loose and fast formations we were attacking immediately and breaking off into pairs. Tommy was right with me as we dived onto them. Suddenly as so often happens in dogfights the sky emptied of every aircraft though in this case not quite. Three of us were still crazily zooming all over the place, one a desperate FW190 trying every trick in the book to shake me off and Tommy Tucker sticking tenaciously behind. I was amazed and delighted to find Tommy still with us. His ability to stay in the number two spot was remarkable, enabling me to concentrate entirely on the enemy in front knowing that my tail was covered.

The 190 pilot made it almost impossible to obtain an accurate deflection shot, added to which was the extreme buffeting caused by the speeds we were flying and the G forces involved. As a result my cannon ammunition was used up by what can only be seen as inaccurate shooting. Strikes were made on various parts of the 190 but not enough to destroy it.

The combat had begun to worry me as we had moved a long way from the original target area and were travelling far into France, inviting deep trouble. We were also down to a very low level. Just as I was about to break away and call Tommy up for us to get the blazes out of there the 190 suddenly slowed right down so that I shot up beside him and could see him silhouetted in his cockpit. I think he was slumped forward but will never be certain.

I pulled away and called out to Tommy to take over and fire. Almost instantaneously the 190 dived down smoking and hit the ground just in front of a church in a small village. It was a vividly haunting picture that will stay with me forever. Tommy and I had a long and dangerous flight back home to Biggin with very little fuel left in our tanks.

The intensity and the entire approach to the air war had changed. There were no longer limitations of distance, of day or night, whether with fighter defence or without. The USA's entry into the European War as a top priority before giving maximum attention to the Pacific brought about this huge increase in intensity. To us some of the tactics adopted staggered us as we knew that there would be appalling losses – there is no doubt that the US High Command was well aware there would be a high price to pay but they just went ahead and did it.

We met Flying Fortress aircrews in the London pubs who boasted to us of the way they were going to fly into the heart of Germany without fighter escort, assured that their perfect tight formations would between them pack all the firepower they needed to blast the enemy out of the sky. We didn't doubt they would present a very dangerous challenge to the Germans but we still felt very concerned for their futures.

Some of those we met a few days later were not quite so jaunty but the fact that they were still alive proved there was some kind of survival rate. The confusion in the air during those battles gave rise to some very distorted figures as to the number of enemy aircraft shot down by Fortress gunners. Numerous gunners would each claim the same aircraft hit by the concentrated fire of all of them. Regardless of probable exaggeration we admired the incredible courage displayed by those crews.

I guess the British including ourselves were highly conservative and tended to understate achievements and abilities whereas the sudden influx of goods and men and abundance of supreme confidence changed the whole ethos and quickened the pace. During that period it was not unusual to come across an occasional lonely Fortress sometimes being harassed by enemy fighters and sometimes simply flying in the wrong direction with their aircraft in severely damaged condition.

Going to help them we were sometimes fired on as the crews were obviously tired and confused, and leading them in the right direction was not easy. Those early Flying Fortress attacks deep into Germany without escort required great bravery and the losses at times were horrific. Only a nation such as Uncle Sam's could have been able to withstand them.

One small consolation was that as these raids were in daylight the number to escape by parachute was much greater than that of the night bombers. Our RAF Lancaster bombers poured over Germany night after night culminating in 1,000-bomber raids. Our aircrew losses were also massive and for those having to bale out with searchlights glaring and guns flashing it must have been like hell on earth at times. Most of our bomber escorting was now aimed at covering US Fortresses or Marauders.

The Luftwaffe rose against us in force because they knew we were most likely attacking their airfields or other sensitive military targets. On one such escort of Marauders part of their formation seemed to become disorientated and flew off and away from the target area. Johnny Checketts, our CO and leading our flight, went after them. This took us well away from the main formations and well inland. However they seemed to discover their error and turned back. It was then that a strange thing happened – the appearance of a very tight formation of eight Me109Fs.

There was a momentary shock of inaction because what we were seeing could not possibly be real. Then a few seconds of waiting while Johnny made an urgent call to Alan Deere for the OK to leave our Marauder responsibility and attack these incredibly enticing targets. Alan Deere replied that he had sighted the Marauders and would cover them and Johnny attacked the 109s still flying as if out for a Sunday afternoon fly past. We watched in astonishment. The carnage was ridiculous. First down went one and then the next and still the remainder were keeping tight formation. I was approaching and Johnny called out for each to take one.

Incredibly when I lined up my sights on the next in the formation they were still displaying no form of evasion. My target aircraft disintegrated. Tommy Tucker was shooting down the next one and Bruce Gibbs the next. Then Johnny Checketts got back into the fray and probably destroyed another. Between us six destroyed and one probable. Later German records confirmed six of the seven claims. That group must have been on a training flight in the wrong place very much at the wrong time.

We had another fierce battle on 17th August when we escorted some 75 Marauders to bomb the German fighter base at Bryas, in northern France a few miles inland from Boulogne. Again the Luftwaffe met us in force with both FW190s and Me109Fs. Lieutenant Travis, the American, was flying with me that day as number two and he proved to be a great companion as we successfully destroyed two 109s.

What we were unaware of that day was that we were taking a very small part in one of the great air battles of the war. We were acting as a diversion to occupy a large proportion of the German fighter force while the Fortresses were fighting their way deep into the south of Germany far beyond fighter protection. The raids were to the ball-bearing factories at Schweinfurt and the Messerschmitt aircraft factory at Regensburg.

The tempo still remained high throughout August right up to the day of the 22nd, a day in which my life would change dramatically.

It was a beautiful sunny day and there was no immediate pressure of combat operations looming. We were told that there would probably be a show later on in the day but in the meantime we could relax. We were fast reaching a stage where we needed to stop for just a while. The strain was starting to tell on some of the chaps and I suspect also on some of our leaders, even though we were able to break now and then for some fun. The squadron was made up of great fellows and morale was high.

We attended a briefing that afternoon and were advised we were to cover an attack by Marauders on an airfield at Beaumont-le-Roger south-west of Rouen. We knew this show would be a hot one. Take-off time was late, set for 1600 hours, as it was daylight until well after 2000 hours.

I went to my aircraft and as usual had a brief chat with one of our wonderful cheery ground crew – to my shame I cannot remember his name. Strange the way words said to you at a special moment can linger with you forever.

"I'll have a good hot cuppa ready for you as soon as you get back – it's a shame you have to fly on a Sunday," he said. My reply was casual and offhand.

"Oh, Sunday doesn't mean a thing to me, it is just another day." He looked a little concerned.

"I wouldn't say that sir," he said.

It was the usual routine squadron take-off but I clearly remember that one in particular and always will. Taxi out onto the field, move into number two position next to the leader, an unusual position for me as it had been a long while since I had flown as a number two. Johnny Checketts had originally left me out of the team for this show but at my request agreed to include me with him.

Years later I was to learn that I had been posted that day to be a flight commander on another squadron and Johnny was uneasy with the superstition that existed regarding putting someone on ops after he has been posted.

The roar from the engines of the twelve Spits was thunderous. From Johnny came the usual rotating signal with hand pointing forward for full throttle. We roared along with increasing speed and in formation, then wheels up and behind us the next flight and then the third until all twelve were climbing to our pre-arranged height where we circled at rendezvous position. A few minutes later the French squadron joined us and then the Marauders flew gracefully below. Other squadrons took their place with this giant gaggle and we set off over the sparkling waters of the English Channel at a height of about 25,000 feet.

Shortly the green fields of France were below as we approached our target area. Warnings had been received that there were large concentrations of enemy fighters building up just south and above us. Next moment at least 30 plus enemy fighters at the same height confronted us. With a slight turn to the right the squadron wheeled to meet them for a head on attack. At a closing speed of about 1,000 mph this type of manoeuvre is usually over in a flash. Instead, as we wheeled a large group of 190s also attacked us from the left.

Utter chaos developed and the enemy seemed as confused as ourselves with one 190 crossing right in front of me, only a few yards away between myself and my number one. I fired at point blank range and the 190 exploded with pieces of aircraft flying everywhere. When forward vision cleared, my number one had disappeared and my only company were numerous most unfriendly 190s. The immediate decision was to get the hell out of there, firstly by diving and then climbing up elsewhere to rejoin my squadron. I was acutely aware that meantime my number one was without me but floating around by myself was certainly not the most useful form of fighting force for anyone.

I was to learn later that in those few moments of chaos the squadron lost Chalky White (later to escape), Mac Sutherland badly wounded and a prisoner, and Fraser Clark shot down and killed. That day was certainly the

Luftwaffe's day. Then for me came the shock of all shocks – something I had never thought would happen.

After the initial power dive I opened the throttle to climb, the engine gave an ominous belch and coughed out masses of smoke. A quick glance down at the instruments told the sad story. My oil temperature was off the clock and the glycol temperature was also very high. Pieces from the exploding 190 must have lodged into the cooling systems, in particular the oil coolant.

I made another attempt to coax some life into the engine but it was not to be. My position was now precarious – what to do? A quick look towards the English Channel showed it glistening in the distance. But the guns of Dieppe were in between and it was clearly far beyond my gliding limits. It would be a dumb choice anyway.

One obvious option was to bale out, not a very pleasing idea. A forced landing appeared to have some advantages. You could choose a more isolated spot with less chance of landing right by a military camp. You could also keep away from main roads. In fact I was thinking of all sorts of clever reasons probably just to avoid making that unwanted jump.

There were much more urgent matters to deal with. I was losing height rapidly; my windscreen was oiling up badly and visibility becoming serious. There were still a lot of enemy aircraft about and my tail needed to be watched. I switched off the motor, which was still spluttering – the prop stopped still in front of me and the oil stopped spewing over the canopy. There was a strange quiet as I descended towards the green fields of France. I had sighted a possible area to land; it was well away from the main roads with only small clumps of trees here and there. I opened back my canopy to give myself some visibility and then, damn it, I was attacked by two Me109s.

To avoid them required a steep vertical dive and then a pull-in with steep turns. This action shook off the 109s but turned my prop over again and great layers of oil spewed over the fuselage and into the cockpit. This meant the canopy had to be closed, as the oil was hot and blinding. It is interesting that those 109s did not attack again – perhaps they had some sympathy for my plight. My only visibility left was the area immediately behind the blister shape in my canopy. In other words I could only see backwards and my height was now too low to risk jumping.

The only option now was a forced landing. This required a number of dangerously steep gliding turns while keeping an eye on a patch of green that could be seen by looking behind me with no idea what lay just outside the circle. The idea was that at the last possible suicidal moment I would straighten out, hold as straight as could be judged and wait for the approaching stall. This took a while because of the speed I had built up from the dive.

The Spit just didn't want to go down so finally I had to gently push her into the ground. After the roaring and banging of the crash I found myself still amazingly in one piece as was the much maltreated Spit though surrounded by threatening smoke. In fact it looked as though she could burst into flames at any moment. Boy, had I made a mess of things. Obviously forced landings according to the book were not my style.

I'd succeeded in doing just about everything wrong. Not only did I not land in that nice isolated area away from military camps, I finished up right beside one in a wooded area from which I could hear the army rushing to action stations, vehicles pouring out to find the crashed enemy aircraft. I had also succeeded in being right next to two major roads. Although I didn't know it at the time and was still naively thinking that somehow I would get back to the squadron, I had flown my last flight as a fighter pilot and the last in my beloved Spitfires.

Getting out of the plane was urgent as the threat of fire was very real. I jumped out into the long grass and legged it for cover in some nearby bush. My life, though I didn't quite appreciate it, was about to undergo a radical change of pace. Strangely, as I sat in hiding among the trees, what came into my mind was the face of that cheery ground crewman with his ready cuppa and his admonishment for my disregard of Sunday. What a time to think such irrelevant thoughts.

XVIII
Enemy Territory

One unprepared but still optimistic grounded pilot sat hidden under some scant bushes trying to decide his next move. My first problem was that the crashed-landed Spitfire had stopped burning. Soon it would be discovered that the pilot had escaped from the crash. Then the hunt would be on. The smart move would have been to use my Very pistol to set the plane fully ablaze. Considering what had gone before, clearly this wasn't my day for smart moves.

Locals, including women and children, were gathering on a nearby lane to stare at the crash site. Military troops could be heard on the move from the other side of the fields. It was hopeless to stay where I was so I opted to make contact with our French friends. Boldness was the only way. I figured that all I need do was run up to the nearest group of French, mix with them for camouflage and hopefully they would somehow whisk me away into hiding.

As soon as I stood up it became obvious I needed Plan B. They made it clear my presence was not very welcome and smartly moved away. Even if they'd welcomed me with open arms there was no chance of blending in. Every French man in that group was wearing some form of hat – mostly of the beret type.

My blonde thatch would have stood out like a beacon. What I needed was a hat. I had all sorts of clever little escape devices tucked away in various pockets of my uniform – a compass, French money, and some vague knowledge of a contact in Rouen – but no hat. Even my flying boots were of the ingenious escape variety in which the tops could be torn off leaving what could pass for shoes. I had already done that but nobody had thought to tell me that every damn Frenchman in this area wore a hat.

My appearance, face spattered with oil and clothes soiled with dirt, hardly helped. My battle dress was now inside out, not particularly effective but the best I could do. I think what put the kybosh on the whole situation was my attempts to communicate in French. Several Auckland Grammar teachers could have predicted this situation, having given me up as a useless language scholar particularly inept in French. Worse still, under the stress of the situation I just couldn't think of the word for hat.

The *pardonnez moi and s'il vous plaît* rolled out in shocking pronunciation but that vital noun just would not come. I gesticulated and waved and must have looked like the proverbial clown as the crowd moved further away. Then a young boy approached on his bike. I tried to take his hat from him to demonstrate my need but it was a lost cause. He peddled away in a panic.

Reviewing the situation later it was obvious I had landed in a place where it would have been impossible for locals to become involved. I was smack bang in the middle of a military area of some kind. My only choice was to try and find somewhere to conceal myself as it was now late evening. To the relief of the French I left them and went looking for somewhere to hide. A large haystack on the other side of a field of turnips looked a likely place, not very imaginative but the best that could be done in short order.

I set off across the field and got about halfway when the sound of trucks pulling up caused me to dive for cover. Damn, a major road lay between that tempting haystack and me. And what seemed like half the Wehrmacht was bustling around there. I lay quite still trying to hide under sparse and not very high turnip leaves, feeling ridiculous. Then came a sharp command in German with the unmistakable words "Halt" and "Fire" mixed up in the sentence somewhere. A look around showed a very unhealthy environment – at least half a dozen pistols all pointing straight at me. I stood up, looked at them and could not help but smile at what seemed like a slightly ridiculous situation. And so did my very impressive group of captors, elegant young officers all. In fact they seemed delighted and highly amused. They were a group of Luftwaffe men who had got to me before the army arrived so were in a great mood.

Obviously not used to the procedure of arresting an enemy – just as we in the RAF would have been back in the UK were the situation reversed – after some discussion they placed me in one of their small cars next to the driver. Just as we were about to drive off an officer came up to the open door beside me, saluted and said – in careful halting English: "Do you know Auckland?"

"Yes, do you?" I said, looking up at him.

"No. Good day," he answered, saluted again and departed.

I realised he must have seen the words New Zealand on my shoulder flash. My delighted escorts then packed into the car beside and off we drove into the local township. None could speak a word of English. They stopped outside a small store where they bought a bottle of brandy and, using sign language, indicated we should have a drink. It was obvious they hadn't a clue what to do next so the drink turned into three or four before I was taken to a very different reception at some form of headquarters.

I should say here and now that my capture in the situation I had found myself was inevitable. The French were a wonderfully brave people in the way they risked their lives to help pilots to escape back to Britain but there is no doubt absolutely nothing could have been done for me at that time. However I was amazed we had never been warned to take some form of headgear.

Incidentally, Chalky White years later used to chuckle at my capture. He saw me coming down that day and claims I acted as the perfect diversion causing the troops to surround my crash site and gave him time to get away. Well, it wasn't exactly the best of days for either of us but, Chalky, you sure performed wonders with your remarkable escape so it wasn't all bad news.

The light-hearted atmosphere of my initial capture disappeared very quickly when I was taken by two armed guards into a large hall, each guard with a gun at the ready. They came to attention in front of a pompous senior NCO. It so happened that I had been marched in just after lighting one of my precious cigarettes.

Our pompous individual jumped down from his elevated platform, rushed over, snatched the cigarette from my mouth and stamped on it, shouting and yelling and pointing to a sign that like many others I would get to know. The sign in large letters said *Rauchen verboten* (smoking forbidden). He repeated the words over and over again. The anti-smoking campaigners of today would have loved his performance.

For me at that time it was a case of being on a fast learning curve. There was no future in arguing, surrounded as I was by guns at the ready and pistols with their holster flaps open. After this theatrical performance the standard Name, Rank and Number were duly given and recorded. Then I was taken by army truck out of the village area and towards the Dieppe coast.

We drove through large areas of fortified gun emplacements and deep into barbed wire entanglements surrounding military camps, finally stopping next to a small building, which I was to discover, had one very secure lock-up cell. It included small separate quarters for the guards plus limited washing and toilet arrangements. There was also a very large and intimidating Alsatian dog. Two guards were assigned to regularly patrol this small isolated set of buildings and at night the menacing dog always accompanied them. Each day I was visited by a *Feldwebel* (approximately equal to a flight sergeant). He was the man in charge who also supervised the provision of food. He was friendly enough but the language barrier made communication difficult. One thing was for sure – there was no way of escaping from this place.

Time started to drag painfully although the stay there was not very long – possibly about four or five days. Before I landed in France there had been time to call operations control telling them I was OK but would have to force-land. I hoped my parents and close friends would have been advised though I realised that for reasons of security the information might be withheld.

It didn't take long to sink in that my chances of escaping through the French rescue organisations were now very remote indeed. I also realised just how little real interest most of us had taken of the plight of comrades who had previously failed to return. We had developed an acquired immunity to losses and taken very little interest in what procedural mesh surrounded a captured pilot.

When told the Red Cross had confirmed that one of our squadron members was a PoW I must confess that with most of us the reaction was: "That's great news, good to know he survived" while promptly putting him more or less out of our minds. This applied even more so with those we knew had been killed.

We who had returned to base had to carry on with the war which was all about survivors and surviving. Thus it was that I didn't have the rosiest of thoughts during my period imprisoned within the defences of Dieppe.

The *Feldwebel* in charge of my over the top security had a very good reason for ensuring I had no chance of escape. I learnt he was going to be in charge of escorting me to Germany and that he would be getting a chance to return to his home for a week's leave. His over-zealous guarding of me never wavered for an instant and, though irritated, I had to admit that if I'd been in his shoes my attitude would have been no different.

He and a second man guarded me on the train to Paris. I must have tried the age-old toilet trick about a half a dozen times but each time he would follow, put his foot in the door after checking that the window was locked, and remove his revolver from its holster while the second guard stood nearby.

When we had to change to another terminal in Paris he was like a cat on hot bricks. He and his mate, with guns visible, kept a clear space around us in the crowded station while hundreds of French men and women swirled past. And while he was having difficulty in a 'phone booth trying to call for transport he stood with the door open and that cursed revolver still at the ready.

Understandably he was most uneasy with the situation and the crowds of French people around us. I felt there was some chance of escape in these conditions and was acutely aware that this might be my last opportunity. A gendarme walked past, made eye contact with me, and then nodded his head in one direction. The temptation to make a dash after crashing into the guard closest to me was considerable, but I knew that within seconds bullets from both guards would have been flying into hundreds of people.

The thought of the horrible carnage, apart from the personal risk, that could result from using the public as my cover made me discard any thought of making such an attempt.

My very jumpy *Feldwebel* finally won his telephone argument and obtained transport plus the help of a couple of temporary guards to transport us across to another main Paris station. It was now dark in the streets and damned frustrating to be so tightly hemmed in with guards when out there were thousands of potential French helpers. Throughout the train journey into Germany continual demands for trips to the toilet were made but not once did that damned *Feldwebel* relax his vigil. He certainly earned his leave back in his homeland.

Well Flying Officer Rae, I thought, you'd better get used to the idea that you are now a prisoner of war alive by courtesy of the German High Command and its recognition of the long arm of the Geneva Convention. I was later to learn how this was formulated by the International Red Cross as the result of the dreams of one man – Henry Dunant – who had been appalled at the suffering of the wounded left to suffer and die on the battlefields.

Now I was in the midst of this paradox of no longer killing the enemy while accepting his more or less grudging hospitality, such as it was.

I was also to learn that there were some basic rules of conduct and if you stepped outside those you could no longer expect to be protected by the Geneva Convention. I had the right to try and escape but I did so under the laws of the captor country. That meant if in escaping I attacked one of their citizens or soldiers – in other words left any form of blood trail – the penalties could be severe.

And if I was caught attempting to carry out any form of sabotage I could expect an extremely stiff penalty. It was also frowned upon by the Germans and prisoners alike to attempt to escape when being transported to or from hospitals, or receiving medical aid, as this could jeopardise treatment of genuine cases of illness.

There were numerous other no-nos but the main over-riding situation that governed the life of 'Kriegies' – short for *Kriegsgefangener* or war prisoners – was the continual attempt to escape. I was to discover that the means attempted to achieve this were unbelievably varied and ingenious.

This massive change in my life situation was not yet at an end and I was to find there were still a few shocks in store for this unsuspecting and very new PoW. We arrived in the early hours of the morning at the station of Frankfurt am Main; myself feeling very dirty, as there had been only face washes since my capture and sporting an impressive growth of stubble. From the station I marched under guard in front of staring civilians to a waiting transport. This took me to the infamous Dulag Interrogation centre where I was placed in one of a row of small cells. There was a number on each door. Mine was number four and a guard told me that if I should need the lavatory I was to call out my number *vier* in German. I soon found this a damnable number to say or shout loudly. Believe me I had to shout the number again and again at times as they would only permit one at a time out of his cell and of course it was part of their amusement to make you wait.

The place was a hive of activity. I could hear the odd shouted conversation between prisoners from one cell to the other as they were obviously from the same bomber crews and checking on each other in spite of the guard's warnings of *verboten*. Food was a very poor form of slop.

A small piece of black bread twice a day became the highlight of our meals. And oh how time dragged. No one came near me for the first seven days. I made up a sort of draughtboard scratched on the floor, broke up small pieces of splinters of wood and played endless uninspiring games of draughts.

The sudden withdrawal from smoking was really getting to me. Fortunately I discovered that the centre of my buckle would, after a bit of struggling, open the locked catch of my opaque window. This gave me a peep through the bars at the blue sky; a glimpse of green lawn and the smell of flowers in a garden just near the window. There was a prisoner working in the garden and a German guard further away. When this chap spotted me he worked over towards me and with a beaming smile said something similar to *"Ruskie, Ruskie"* pointing to himself. Then he took a quick look about, dashed up under the window, passed me a bright red apple and shot away. Unfortunately he must have been seen because I had only had about half the tasty apple eaten when the sound of thundering boots sounded outside the cells and next thing my door burst open.

The guards, one of whom spoke excellent English, examined the window with great puzzlement, demanding to know how it was opened. The room and myself were searched on the insistence that I must have some form of lethal weapon (they never gave my belt buckle a second look) while mumbling about sabotage and punishment. Then once again I was left to my isolation having at least achieved some variety in the soul-destroying monotony of the cell routine.

Just to defy them I again worked on the window but with much more caution at opening it. When it was open the sounds of voices calling out in English could be heard, light-hearted laughing sounds coming from some sort of sports event. I just could not figure it out at the time.

What I thought it sounded like seemed far too ridiculous even to consider but I was later to learn that it really was the sound of a game of cricket. I never saw my friendly Ruskie again and hoped that he did not suffer any reprisals for his impulsive act of kindness, for he did not have any Geneva Convention to protect him.

A couple of days later my first visitor arrived. We had been warned back in the UK of the skills used during interrogation. Under the Convention we were obliged to give only our name, rank and service number and should avoid giving any other information no matter how trivial it might seem. My interrogator was dressed in the uniform of an *Unteroffizier* (corporal) and spoke quietly with a pronounced Irish brogue. His first action was to offer me a cigarette which I took, trying hard not to let my hand shake while extracting it from the packet. He lit it for me. My first draw from the coarse German tobacco – although it tasted lousy – sent me to 'cloud nine' and made me slightly light headed.

Any heavy smoker who has been without for days would know just how exquisite that first puff was. What a hell of a way to meet a skilful interrogator – he now knew that I was vulnerable with a smoking habit. He pulled out a sheet of paper and read from it. First telling me what squadron I had come from he listed my service records, my citation and told me who was the squadron CO. This was his first error. He was a few months out of date, naming Reg Grant. I was still trying to remain aloof and uninterested – any flicker of interest or a change of expression would have indicated he had scored a response.

He pointed out that all he wanted from me was confirmation that the information he had was correct. He also asked if I could confirm the crystal frequency used for our radio. That was a real optimistic try-on, not that I had the faintest idea of the frequency. Fortunately the crystals were rigged to self-destruct in a crash.

He then changed tack, shrugging his shoulders as if shaking off all responsibility for me and said that he was sorry but if I would not endorse the information as correct he was compelled to leave me to remain in this cell. Adding that, as there was no confirmation of my capture I was technically not yet under the protection of the Red Cross, which meant he could call in the Gestapo.

He also pointed out that until I was transferred to the Dulag where "all your friends" were living in comfort with showers and sheets to sleep between and Red Cross food parcels to enjoy he could do nothing to help me. Before leaving he returned to his threat mode.

"You do realise," he said, "until we notify the Red Cross you are a prisoner there is no one that will know if you are alive or dead. As a fighter pilot you are completely alone – not like those bomber crews that you can hear. Do you really think we are going to send a special spy all the way to New Zealand to spy on your family? If you give us your home address we can arrange for a message to be sent."

My stock reply which sounded so stupid following the remarks of this smooth-talking Irishman was, "Sorry. Name, rank and number only." He left me with about four cigarettes telling me that the guards would give me a light when asked. Some days were to elapse before he came cheerily in to see me again. More or less the same routine again except that he now told me that Johnny Checketts was on the loose in France but that he would be caught (he wasn't).

But his information was good. He also told me about the time that Ray Hesslyn and I stayed at the Savoy Hotel when we spent some of the profits from his Malta book, then he handed me a small top secret handbook on the new Griffon engine just installed in Spitfires and went on to chat about some of the squadron members including comments such as "Lindsay Black likes the girls doesn't he?"

He reminded me again of all the comforts I was missing, shrugged his shoulders at my stock reply, said, "Sorry but I can do nothing for you" and left. I felt dirty. My teeth felt horrible. I was getting very cross with the stupidity of the situation. Another two or three days passed and then suddenly the door was flung open.

"*Heraus! Heraus! Heraus!,*" shouted the guard and I was escorted into a small room in which there were some other Kriegies. They were all talking to each other as if there was no time to waste and there was so much to be said. It was an incredible feeling to be no longer locked in a solitary situation, to suddenly meet others and talk to them; simple pleasures that felt almost overwhelming. We were marched as a group across to a compound – my first sight of Dulag Luft with its high barbed wire circumference watch towers and patrolling guards.

On entering we were welcomed by other air force officers and each given a bundle of clean clothes, a toothbrush, tooth powder and a towel, and told where the showers were. For a few moments I stood still, confused and trembling with anticipation. Which first? Clean my teeth? Jump under the shower? Shave? Then some clean clothes. Wow! Isn't this just great! And at precisely that peak of anticipation two guards rushed into the middle of the celebrations and called out my name. *"Heraus! Heraus!"* they yelled, insisted that all my goodies be left behind, told my newfound friends there'd been "a mistake" and marched me back to my cell.

That in my opinion was their smartest move in our little game of interrogation. Suddenly the whole business of refusing to confirm what they already knew, of having my parents back home not knowing, of living like a pig in isolation, seemed like the height of stupidity.

The hell with it, I thought. I'm not playing this smart. I sat and fumed throughout the rest of the day and I'm quite certain that if my Irish friend had come back during that time of incredible depression he would have gained my confirmation.

However by the next day I had recovered enough to stick it out a while longer. As it happened, a few days later I was again taken to the Dulag – this time without further trouble. Somehow my Irish friend had arranged a cunning manoeuvre but tripped up in the execution. My memories of the Dulag are very sparse except that the short period there did help to restore a sense of well-being and to feel clean again. When the normal pleasantries of life are suddenly removed, and when compliance is demanded at the muzzle of a gun, the experience is difficult ever to forget.

My stay at the Dulag was very short as it was only used as a temporary transit camp to house the vast numbers of RAF being taken prisoner as our attack on Germany intensified. As soon as the camp filled up with prisoners they were moved on to larger camps. We were loaded onto well-guarded trucks and taken to the railway yards. There we had our first sight of our destined form of transport. It was a distinct physical shock. In front of us were rows of large closed railway wagons with huge sliding doors. Written on the doors in large letters were the words: *"7 Chevaux/48 Hommes"* (seven horses or 48 men). We were herded into these cattlewagons until we could hardly move; the large doors were closed on us and then the next wagon filled and so on.

The heat was considerable and trying to find a few precious feet just to sit down was extremely difficult and probably meant that someone else got squashed. It was hours before the train, after jolting and crashing, finally started to move. Two armed guards were assigned to each wagon. They appeared during stops for everyone to get out to pee beside the tracks.

As the heat increased we persuaded one of our guards to leave the huge sliding door partially open. He agreed to do this and chose to sit by the door to watch us. This did improve the conditions considerably as the air started to flow through the stifling interior.

I found myself seated beside this fairly young alert-looking German soldier. I was just itching to have a go at one of these poor misguided, misled Nazi soldiers that could speak English. After all he must know that the writing was on the wall, that they were entirely in the wrong for plunging us into this war etc. etc. My first question, designed to open the conversation on a friendly basis, was to ask him where we were going. He told me that it was to Sagan, south of Berlin in Silesia, that they were very good camps and we would enjoy staying there.

"You are safe now – for you the war is over," he added.

Oh, how I hated those words. I asked him what the prisoners did there.

"You will dig tunnels and we will find them," he laughed.

I then asked him why the devil Germany ever started this war.

"We did not start this war with you, you declared war on us," was his reply.

I wasn't doing very well so I started on a different tack. "Why did you bomb the innocent civilians of London and other British cities?"

He answered with a question. "Did you not bomb Berlin first?"

I checked this out with some of the bomber boys and they agreed he was right.

"This made Hitler angry and he decided to teach you a lesson," he continued.

I began to realise that this committed Nazi had been questioned many times before by previous PoWs and had well-rehearsed answers ready. It was the first of many lessons that made me realise that to a vast number of Germans Hitler was their saviour, the Gestapo was there only for the enemies of the state, and Germany was on the side of right and morality. Every clear-cut argument I thought to make could be equally countered.

I sat a little quieter after that as our slow painful journey crossed Germany and on to Silesia near to the border of Poland. Once we stopped close to an industrial area and saw dozens and dozens of white-frocked factory girls resting in the sun. Some looked topless but the train did not stop long enough to check this out. One thing did sink in, which was contrary to any previously misinformed ideas I must have had: Germany in September 1943 was still a very potent and powerful enemy and a long way from collapsing. We knew that we would ultimately win but somehow the Germans didn't seem to have got the message yet.

Without going into sordid detail readers could imagine what the conditions in those tightly jammed wagons were like before, thankful for small mercies, we reached Stalag Luft III, Sagan, Silesia. Though we didn't know it then, the camp would become a part of the history of World War Two, a place in which many of us would be contributing to a unique human endeavour created by the bottling up of so many highly intelligent and imaginative young men into one place.

We certainly didn't subscribe to the guard's view that we were entering a place where, as they kept repeating, "For you the war is over," and we could wait safely for hostilities to end. This was a place where we could be a continuous problem to the enemy, forcing them to retain large forces of men to guard us and so strain their resources.

These were the main objectives in the PoW camps of Sagan and many other places. It was well known that the chances of a successful escape back to our own side were remote in the extreme but to continue trying to escape was an accepted duty for a large number of the prisoners. There was of course a small group opposed to any disturbance of the peace and who wanted to just wait for the war to end. Its opinion was accepted and tolerated but not respected.

Travel-weary, bedraggled and dirty, 300 or so of us climbed out of trucks and, surrounded by armed guards, had our first look at Stalag Luft III Sagan North, South and East Compounds. We were marched to the first set of heavily barbed wire gates in front of North Compound and halted again for the first of a series of tiresome counts and recounts.

The enemy, we realised, was leaving nothing to chance. Behind these gates were another set, equally large and barbed wire festooned. Again a recount and then we were finally marched into our future prison.

With typical German thoroughness names were then listed, personal items examined, and some confiscated after being carefully noted and labelled. Among things *verboten* was my lighter which was handed over reluctantly. We were then assigned to various huts and I had my first exposure to the various devious activities, which abounded within this compound.

Just as I was settling into my new accommodation a smiling fellow came up to me and handed me my lighter.

"I believe this is yours – it seemed to fall out of the goon's file," he said (a 'goon' was a camp guard).

Sleight of hand was, I learned, both highly skilful and ongoing. Apart from that incident, there was no great rousing welcome for us from those already there. But for an initial quick scrutiny for familiar faces, with here and there the odd yell of recognition, most people went back to their own routines.

The first impression of the compound was its colourless sandy soil completely devoid of any grass. There was a scattering of uninteresting pine trees and rows of dull-looking huts. The perimeter looked menacing with double rows of high barbed wire and an overhang of further barbed wire broken here and there by towers bristling with machine guns and searchlights.

Not seeing any familiar faces I set off for a look around and hadn't gone very far when to my astonishment I sighted Mick Shand, one of our most extrovert and popular squadron members.

It was great suddenly to see someone you know especially from your own squadron so I went up to him in delight. He welcomed me with pleasure but after the first burst of conversation I found myself trying to maintain the chatter. He seemed to become strangely pre-occupied, continually glancing away from me and concentrating on some distant activity. The latest news of mutual friends didn't seem terribly important to him.

Poor Mick, I thought. Prison camp seems to have got to him. Where was his usual hearty laugh? His expression was so serious and intense that I was about to ask him if he was all right when he turned and ran, yelling as he went: "Sorry I've got to go." I stared after him in astonishment and for the first time noticed he had what looked like a roughly made hand-shovel with him.

He continued his mad dash to a horse and cart, which was beside a rubbish bin. The horse was just lifting his tail as horses do to relieve themselves. Mick, the first there in a remarkably close race against other Kriegies, scooped up the prized droppings and went off to bury them in his own special tomato plot.

I learnt one important lesson from Mick that day. If you want to survive successfully within this harsh environment you had to adjust to an entirely new set of values.

Each hut of 12 rooms contained the basic needs of over 100 prisoners. The rooms were just large enough to take four double-tiered wooden-slatted bunks with a small coal-fired heater in the corner. Each bunk had straw-filled mattresses, a sheet palliasse and two fibre blankets. A single cold shower and a toilet sufficed for all in the hut. Eight of us were jammed into each room knowing we had better get used to each other or else.

No group of men could have been better prepared for future years of marriage as they were compelled to recognise their own irritating personal habits, the small things that drove the others to distraction, and were forced to correct them. Sometimes they failed and moved in with others more prepared to tolerate their failings.

At times the silliest things could drive the atmosphere to explosive levels. I could fill a couple of pages with just some of the stupid niggles which sometimes brought our room of eight to a pitch of high tension. However, we as a group learnt to deal with them, discuss them, try to adjust and change. I discovered I had quite a few irritating habits that had to be curbed. One in particular had the entire room in a state of extreme tension.

My lighter had quit working and matches were a scarce commodity. I learnt from older Kriegies that each match could be cut with a razor into at least two and the thick ones into four. You had to be very careful and stroke them gently when lighting. When the lights went out, usually about 2200 hours, we settled into our spartan beds for sleep.

But not me, I always had a last peaceful relaxing cigarette before sleep.

This meant sitting up and carefully stroking one of my precious matches across the matchbox. They rarely lit immediately and the stroking action had to be repeated again and again until at last the match flared and I could lie back to enjoy Dame Nicotine's persuasive poison.

Until the match was lit the tension within that room was explosive. I was aware of it but initially determined to carry on. It became much worse when I decided I was not going to damn well light a cigarette at all. As I lay in my bed willing myself not to light one there was finally an explosion of wrath from all the seven hutmates.

We finally called a truce and that luxury of mine was cut out. All the others had their problems – sniffing at food, irritating coughing during every meal, constant complaining, talking too much, dodging their share of chores, surliness, hygiene problems – whatever they were, each was discussed and rectified or else. As a group of three New Zealanders, one Rhodesian and four Australians we enjoyed much humour between us.

When we first arrived the camp's 'X' organisation made careful checks of each of us. X was an important highly secret organisation that controlled all escape attempts, helped to plan them and provided necessary documentation.

Security was naturally a high priority. This made it important to check that all incoming prisoners were genuine, as it had been known for the Germans to plant fake PoWs as spies to report any planned escapes. As a result each of us was interviewed and required to provide the name of someone who could verify our bona fides or answer some very searching question if we couldn't.

With that procedure over the next was a much more informal affair where each of us was invited to have a cup of coffee in someone's room so that the occupants could gen up on the latest happenings in the RAF and the UK.

I was invited to one of these gatherings, all strangers to me and all English. The conversation drifted from one thing to another, as they were hungry to hear of the latest development in aircraft, what it was like in the UK now and how things were affected by the influx of Yanks, etc. It was a pleasant general chat until one of the fellows voiced what at first seemed like an innocuous query.

"Do you know a New Zealander named Jim Gunn?" he asked. Hearing that name popped at me from a group of Englishmen was quite a pleasant surprise.

"I certainly do," I said with enthusiasm, and then burbled: "He was on my course, the whole six feet three of him. And would you believe, I only saw him about a week before going into the bag. In fact just missed him up at Ayr where he had his wedding on the station. Everyone said it was a cracker." I looked around the group. It was rapt, so I blundered on.

"When I caught up with him in London you should have seen him. He looked worn out. He must have been having one hell of a honeymoon," I added, delighted to be able to answer the question so fully. There was a slight pause.

"Where did you know Jim?" I asked.

"I've never met him – but he married my fiancée," was the reply. There was a very awkward silence before somebody leapt in to save the situation. As soon as possible after that massive blunder I excused myself from their hospitality.

The world can be far too small at times, I decided, even in the middle of wartime Germany.

XIX

In the Bag

Coming to terms with being a PoW was for me far from an easy process. The sudden loss of freedom was only one of many shocks. To be plunged into an oppressive mass of males in permanent close proximity was in itself stressful but added to this was the depressing atmosphere of the place. Yet as PoW camps go this one was way above the average, we were informed by some of the older Kriegies.

In comparison to many scattered around Germany it seems we were indeed fortunate. The camp had only recently been opened. In fact construction was still going on, with the first prisoners having been moved in just months before I arrived. The camp was over 350 metres square within the warning wire which was set 10 metres from the double perimeter wires. These were over two metres high with barbed wire at the base, a sloping barbed wire overhang and between them further rolls of barbed wire.

The Germans didn't do things by halves. At intervals of 170 metres there were 5-metre observation towers, each with a machine gun and a search light manned 24 hours a day by regularly changed guards equipped with rifles. Armed guards patrolled the entire perimeter from the outside, day and night.

Prisoners were housed in three rows of five huts, each hut being 33 metres in length. All huts were built off the ground so that the ferrets and goons as we called the German guards could constantly check for possible tunnelling activities. The ferrets (they didn't like the name when they learnt its meaning) wore dark blue overalls and carried a long probing metal spike. However they were a big problem for us and needed to be kept under constant surveillance.

Each hut of 20 rooms was built to house four persons per room. So much for German planning, however, for our room already held eight prisoners. It didn't require too great a knowledge of arithmetic to realise our numbers by now exceeded 1,500 and there was another camp immediately behind ours rapidly filling up with US Air Force bomber crews. The cookhouse had been built to supply 1,000 but already could only sometimes provide a thin soup and very occasionally some cooked potatoes.

When we arrived a theatre was almost completed. This was a remarkable achievement as it had been built by our own voluntary prisoner labour and materials purchased with our own funds and supplied by the Germans. Tools for the construction were provided on our solemn assurance as officers that none would ever be used for any escape attempts. It was an interesting form of trust that was rigidly adhered to and never broken.

I had occasion to witness this same form of trust much later on during the war with the same strict adherence. Our ability to purchase various approved items within Germany was part of the Geneva Convention which entitled each officer PoW to receive a complicated payment of about 10% of that paid to the German equivalent rank. There was no payment made to our sergeant pilots so we arranged with the Germans to transfer part of our funds to them. These funds were not paid individually but collectively.

One side of the camp was bordered by the German administrative area in which German troops were housed and from which the Commandant's headquarters and office staff operated. There was also an armoury for the guards' rifles and other weaponry. Our negotiator and camp representative was our senior officer, Group Captain Massey.

To a newcomer the internal organisation was complex and highly efficient but with a cloak-and-dagger atmosphere more *Alice in Wonderland* than MI5. Although developed out of necessity it did at times border on the ridiculous. I was also amazed to see prisoners strolling over to a building with various musical instruments. Out of curiosity I followed and found quite a practice jam session going on using oboes, trumpets, clarinets, saxophones and just about any instrument you could imagine. I'm no music buff but I feel safe in declaring that the noise was terrible.

On inquiry I was told that if I wanted to learn an instrument all I need do was make an application. As soon as one was available I could have it for my personal use. So I made a request for a sax and within a week or so was the proud possessor of a tenor instrument. Thereafter I spent many pleasurable hours playing it and just about blowing my addled brains out on the low notes.

I think it was Danny Kaye who said that an oboe is an ill wind that nobody blows good. He only said that because he never heard me on the sax. In the same breath (no pun intended) it surely alleviated much of my frustration. I did learn to appreciate the talents of some of the other musicians – in particular one Canadian who used to sit and listen to Glenn Miller records (yes, we had one or two gramophones in the camp as well). He would then play back each part on his sax, look at where his fingers were and read out the notes to a fellow Canadian.

Using this method they wrote out entire scores of music just playing the music by ear. Later the Americans from the adjoining camp came over with the agreement of the Germans and together with some of our members produced a magnificent evening of Glenn Miller and Tommy Dorsey – in fact all the well known Big Band music of those days.

Senior German officers attended as special guests. They seemed to have great difficulty in understanding what we thought was damn good music. I should add here that for weeks I was completely thunderstruck at all these activities. Within a few days of being in the camp I found myself playing rugby for New Zealand against our traditional foes of South Africa. It so happened that the New Zealand team needed a hooker and so I was plunged into the battle in my familiar place.

The rugby contests were fought out with great intensity in national teams, representing not only England, Wales, Scotland, Australia and New Zealand but also the USA, Canada and Rhodesia plus any others such as Poles and Czechs who formed the Exiles. We also had teams representing each hut. We discovered that many of the Canadians made great rugby players, in particular those who had played American gridiron football. Despite all that, rugby was a game that left the Germans unimpressed.

Later when the weather warmed up we were all involved in softball much to the delight of the Canadians and Americans. And when the bitterly cold winter hit us a few enterprising prisoners played a water hose over a levelled-off area and bingo we had a skating rink. Ice hockey was then the game, enabling the Canadians to walk all over us. In fact most of us from down under were utterly hopeless at it.

To my eyes the whole situation seemed a bit ridiculous. Here we were in the middle of Germany being housed in relative comfort by our mortal enemies of yesterday and also partially fed by them. We certainly would have been in a starving condition if it had not been for the Red Cross food parcels. However we must have been draining their resources considerably. Reasonable heating was provided, also large quantities of bread and potatoes.

All our musical instruments and food parcels were transported from Switzerland. When theatrical costumes were required for our various classical plays they were obtained on request – at a time when Germany was in the midst of a life and death struggle deep in the interior of Russia, which required trainload after trainload of desperately needed soldiers and supplies pouring eastward while enduring the ferocity of our increasing round-the-clock armada of bombers.

On many nights we lay in our beds and listened with pleasure to the sound of bombs crashing on Berlin and the thunder of Berlin's anti-aircraft defence system in reply. And then after the all-clear sirens sounded we could hear with some frustration the trains start rolling again. The German people must surely realise what their crazy leaders had done to them, we reasoned. To our puzzlement they just didn't seem to see things that way. The Nazi propaganda machine was clearly immensely powerful.

The escape organisation within our camp was highly efficient and had evolved through the years. Many inmates had now lived as PoWs for over three years. Many had escaped before and learnt from mistakes made. Many tunnels had been painstakingly dug and discovered when almost ready to 'break'. Both we and the Germans were now far more wary and devious.

In our camp we had Big X as the head of the organisation. This was Squadron Leader Roger Bushell, a dynamic man, a South African by birth and a pre-war London barrister who fought in the early air battles over France and Britain. Roger had made a successful escape from the Dulag Luft and for some time lived in Prague before being recaptured. There were also 'Little Xs' within each of our huts.

These were our escape contacts who also oversaw security for each hut during such times as the daily reading of the latest news (mainly from the BBC). Yes, we had radios within each camp, which amazingly were never discovered in spite of the many surprise raids mounted by the camp guards. These searches could occur without warning at any time of the day or night.

There were parades every morning, and sometimes also at night, where we had to form up in lines out on the open grounds which was quite often windswept and snow-covered in winter. These parades were arranged in hut groups. We were very carefully counted and then recounted. To frustrate them we often shuffled about to upset their counting. Sometimes this was purposely done to hide the absence of an escapee.

We had an interesting and quite simple way of frustrating one of their forms of punishment. If they decided as a punitive measure that parades were to be held one hour earlier and our lights would be turned off one hour earlier at night then we just altered our 'camp time' by advancing one hour and 'slept in' to our usual time and had our lights on to our usual time at night. The only ones to suffer were the German guards who had to struggle out of bed one hour earlier. Eventually the Germans ultimately resigned themselves to this problem and reluctantly referred to our time as "camp time".

Many of us wanted to participate 'at the coal face' of tunnel digging activities but to our frustration found we were not needed as the escape committee had hundreds of volunteers. The really important jobs had fewer applicants. These needed highly skilled men with long experience behind them.

For example if you were a brilliant artist who could create perfect identity passes, or mould perfect compasses from melted down gramophone records, or sew a perfect imitation of German uniforms and civilian clothes, or make perfect imitation rifles and pistols out of wood then yes your services would certainly be welcome.

And of course if you happened to be an experienced mining engineer you would certainly be welcome to the inner circle. Another very valuable skill used with great success was found amongst the Polish group. Some of the Poles were able to cut out patiently the vital trapdoors through the concrete blocks. These had to be perfect and, when filled with dust, undetectable.

No one ever spoke the word tunnel in the camp, as there was a danger that our conversations might be overheard particularly at night from outside our windows. The escape committee decided that three tunnels, codenamed Tom, Dick and Harry, would be started at the same time. All offered help would be required and needed for the less spectacular but equally important job of 'stooging'. This involved standing about pretending to be doing something while keeping a constant watch for any unusual behaviour by the 'ferrets' or guards, or for any apparent interest from outside the wire such as the use of binoculars.

Other help was vital in getting rid of the recently dug sandy dirt which unfortunately stood out as a much brighter yellow colour when first distributed. Some was spread under the huts and brushed over. Unfortunately after a while the height of the soil under the huts rose noticeably so 'penguins' were created. These were Kriegies allocated the difficult task of carrying bags full of the freshly dug sand inside each trouser leg, resulting in a distinctive penguin waddle.

The bottoms of the bags were held closed by a string, which could be released by pulling it from the top of the trouser. This allowed sand to dribble out from under the trouser cuffs and be idly scuffed around by the penguins' feet to ensure an even spread. While doing this they nonchalantly strolled along or pretended to kick a ball about, as any action that looked normal was essential.

Within my own room I became one of the 'tin bashers' who undertook the making of various important items for our use. Thanks to our Red Cross parcels we received the raw material in the form of hundreds and hundreds of various sized cans. We had no familiar tools and had to improvise. For example our only hammer was the handle taken from the door catch. Suitable knives were fashioned from kitchen table knives.

Solder, melted from the seams of the cans and resin from the tree stumps in the camp, provided the fusion. We made very effective heat using small cans with wicks from a pyjama cord and a thin tube soldered on the top. This had a chin rest attached. Blowing through the thin tube produced a very effective hot small flame.

Larger scale items were made by joining can after can with double type waterproof joins to create complete ovens, trays and pots. Sometimes the skills of the tin bashers were called on for items required within the tunnel activities. My hands became covered with a myriad of tiny cracks from handling the sharp tins and looked far different to those of a pilot's hands.

Then there was the question of the timber needed to shore up the tunnels. The amount required was considerable. To meet the demand double floors were stripped and the precious bed boards on which we slept got fewer and fewer while the spaces between increased to the point of discomfort. This brought the occasional protest particularly from those opposed to any escape attempts.

Surprisingly all this intense activity did not ease my personal frustration at being enclosed in this prison environment. I dreamed day after day of escaping although acutely aware that hundreds and hundreds around me also planned and schemed without success. The Little X for our hut was an outstanding Canadian called Red Noble. He and I had many discussions of various hare-brained ideas for escaping. He well knew my frustrations and gave me one very good piece of advice.

"There are many that feel like you who think of nothing but escaping. For your own sake and your sanity, don't do it! By all means, if you have a plan, think about it with all your efforts. Go over every item and if you think it will work go for it. The chances are like most attempts it will probably fail but if it does, for goodness sake just forget all about escaping for some time. Go away and blow a bugle or take up some study but get your mind right off escaping. Then later, when you have shaken off your frustration you will be ready to have another go. Many Kriegies in this camp have gone round the bend through continually dreaming and scheming of nothing else but escaping."

It was sound advice, which led to me taking up daily practice on my beloved saxophone. I also read right through a book on the law of tort and was as completely ignorant of the subject afterwards as before. The interminable question on everybody's mind was how long this war was going to last. Without any real answer we just had to settle down somehow and endure.

The only war effort left for us to do was to harass the enemy as much as possible. That this collective ambition was ultimately to have terribly tragic results was never foreseen by any of us. And I doubt whether it would have changed our plans even if we had.

XX

Tunnel Mania

Two major events happened within our North Compound just prior to my arrival. One was a tremendous success as far as the Kriegies were concerned and the other a catastrophic setback.

First the remarkable success story, brilliantly conceived and executed. For weeks the 'tailoring section' had been patiently making a few *Unteroffizier* uniforms while others had been involved in making wooden rifles, the stocks polished with boot polish to look like steel. The escapees, confident they would be authentically dressed and armed, were just waiting for the right moment. Suddenly all plans were dashed – the *Unteroffiziers* were issued with revolvers and holsters.

Undaunted, the Kriegie production system went back into action. Authentic-looking guns and holsters were made while the forgery department replicated gate passes for the escorting guards from an original filched by devious means.

The plan devolved on the fact that occasionally 'delousing' parties were allowed to use showers in a building near the Eastern Compound. On this occasion immediately after a change of guards at the gates a group of 24 Kriegies were assembled in front of the gates by the bogus *Unteroffiziers* who spoke fluent German. They then marched the Kriegies through the gates after showing their very convincing passes, continued marching smartly up the road and dispersed into the woods.

Most of them were soon rounded up again and sent to the cooler for a spell of confinement but one, Johnny Stower, succeeded in walking 90 kilometres down to the Czech border undetected where he was helped with money and a smarter set of clothes. He then travelled by train nearly to the Swiss border and crossed on foot into Switzerland which was where his luck ran out.

He had entered onto a narrow strip of Swiss territory where the topography was so confusing that he accidentally crossed back onto Germany only to be caught by a frontier guard. Before being returned to the camp Johnny had an unpleasant period with the Gestapo. Tragically he was shot by the Gestapo a year later after taking part in the 'Great Escape'.

Two other escapees had a very near miss in this cheeky daylight break.

Morrison and Welsh were close friends who tried to steal an aircraft – a remarkable effort that came very close to succeeding. They managed to enter an old Junkers training aircraft and had started one engine when the pilot arrived. At first he thought they were ground crew and then realised that things were very wrong and gave the alarm.

For this effort, which was regarded as sabotage, they were given a lengthy solitary confinement and then sent to Colditz. Another similar daylight escape attempt was made shortly after by two Kriegies carrying the rifles not needed in the previous break. The bogus guards carried passes but unknown to them the Commandant had made a slight change to their format. The difference was noticed and the two were marched off to the cooler.

The catastrophic setback was the uncovering of tunnel Tom which had been so close to completion. A series of factors brought about this discovery. Firstly summer was waning, creating an added urgency for the tunnellers. This was because the majority of escapees would be walking (or "hard arse-ing" in Kriegie terms), a purely summer weather form of travel. Walking at any other time of the year in this severe climate would have been near to suicidal.

Another important influence on the tempo of tunnelling was that an American compound on our south side was nearing completion. When that happened all Americans in our compound would be transferred there. We still had 300 Americans in our North Compound who had helped in many ways with the creation of two of the three tunnels and wanted to be in the escape. These two factors forced a rather hurried time schedule for the completion of Tom.

Just as the tunnel was reaching the edge of the woods and ready to surface a group of German workmen arrived and cut back the woods another 50 metres. Escape organisers were convinced this was just a fluke on the part of the tidy-minded Germans and not done with any foreknowledge of the intended break. However all the intense activity within the camp was difficult to conceal and the Germans, sensing the atmosphere, stepped up their tunnel-hunting operations.

The extra haste had forced the tunnellers into taking more chances with the distribution of the freshly dug soil and the ferrets finally found a few traces of it. The Commandant immediately ordered day and night snap searches with Kriegies shut out of their huts for hours. In particular they concentrated on Hut 123 from which Tom originated.

Readers should refer to the plan of the North Compound showing the placements of Tom, Dick and Harry to appreciate the strategies involved. The extra haste had forced more chances being taken in distributing the freshly dug soil and the ferrets finally discovered some traces of it.

As a last resort tunnel Dick was used to dump back some of the soil. Also, in desperation, empty Red Cross boxes were filled with soil and stacked under beds. These were discovered and angry camp staff threatened to stop the issue of any future boxes. Finally after continual searches concentrating around Hut 123 a ferret felt his spike slip into the covered crack of Tom's trap opening.

The slab was ripped up and there was the tunnel in all its secretly engineered glory. Tom's ending was ignominious. It was filled with sewage and dynamited. The Commandant was so delighted with the discovery that there were surprisingly few reprisals. Possibly he thought his promotion to general, lost through the earlier daylight break, might with luck be back on track again.

Those were but a few of the happenings within this astonishingly active North Compound of Stalag Luft III. Other interesting situations had also evolved within this camp. One was a central trading unit where items – anything from food to clothing – obtained values based on demand. Each item through bidding gained a points value. Points could be recorded and accumulated for a later purchase.

For example, I never took sugar in my tea or coffee so my entitlement was carefully placed in a separate tin and, when accumulated to a worthwhile quantity, exchanged for points. Those points in turn could be used to purchase other items such as chocolate or anything else you might fancy.

I found the only problem with saving sugar was the high demand for its use in alcohol production, quite a quandary for a booze-deprived Kriegie. That said, the system was a surprisingly efficient way of redistributing unwanted goods and meeting various needs.

Sometimes there were surprising purchases and sales made. One of these involved myself. Every new Kriegie longed not only to get a letter from home and to be reassured that all was well with loved ones, but also to get a parcel of extra clothing. Clothing that was often desperately needed with the approach of winter. In the case of New Zealander prisoners, clothing from our personal baggage held by the squadron was sent to New Zealand House in London and then on to the camp. I was aware a parcel was on the way and waited with great anticipation.

Others in my room had all received theirs but mine seemed to be taking a dreadfully long time. At long last a bulky parcel arrived, bearing my name. The entire roomful of Kriegies stood around me, as excited as I was at opening the parcel. It was a bitterly cold day and the parcel couldn't have come soon enough. The first garment to appear was a pair of silk underpants, then another and another, followed by the silk singlets. All those silk goodies that I had so long ago bought in Gibraltar but never worn were displayed in front of the assembled hut.

After the first surprised silence there was a roar of laughter in which I had to ultimately join even if perhaps sounding slightly hysterical. What I said about those dumb fools back in New Zealand House who packed this parcel was unprintable. It took the rest of the day to recover from the shock and after lights out I could still hear the odd chuckle. Dammit, I thought, I think I will light that hated after-lights-out cigarette.

The next day I was still so embarrassed by those damned silk garments that I marched over to the exchange centre and dropped them off for immediate trading. There was an auction that day but I didn't bother to go back. Imagine my astonishment when I later discovered they reached an unprecedented price after enthusiastic bidding. As a result I found myself with enough points to purchase woollen socks, long underwear, warm shirts, bars of chocolates, and still have a very healthy 'bank balance'.

The chuckles in the hut stopped. I wrote home to my folks asking them to only send silk socks and silk underwear in future. They never did. I guess they thought I had gone completely round the bend.

Within our camp was another group of people for whom the prison situation brought out latent interests in unexpected ways. As I mentioned earlier we had a very good theatre and excellent plays were produced. This required some of the men to take female parts, and some of them did so very convincingly. They grew their hair long and flowing, and walked gracefully around the perimeter sometimes attracting wolf whistles. I gathered that the appreciative recipients of my silken garments came from this (very) camp group.

Around about this time I became the hut's number one bread-cutter. Just how that happened I'm not sure but perhaps it had to do with my ability to cut consistently 68 slices from each loaf of the solid dark brown German bread. It was important to save some of our bread so that we could every now and then make a thick 'plonk' mixture with bread and Red Cross milk powder.

Our best cook was Clay Beckingsale, an Australian who concocted a very palatable pudding from this mixture with perhaps other mystery ingredients. However the taste was not as important as the fact that it gave us the rare feeling of being full even if for only a very short time.

Food had to be carefully managed as one Red Cross parcel between the eight of us sometimes had to last two weeks or perhaps considerably longer. At other times supplies improved, as did potatoes. As the weather got colder a very welcome soup was collected from the cookhouse by one of our room members.

New Zealander 'Pop' Collett, who proved to be a good friend to us, supervised the cookhouse. Key positions are important in any organisation and prison camp was no exception. Clay, not content with extending his cooking talents, landed what turned out to be an incredibly good post, administration of the newly constructed hot shower building. Although when he first told us of his undertaking we failed to appreciate its value. It committed us to take turns at unlocking, supervising and allocating shower usage which we found irksome. The far-sighted Clay however fully appreciated its importance.

The incredible value of what we had obtained soon became apparent as the days got colder and our fuel supplies (oversized coal dust brickettes) dwindled. The shower building turned out to be a virtual gold mine, an unlimited supply of fuel that we controlled. Ostensibly it was there only to maintain the heating of the water but as we had the keys to the building it was not very difficult to smuggle a few blocks at a time to our hut. Good old Clay, we thought, that really was a smart move.

We finally had to use a little caution as it became embarrassing when the entire camp were all out on early morning *Appell* (parade) to look back at the huts and see only one chimney, ours, emitting smoke. However we did get numerous comments from visitors as to how delightfully warm our room was. Ray Hill, our delightful Rhodesian member, was most appreciative as he suffered from malaria and the cold made him miserable.

Ray was in poor health, not least from the stressful events which surrounded his capture. He was injured when he took shelter with a Frenchwoman who nursed him. She turned out to be Jewish. They were both later betrayed by her own nephew in a forlorn attempt to save his own skin when caught out not wearing his compulsory yellow star. Ray was forced to watch her being horribly tortured by the Gestapo.

Each member in our room was interesting yet all so very different. The oldest Kriegie (in years as a prisoner) was Bjelke Petersen – no relation to the well-known Brisbane Premier. Bjelke as we called him (or sometimes Pete) was a wonderfully dedicated person. He had been a prisoner from soon after the outbreak of war. Originally from Sydney where his family ran a huge gymnasium, he had been studying physical education in Britain and amongst other qualifications he was a masseur.

His skills were in constant demand throughout his years in captivity as wounded and suffering prisoners sought his help for relief of pain. We used to watch Pete as day after day he would come back to our room, climb onto his upper bunk close his eyes and be instantly asleep. I asked Pete how he was able to relax so completely in spite of our spartan conditions. He laughed.

"I have always managed to do this because if not I just couldn't keep going. All I do is cast my mind to a beautiful warm sandy beach with the soft sound of the sea, close my eyes, imagine I am there and then drift into a beautiful relaxing sleep," said Pete.

I tried to copy his technique. Dreaming of my beautiful Piha surf beach back in NZ was easy but drifting immediately off to sleep just didn't work for me. I remained acutely aware that I was lying on a very hard uncomfortable bunk, in a depressing wooden hut surrounded outside by menacing barbed wire.

One invaluable item given to each of us on arrival was a small blank-paged booklet labelled *A Wartime Log*. I still have that booklet in fact it was the only item I held on to throughout the chaos of the closing weeks of the war. One of my first efforts as an artist of very limited ability was to copy an illustration seen in someone else's booklet. I thought it perfectly summarised all of us in that camp. When I open the booklet today and look at my drawing I still think it wasn't a bad effort. Even today it brings back chuckles as I recall just how truly that picture portrayed our complete and utter frustration.

It is a drawing of Donald Duck with an intense frown. He is looking out through a barred window, wearing a flying helmet with goggles up on his forehead. The caption reads: "I wanted wings".

We used milk powder as glue to stick various paper cuttings in our wartime log. As a result many have been lost but I still have some outstanding poems written by deep-thinking men in that camp. There are also extracts of unbelievable statements received in letters from wives and girl friends. Just as my valuable flying logbook recalls memories so does this incredible little booklet.

There are signatures of many friends from the USA, Canada, Britain, Australia, New Zealand, Southern Rhodesia, Norway, Argentina and France. I never contacted most of them again, nor they me. Just why that was I'm not sure but possibly because lives had to be radically re-adjusted after our PoW experiences – at least that was my experience.

The one reality in Stalag Luft III during December 1943 was the bitter cold of the winter that held Silesia in its grip. There had been many changes in the war situation. Germany was fighting a desperate rear-guard battle with British and American troops in Italy and the tide was turning against them in Russia. There was no doubt that Germany was going to be defeated.

"But when?" was the constant question asked by every PoW.

We began to think that the Germans must like collecting prisoners in the thousands. Perhaps it boosted their collective ego, we thought. Why they wanted to saddle themselves with the overwhelming problems of feeding, sheltering and guarding them seemed ludicrous and lacking in common sense to many of us. In particular what intrigued us was the massive transfer of prisoners from Italy after that country had surrendered to the Allies. Add to that the many thousands of miserable half starved Russians. True, these were dumped in sub-standard conditions but nevertheless still required constant surveillance and some token of food.

We were astonished at the large numbers of prisoners who arrived in our camp who had previously been held by the Italians. In some cases they had been in the midst of celebrating their expected release when instead they were suddenly surrounded by German troops, bundled into trains and transported all the way to Silesia.

One of these was Humphrey Jowett, a very tall, six foot eight, lanky Australian. Humphrey arrived in our room after being recaptured by the Germans. He had been hiding out in Italian villages for many weeks in an area with an acute shortage of food and salt.

His towering bulk seemed to fill our room but what struck us most was his almost pathological need for salt. We watched in amazement as he covered his food in layers of the stuff.

"It's alright for you to talk. You just don't know what it feels like," he growled when we commented on his food habits.

He was continually starving and when I was cutting the bread he would hover over me, wet his finger and pluck up any minute crumbs. In other words we had amongst us a very hungry man. The salt problem didn't worry us initially until all of a sudden we ran out of it, only to find that salt supplies to the whole camp had stopped. It was weeks before we were able to get any more for our room and, would you believe, for the first few days we were all as bad as he had been – smothering our food to satisfy our salt craving.

We all learnt one important lesson – your body tells you what it needs. Our bodies sure screamed out the same message on that occasion.

"I told you so," said Humphrey.

Winter seemed to be regarded as the off-season for tunnel operations. The Germans relaxed their surveillance and movement between huts was permitted for a short time after dark. The X organisation decided to recommence digging during late January. Discreet dispersal of the freshly dug sand on snow-covered ground was impossible. Dick was already full so that was out of the question.

Everybody mulled over the problem. Then some bright spark suggested putting the sand under the theatre. The building had been constructed by the Kriegies and no inspection areas had been built. So after an access trap had been made in the structure digging started apace and the sand was carried to the theatre after dark.

We also felt that the Germans would not expect plans for an early summer break. During this quiet period there had been a couple of attempts at 'wire jobs' usually attempted during air raids when all lights are out. The problem at those times is that the guard complement is increased for the duration of the raid. No one had ever succeeded in escaping through or over the wire from Stalag Luft III. It was always certain to earn a period in the cooler and the risk of being shot during the attempt was very great indeed.

Amongst our many flamboyant Kriegies was Wing Commander Bob Stanford Tuck, a well-known fighter pilot of high renown from the Battle of Britain days. He had participated in numerous escape attempts with the X organisation and should have known better but his next trick must have been taken on impulse. The often seen horse and cart with a Russian shovelling and German guard as escort was doing its usual rounds of rubbish collection. Stanford arranged for a distraction of the guard, dived into the truck and the Russian shovelled rubbish over him. I should add that when this truck is trundled through the gates the guards check the rubbish by thrusting their rifle bayonets again and again through all parts of the heap.

Such an attempt is suicidal in the extreme unless there is some arrangement with a guard or a major diversion as the truck goes through the gate. Anyway on this occasion X was unaware of this crazy attempt and the truck continued its slow trundle around the rubbish collection places in the camp.

It stopped outside the theatre and a couple of busy Kriegies came out with boxes of rubbish and a bucket of ashes cleaned out from their stove. The truck slowly moved on and as it started to approach the gates there was a noticeable plume of smoke rising from the rubbish. All of sudden poor

Tuck jumped out of the truck with his backside burning.

Who knows, perhaps that small fire saved him greater injury? Many years later at a function in London I made casual mention of that occasion to him but discovered he didn't appreciate my comments.

Chance situations can sometimes set one alight with fresh enthusiasm and suddenly I found myself again thinking about nothing else but escaping. For some time I had known that my name would be in the draw when Harry was opened with perhaps a less than fifty-fifty possibility of being selected. However we all knew that with any large mass break the chances of escape were very small except for the few who spoke fluent German and could immediately travel by train out of the search area. As for the 'hard arses', the foot walkers, every member of the *Hitler Jugend* (Hitler Youth) in the country would be looking for them. A smaller break was preferable as it generally didn't trigger a nationwide hunt, as the German view was that normal security would always net the one or two escapees.

"Have you ever noticed how the surface of the ground here has sunken slightly?" Rex Probert, a Canadian, asked me while standing next to me during the morning *Appell*.

"Probably caused by the trenching for a large drain that must have been laid along this part of the ground," he added.

I looked at the ground surface and saw it was certainly slightly lower and had sunk for a long way running parallel to the warning wire – in fact the slight depression extended right through to the new American camp. The width of the subsidence was just over a metre and the depth at the centre perhaps 15 centimetres. After *Appell*, Rex and I took a closer look. As we walked along this indent and passed the watchtower we noticed that about twenty yards further there was a large old tree stump hard up against the inner perimeter wires and another nearby.

This was unusual, as all old stumps had been carefully cleared away from the perimeter wires closer to our huts. This walk completely unsettled us both, particularly Rex who was an extremely intense and very determined young man. Together we seemed to set each other off. My 'escape vibrations' were again at maximum pressure.

To have any chance of success certain basics were essential. Firstly we needed the approval of the X organisation and its support. To gain this we had to provide a convincing plan of operation. This required us to show how we would tackle such requirements as camouflage to enable us to reach the wire, how we proposed to crawl through the coils of ground level barbed wire and how we would handle other problems not even considered at this stage.

We decided the most effective method of camouflage would be palliasse-type sheets – that is two sheets sewn together and closed at one end – part painted and part rubbed in dirt until they matched the colour of the ground. Peepholes would be cut where the sheets joined together and also holes for the arms to protrude if need be. Long internal pockets would also be required to carry the wooden stakes needed to hold up the coiled barbed wire as it was cut.

Between busily operating as a stooge covering covert X operations, practising with the sax in spite of the intense cold in the practice room, carrying out my room duties and now into sewing operations with our weird ghost-like hoods, my days were exceedingly full. My roommates thought we were completely mad and perhaps they were right but the two of us now had outsize bees in our bonnets and ignored all negative comments.

The big question was would the Escape Committee approve and support us. They examined our plans, asked a few questions, and gave their verdict, a qualified yes. If we did a successful test run they would support the escape. To determine the effectiveness of our camouflage under the searchlights we must crawl out to the warning wire, work our way along it for a few yards, go directly under one of the towers and return. If we made it without detection they would back our attempt.

Arrangements were made to carry out the test the very next night. At the appointed after-dark hour four of the Big X members met us behind the back entrance to our own hut. We stood there bedecked in our ghost-like outfits. They checked us out and gave us the go-ahead. I have been mighty nervous at times during many of my flying days but none of those moments matched this one as we set off, crawling on hands and knees away from the cover of our hut and out into the open.

That short distance, walked often in daylight, seemed like forever when crawled in the dark. Slowly and awkwardly we neared the warning wire, then flattened and froze as the sweep of the searchlight approached our position. The blaze of light seemed to hesitate for a moment. Had we been seen? The searchlight operator answered our question by moving the beam away and then snapping quickly back again. Neither of us moved a muscle.

The searchlight again swept away and we resumed our slow progress, reached the warning wire, paralleled it for a few metres, turned and slowly crawled back towards our hut. The searchlight swept over us again and again but did not detect us. Finally we thankfully reached the shadowy watching group behind our hut. While we disrobed they had a quick discussion.

"You're on," they said, finally. "We'll be in contact."

Next day a couple of escape committee representatives came to see us and ask what our plan of operation was once we had escaped from the camp. With Rex Probert as a navigator and myself as pilot our first plan was to attempt to steal an aircraft. The committee said they would give us cockpit plans and necessary details of the various planes most likely to be available at the nearby aerodromes. They could also supply a plan of the layout of the local aerodrome.

As we spoke very little German, papers would be provided showing us as Spanish workers so off we went to swot up on some basic Spanish. All necessary papers plus concentrated food, compasses and other escape items would be given to us on the night of the break-out. We made the point that for this attempt to have any chance of success we needed a very dark night with low cloud and storm conditions, the better to cut through the wire without detection. The committee agreed and said we should stay ready. When the right weather conditions arose they would bring our gear and give us first escape priority.

Within a couple of days I had pages of information on various German aircraft together with detailed information on their fuel systems. Some of it worried me. Apart from needing to learn the German words on the instrumentation panel and remember that all figures were in metric measurement, I found a few of the fuel systems looked very complicated. This applied especially to the Ju88 and I secretly hoped I wouldn't have to deal with such an aircraft.

As a single engine pilot I knew we could strike some problems in our choice of aircraft but didn't worry Rex with these thoughts. The poor guy probably had some ill-informed confidence in my ability and I would have hated to disillusion him. I was still imbued with the supreme over-confidence of youth and completely ignored the dangers of the entire proposition.

Big X checked with us to see if we were ready and advised that the weather forecasts predicted bad weather approaching. On the first 'wild weather' night they would be around after dark with all our gear.

One other hazard we knew we would have to face but hoped that somehow we'd be out of the way before it arrived was a very large Alsatian dog named Heidrich. Every night at widely varying hours a guard brought Heidrich into our camp and he walked him around the entire perimeter. At intervals he let him loose to roam and hunt for any possible Kriegie that might be silly enough to be out there.

We had done our best to study the habits of the guards who patrolled just outside the perimeter but the corner to which we planned to go was too far away to see properly, or to make any reasonable assessment of their pattern of movement. We were fairly certain that the guards would be more casual in that area as it was so far away from any likely attempt at escape.

Based on what we could see, we knew that we could expect at least a five-minute period each way when they would have their backs to any given point. Not a lot of time but with luck possibly enough.

Then one afternoon the weather deteriorated. It started to rain, turning to cold sleet and rising wind. It looked as if we were in for a storm, absolutely ideal. The two of us had the feeling this was going to be the night. Our hut faced the outside perimeter, which we intended to penetrate, but my particular room faced inwards and our window, sheltered from the searchlights, was our planned exit point. Just before 10 p.m. when all hut lights would be switched off there was a tap on our window. I opened it and found a couple of chaps from Big X standing outside.

They handed me our identity papers, a map of the local aerodrome and also a local map, a compass and some emergency concentrated food. Red

Noble, our hut Little X, came in and gave us our wire cutters. They had very long handles to give us maximum leverage. My roommates assisted us into our weird apparel and then tried to help us out through the window. But the half dozen wooden stakes we each had hanging around us on the inside of the sheets proved so heavy to climb with, however, that we decided instead to get ourselves dressed in them outside the hut.

We tossed up as to which one would use the wire cutters. Rex won so he led the way. The lights in the huts had just been turned off. It was now pitch dark and the wind was blowing hard enough to drive the sleet almost horizontal. We moved quickly along the side of the hut away from the searchlights. Our next move was to get around the inside end of the theatre. This meant a short distance under the full glare of the searchlights so our careful crawling action commenced. We made the distance which was about 75 yards without the lights even pausing over us.

We were then moving out from the end of the theatre into a completely open area where we were exposed to two direct searchlights, one quite near and the other beaming in from the more distant perimeter. We had at least 100 yards to crawl before we would reach the partial safety of the deep indent in the ground. We had just started on this very exposed portion of our crawl when the unbelievable happened. The rain and sleet stopped, the wind dropped, a bright full moon appeared and lit up the camp almost like day.

Without the wind and rain noises the scene was terribly quiet. We could hear the guard coughing in the tower above us and also the footsteps of the guard patrolling outside. To us the worst problem of all was that each movement we made created what seemed like loud scraping noises. In fact they definitely were very loud and our movements now had to be very slight and careful. The air temperature was plunging and the night becoming bitterly cold. We were now right out in the open. We reasoned that if we turned now and went back the stormy weather might suddenly return so we pressed on, inch by inch.

Being forced to lie on the freezing soil while bathed in bright moonlight and fearing to make a sound made it a highly uncomfortable operation indeed. At last, after we must have been going for at least a couple of hours, we finally reached the area of depressed ground which would provide us with the much needed extra cover. Then we heard the dreaded sound of another guard calling out.

"Hier Heidrich! Hier, Heidrich!" The giant dog's paws clumped on ground about 50 or so yards away. I certainly wasn't going to lift my head to take a peep.

Then Heidrich came into view. I could see him with his nose down, zig-zagging over the ground. He paused, lifted his nose and started clomping his way towards our position. I'm sure my heart must have momentarily stopped. The guard, who was quite a way behind the dog, called out to him to come back. Heidrich paused and then trotted off in a different direction. Words were exchanged between the guards and then it was back to the terrible quietness. We continued again.

I had completely lost any concept of how long we had been going but we heard two changes of the guards so it must have been a fairly long time. Finally we reached the place well past the watchtower, cut the warning wire and started our extremely careful approach right beside the tower and then towards the large tree stump. At long last we reached our first goal. Out came the wire cutters and in the still night air we could hardly credit how loud each snip of that wire sounded. A few were successfully cut and a couple of stakes placed under the coils of barbed wire.

Then we heard another set of guards taking over including the one above us in the tower and the guard outside. The outside guard had proved helpful as he took quite a long time between walks to return to our position. But, we couldn't believe our damnable luck, his replacement was a blasted fitness freak or perhaps he was just extremely cold. Whatever the reason, from the moment he took over he started jogging along his patrol area, backwards and forwards in a steady jog trot.

Each time, just as the wire cutters were about to snip, he would be coming back towards us. The situation was now becoming desperate. We had run out of time. It would be daylight very soon; in fact there was a slight hint of daybreak in the eastern sky. The cutting just had to be made quickly. Sure enough, the jog-trotting nuisance spotted Rex Probert as he lowered his wire-cutters and suddenly there was loud and excited shouting.

The guard up in the tower got extremely agitated as he demanded us to raise our hands while Rex, who claimed to speak better German than me, was trying to tell the guard that we were unable to raise our hands while in fact we were trying to place some of our papers into our mouths and swallow them. Unfortunately what Rex in the excitement kept telling the guard was that we would not raise our hands so we got very close to being shot.

With the wisdom of hindsight we should have turned around and gone back to try another day. Instead, after crawling under those searchlights for probably close to eight hours, we found ourselves marched off to the cooler in the dawn light. A small crowd of fellow Kriegies gathered at the gate to watch the entertainment. Very soon after that escape attempt the surface depression in the ground was filled in and the two large tree stumps removed.

Our attempt had been made at the end of February. We hoped fervently that we would be out of the cooler in time for the draw for the big break-out through tunnel Harry. We knew it was almost ready and tension in the camp was building. I still vividly remember my great Maori friend Johnny Pohe, who had shared some exceptional fun times in London with me, standing watching the comic opera of our return through the gate still dressed in our ghost-like camouflage.

"I'll bet I'll be in London before you," he called out to me with a happy grin on his face.

That was the last time I saw Johnny. He did get in the draw and went out through Harry to become another Gestapo victim of the Great Escape.

XXI

The Great Escape

Our escape attempt gave the Commandant a couple of problems he didn't need. One was that we were undetected during our approach to the wire. We were questioned long and hard on that. But it was the plan of the aerodrome, which he found difficult to swallow (we did too, that's how it was found by the guards). He decided the escape had the intent of sabotage.

That meant three months in the cooler, although we were only told the length of the sentence informally by the guards. This news was a shock. We had expected only the usual month in the jug. Such a sentence would almost certainly exclude us having any chance at the big escape which we knew was very close now; in fact most of us had reckoned on the break taking place in April.

The cooler was a fairly secure building which contained a front guardroom area, a corridor with lock-up cells on both sides and a toilet together with a wash-up area adjacent to the guardroom. The cells had quite impressive solid doors boasting a peephole protected with bars. A signal flap could be actuated from inside to call a guard for such things as toilet requirements. The most surprising addition was that next to each cell door on the outside was a built-in compact fireplace.

This was regularly stoked and fuelled by the guards which kept each cell pleasantly warm, making the name "cooler" a complete misnomer. We were provided with a comfortable bunk, a pillow, a couple of blankets, a chair and a small table. No Red Cross parcels were provided but reasonable and varied food came to us from the camp cookhouse.

In stark comparison to our relatively comfortable isolation were the conditions of the Russian prisoners used on cleaning detail. Every day a guard would bring a Russian into each occupied cell to sweep the floors. The man would also sweep out the guardroom, clean the toilets and carry out any other menial tasks needed. He was watched at all times by the guard, afterwards being locked back in his cell.

But what a contrast: his cell had no heat or blankets, no chair or table, certainly no pillow and the temperature was extremely cold. The comparison between this prisoner unprotected by the Geneva Convention and our situation was a reflection of the stark brutality that can develop between enemies. The treatment by both sides, Russian and German, of each other's prisoners of war was at times unspeakable.

We learnt that our cell sweeper was a Russian officer with the rank of major. He had been a fighter pilot in the Russian Air Force. The story he gave was that he had crashed one of his planes through forgetting to put his wheels down, shortly after damaging another aircraft while taxiing. For these two serious mishaps he was sure that he would have been shot so he took an aircraft and flew across to the enemy. He was quite certain he would not live if the Russians defeated the Germans. It was interesting that most of the Russian prisoners feared for their lives when released as becoming a prisoner was considered by them as a disgrace.

Regardless of the conditions in this three-star cooler, it was still damnably difficult to live in a state of solitary confinement while we knew so much was happening in the camp. Quite fortuitously one solution presented itself, staving off the boredom and frustration for quite a few weeks. The unlikely interventionist was the *Unteroffizier* in charge of the guards, a typically ardent brainwashed Nazi, arrogant and excitable.

He came into my cell to hold forth on how he had been part of a group that had raided some Jewish premises. According to him the raid had uncovered secret documents that proved the Jews were conspiring to destroy the Third Reich. He rambled on, describing other raids and various secret plots and sabotage groups discovered, clearly his favourite fantasy which obviously got more lurid in the telling.

When he stopped to take a breath I told him I didn't believe a word. I'd hate to try and repeat the torrent of German unleashed in response to that. Fortunately he understood a fair amount of English so again I suggested that perhaps he was not quite correct; and questioned his accuracy on some points. The result was quite amazing – each day and sometimes two and three times a day this misguided man would come back, trying to convince his captive audience and possibly also himself that his beliefs had no flaw.

Whatever his intent, his tirades helped pass away some of the dreary hours. I doubt if he ever realised he was being baited but he must have seen he wasn't making any converts. Eventually his visits became less frequent though every now and then, having recalled some new piece of Nazi doggerel, he came back with renewed enthusiasm.

On occasion we were taken from our cells and mustered in the open air for exercise. Unfortunately our mustering place was on the side away from the camp facing the perimeter, which bordered the road. There we were allowed to walk around in a restricted circle – spaced apart so it was difficult to speak to each other except spasmodically. Three of us were in the cooler at the time, the third prisoner being an American. Very short in stature and lightly built, he was placed in the cell next to mine.

This was a great boost as we discovered that a message shouted through the barred window could be heard by the other (and probably half the camp could too). We had some great conversations. I found him an interesting man. He came from New York of German parentage and spoke fluent German. He had escaped from camp at least twice before, leaving the Germans completely mystified as to how he did it.

The secret, he told me, was his light weight. So light in fact that the overhead telephone wires which crossed into the American compound could support his body. On two occasions he had taken advantage of night air raids when all the lights were out to jump up and grab the phone lines. Then it was just a matter of swinging along them hand over hand, over the perimeter wire and out of the camp.

Unfortunately the American compound had yet to organise a good forging system of identity papers and he had been caught out each time. With passable papers and his fluency in German he would certainly have got completely away.

He proved to be good company and together we devised a complicated plan of escape from the cooler. After probing our ceilings (made of a type of plasterboard) I found an area in my room could be cut through large enough for a trap door. What I needed was something to plaster over the cuts so they couldn't be seen during cell inspection. We discovered the ideal material was toothpaste. For some strange reason British prisoners were only allowed tooth powder whereas the Americans were allowed paste, so my American friend passed his toothpaste to me.

This worked well, patching the cracks so firmly they were barely visible. I now had a complete trap door just waiting for the night. It was a completely crazy venture but plans went ahead regardless. Rex Probert was to kick up a great fuss and divert the guard while I was returning from the toilet.

This would enable the opening of the American's door and his joining with me in my cell. Together we would then climb through the ready-made trap door. Looking at the plan years later it was more wishful thinking than anything else but there in that crazy environment it seemed quite rational.

However, at the critical stage things went horribly wrong. We probably will never know exactly what triggered the actions of Rex Probert that night. I can only surmise that the tension preceding the deadline must have played on his mind and worried him, because without any warning he decided to charge the guard who was then forced to shoot him.

Rex was seriously wounded, rushed to a hospital and not seen back in Stalag Luft III again. However reports were received that he subsequently made a full recovery. This of course put a stop to our very naïve plan. In retrospect I question whether our thought processes over that period were really operating in a rational manner.

As we neared the last week in March our thoughts turned more and more to tunnel Harry. It was exciting, and frustrating too, to think that some thirty feet below us there was an almost completed tunnel. We knew tensions would be rising within the camp. The ferrets were convinced that Hut 104 was the centre of activity and concentrated search after search there.

Through much use, the entrance trap to Harry was starting to get slightly wobbly. Discovery could come at any time prompting the X leaders to meet urgently. They decided that although the weather was still very cold with up to six inches of snow on the ground, the risk of waiting any longer was too high. The date was set: a breakout on 24 March, the next moonless period. Any idea of waiting another month could not be considered.

Sometime later we were given graphic descriptions of the drama that took place from the moment the decision was made. It required a massive amount of last minute organisation especially by the forging group who had to prepare all the special passes with the correct date. The draw was made. Three hundred were selected to make the escape.

Each man was briefed on the order of procedure and told in which hut to assemble. As they could not all congregate in Hut 104 at the same time some had first to stealthily move to 109 and, when signalled, from there to 104. On the day each was given the necessary papers, concentrated food and compass, and again briefed as to the procedure within the tunnel. They were also asked to take the minimum amount of bulk, as the space inside the tunnel was limited.

The story has been told and retold of the happenings that night but I believe the following is a reasonably accurate account of events as they unfolded. Initially everything proceeded like clockwork. The very nervous escapees gradually congregated in their allotted huts while down below in the tunnel the drama intensified. Slowly and very carefully the tunnel was opened, an operation that had to be done in complete darkness.

To ensure that no light would show to the outside two blankets spaced apart had been hung in the tunnel. Johnny Bull climbed the ladder to the point of opening while five others jammed in the small space below. He wrestled and tugged and fought for nearly thirty minutes with a section of the timber braced above him but just could not shift it and gave up exhausted. He intended to travel as a workman so the fact that his clothes were getting dirty was not critical but the others waiting below were all in immaculate civvies.

One of them, Johnny Marshall, stripped off his clothes and climbed up to attack the timber in his underwear. He worked on the swollen timbers and at last broke one free.

The opening had been planned for 8.45 p.m. but it was 9.30 before a blast of cold air told those waiting that the tunnel was in operation.

Then came the shock to beat all shocks. The point of exit was not as planned. Instead of surfacing just inside the woods it fell short, giving no cover at all. The opening was only a short distance from the road and in full view of the perimeter watchtower just behind the cooler building.

Decisions had to be made. Roger Bushell, one of the group of train travellers at the entrance, insisted that closing the opening and digging the extra few yards would delay the break to the point where discovery was almost a certainty. The odds, everyone felt, were better on the escape continuing.

A rope was strung from the exit opening to just inside the woods, laid by the first man out of the opening. Each escapee at the tunnel exit was to take hold of the rope, which extended to his predecessor hiding under cover in the woods. If all was clear the one in the woods would signal with a tug on the rope. It went like clockwork. Tunnel Harry was in full operation.

Just then the air raid warning sounded. The RAF had chosen that moment to mount a raid on Berlin. All camp lighting went off immediately, including the tunnel, and sounds of the guard being doubled could be heard from the staff quarters. The escape barely paused. Preparation for just such a possibility had been made and fat-burning emergency lamps were brought into play.

Meanwhile the reception huts were crowded with escapees, some in 'civvy' clothes with suitcases, others in barely camouflaged RAF uniforms with bundles of blankets and some in disguised German uniforms. Each slowly moved in stages towards Hut 104. Traffic in the tunnel itself was effected by means of a trolley with flanged wheels, which ran on rails. The plan was that each escapee would lie flat on the trolley while being pulled by rope from one 'station' to the next. Body size and bulky baggage conspired to cause frequent stoppages as escapee and baggage jammed against the tunnel sides, sometimes derailing the trolley on which the escapee lay.

When this happened the escapee was often unable to move. To get things back on track – literally – the 'puller' from either Piccadilly or Leicester Square (the half-way stations) had to crawl along the tunnel to the blockage point, free the escapee and lift the trolley back on the rails. Being in the tunnel at all was a highly claustrophobic experience for many and the frequent hold-ups didn't help this problem.

It was intended that escapees would proceed at the rate of one every two minutes. Already, apart from the late start, the average was closer to five minutes or more. Yet in spite of all these problems there was a steady flow of escapees into the woods.

However, at 5.30 a.m. the escapers' luck ran out. A guard chose that moment to walk along the road and then towards the area where one prisoner had just left the opening and was about to crawl towards the woods. Another, my squadron friend Mick Shand the enthusiastic tomato grower, had almost reached the woods.

The guard seemed to be lost in thought and walked right past the escapee lying on the ground. Suddenly to his astonishment he saw Mick Shand and grabbed at his rifle which he'd been carrying slung from his shoulder. Another escapee behind a bush jumped up yelling out to him not to shoot.

The guard was utterly astonished and confused and when another Kriegie rose from almost at his feet the confusion was just too much for the poor man and he fired his rifle into the air. This alerted the guard in the watchtower who phoned the guardhouse for reinforcements. In the resulting chaos Mick Shand ran away in great haste – the 76th escaper and the last to get away that night by way of the famous Harry.

This account of that remarkable escape operation can only be secondhand. However from my personal experience I can say our cooler that morning became a place of bedlam. There was the tramping of boots, the shouting of commands, the opening and shutting of doors, and prisoners being packed in four to a cell.

We later learned that what we were experiencing was really a very small backwater compared to the chaos within the camp, and Hut 104 in particular. There have been excellent books describing in detail all the intricate preparations, the escape itself, the frantic and angry reactions by the camp guards and a deeply upset Commandant. I can give only some very brief account of the aftermath. Because of the demand on cell space I was immediately removed from the cooler and sent back to my hut with the warning that I would later have to resume my sentence.

The entire camp was in upheaval as every prisoner had to be checked against his photo so that the Germans could determine who had escaped. This took many hours and the guards enjoyed keeping the prisoners out in the cold for this lengthy period. During this time the guards were in full combat clothing, wearing their 'coal scuttle' helmets with rifles at the ready.

One interesting event which occurred immediately after the discovery of the tunnel was that a ferret entered at the exit end and crawled back through the entire length to find its entry point. From that point he found he couldn't return. Unfortunately for him the Kriegies had in the meantime shut down the entrance and lit a fire in the stove. For camouflage reasons the stove normally stood on top of the trap, being moved aside only when access to the tunnel was needed. Deep concern and anger arose from the Germans when they discovered their ferret was missing. They finally appealed to camp adjutant Squadron Leader Bill Jennens – not the Germans' most favourite British officer in the camp – to open the tunnel entrance as their very successful (to us infamous) ferret named Rubberneck was missing.

Bill discussed the matter with a few of the X group who decided there was nothing to lose by revealing the entrance to Harry. He went to the fireplace, extinguished the fire, removed it and lifted the trap to reveal Rubberneck, our ferret-in-chief and old bugbear, looking up with great relief.

Ultimately a dreadful price was paid for what we at the time regarded as a major achievement, the causing of a vast amount of disruption throughout Germany. Until then the German High Command had kept to the spirit of the Geneva Convention. This time there was a grim break with this tradition. Himmler, the head of the Gestapo, issued orders that 50 of the escaped officers were to be shot when re-captured. It was later found that the orders originated from Hitler.

Of the 76 escapees only three succeeded in returning to the UK. Most of the others had to endure long and tedious interrogation by thuggish Gestapo agents. From what they recalled afterwards it seemed a matter of luck rather than what replies were given to their questions whether one lived or died. At first we in the camp did not believe they had really been killed. We thought it only a bluff to stop further escape attempts. The Luftwaffe High Command were obviously deeply upset at having to pass on the news and only when some of the victims' belongings were returned, some with bloodstains, was the terrible truth accepted.

Permission was granted for prisoners to build a memorial in Sagan for those fifty officers who were shot, among them Roger Bushell, our Big X, and also, to my personal sadness, my smiling Maori friend Johnny Pohe.

Life had to go on in the camp. When the number of prisoners in the cooler fell to normal levels the guards again appeared at my room to escort me back for another month or so of isolation. With all that had happened I'd been hoping my offence would have been forgotten. Not so. The German penchant for thoroughness ensured there'd be no stone left unturned, or in this case no escapee unpunished. Thankfully someone (I never discovered who) had smuggled a book into my cell. I found it there under a blanket. It is difficult to describe just how dreadful life in isolation can be and what a pleasure it was to find something that would pass the leaden minutes.

In this case it was a copy of the collected works of O. Henry. It gave me hours of enjoyment. I savoured those pages. Chock-full of humour, they helped ease the days until, at long last, my sentence was completed and I was released back into the camp.

If the appalling crime committed by Hitler and Himmler had been aimed at stopping us from digging another tunnel it had completely the reverse effect. The underlying need for a new escape tunnel gained strength by the day. As the war progressed and the bombing of Germany intensified there was a growing animosity among the German civilian population towards captive British and US Air Force crews. The newspapers carried a constant barrage of propaganda in which we were constantly referred to as Luft Gangsters and Murder Fliers.

Unfortunately for us, this propaganda campaign gained powerful support from an incident in which a downed American Fortress crew were found with the words "Murder Incorporated" inscribed across their flying jackets. The pictures of these airmen and the slogan on their jackets were published throughout Germany and the Axis partner countries.

We felt there was a growing threat of a backlash against prisoners of war in general and airmen in particular as the inevitable collapse of Germany drew closer. Already we detected some hostility among the guards although fortunately only a few.

For that reason it was decided to push forward with as much speed as possible on another tunnel named George. The take-off point was in the theatre. It was also agreed this tunnel would not be used to make a general escape but only in emergency for our own protection. Core defence groups were formed. The rugby players and other athletic types were instructed in basic combat tactics. The main instructors were ex-paratroopers in the camp.

Tunnel George went directly towards the central German Camp Command headquarters with a breakout point planned for near their central armoury. In the event of any threat or danger from the populace we would desperately need to arm ourselves. The defence unit was called the Klim Club after the well-known American milk powder. It was an organisation we hoped would never be needed.

George was dug rapidly and completed as planned. As events transpired it was never used. I have often wondered over the years if that tunnel was ever discovered. The opening trap was situated under a set of theatre chairs. And possibly due to some perverted sense of humour our German guests to the theatre shows were placed on those particular chairs.

There was a strong reason why that tunnel would not have been used for general escaping. The theatre was very important to the morale of the camp. It would have been closed as a first reprisal if found to be part of an escape attempt. We didn't dare risk the possibility.

As for the arts, many groups flourished in the camp. One camp artist in particular, Bjelke Petersen – Pete for short, whom I mentioned earlier, had another remarkable talent. He could rapidly draw cartoon type figures and create compellingly dramatic sketches. Pete finally made his name among other artists in the camp when he decided he would try oils as a medium. He put in his request through normal Red Cross channels which meant going on a waiting list.

One day a canvas and a frame arrived for him, but no paints. He was rather surprised at the large size of his canvas but it certainly served to whet his excitement. From then on he spent his time talking to arty types who kept bombarding him with all sorts of advice on what to do and not to do with colours in the medium of oils.

Despite being a fairly pragmatic Australian, Pete's excitement grew as the weeks passed. At last his oils arrived. To our surprise he decided his first subject would be Percy George. Percy, also an Australian, had many likeable qualities with a great sense of humour but at times a bit acid-tongued. Generally he was one of the quieter hut members with a depth of thought very rarely expressed. In appearance he would probably be described as rugged.

Pete started on the portrait, splashing his oils around with a great confidence and bold strokes. I'd heard some of his many advisers telling him never to use blue as a main background when doing a portrait. To my surprise he did exactly the opposite and started off with a deep blue background.

How he was able to paint at all with a constant group of four or five viewers standing around I couldn't imagine but paint he did, and with some degree of flair. As early as the second day of work he was producing very interesting material, and by the third day we had an almost visual shock when the likeness of Percy stared at us from the canvas.

We who had lived with Percy at close quarters for quite a long time thought we knew him well. But the portrait that Pete was creating seemed to show aspects of his personality that until then we had only glimpsed. It was an incredibly insightful portrait of someone we all knew.

Pete continued with the painting for a few more days, applying finishing touches here and there. His various artistic advisors came to inspect and comment, and spread the news. Soon the art lovers were coming to our room in droves. Everybody admired the work. Pete seemed transformed, flushed with pleasure and pride in the talent he had so long suppressed. I hope that wonderful painting survived the chaos of the Russian advance – because eventually our camp and all that territory were to become part of East Germany.

In early June we had momentous news. The invasion of France had begun and the long awaited Second Front was now a reality. Predictions as to the length of the war were rapidly revised. Some suggested it could be over by Christmas. We knew from our daily BBC news bulletins that Russia was rapidly advancing through Poland and towards Silesia.

Some of us were convinced that we might have to survive on our feet so a few in our room developed a mania for applying Dubbin, a leather polish and water repellent, to our boots. We worked constantly on the leather, trying to make it as soft and waterproof as possible.

Long discussions on what we would need to do in various circumstances filled our days. We sensed the approach of chaos and felt strongly that precautions taken now might perhaps make life just that little bit more bearable.

XXII

The Long Journey

The atmosphere in the camp during the latter months of 1944 was a strange mixture of relief and apprehension. Relief that at last the war was reaching its final stages and apprehension as to how this craziness would finally end. Every action and reaction of this titanic struggle had been watched and studied in particular by the older Kriegies amongst us. Armchair strategists abounded.

Some rooms had large maps of Europe and others of Russia. Each day arrows depicted the advances and retreats. Bets were laid, some quite large, as to the month or even the day the war would end. Cheques were written out on pieces of paper, which, we were assured, were quite legal and acceptable to banks. That was the lighter side of the picture.

A more ominous, constantly recurring theme was the possibility that PoW Allied Air Force personnel would most likely be held as hostages. It wasn't a particularly pleasant thought.

At the end of 1944 tunnel George was virtually complete but remained unopened, awaiting the emergency we hoped would never arise. Winter temperatures were already plunging when there was a new development. Faintly at first but growing by the day, the sound of the Russian guns could be heard in the distance. They thumped and rumbled their message that the fighting front was getting closer.

Reports indicated the Russians were approaching the Oder River and would soon be entering German territory. The prospect appeared to have little effect on camp administration. Guard changes came and went as always.

Outside the perimeter fence German workers could be seen going about their normal daily routine of maintenance tasks as if nothing had altered. Guard duties did not vary, giving the impression they all expected the Führer's promises would be fulfilled. This of course had always been a constant refrain of guards' conversation, a fixed belief that German science and technology in the form of a secret weapon would save them.

Their faith seemed incredible. Were they really that stupid? I doubt it. Perhaps the real explanation is that they were simply stoically, and certainly courageously, resigned to the inevitable. And with typical Teutonic attention to detail they were carrying on with the job.

It all came to an end with maximum drama on the night of 28 January, 1945. The snow was deep on the ground and partly frozen to ice when guards rushed through each hut in our camp calling out: *"Heraus! Heraus! Efferybody heraus!"* To a pounding of boots and yelled orders we learned that we had about an hour to pack up our belongings and move out onto the road.

We were not going to be left behind for the Russian advance troops to liberate. Instead we were to be evacuated, on foot. But to where? Nobody seemed to know. And why the hell a night march? Though never officially announced, we all assumed it was to avoid strafing from Allied aircraft. As for the small group in our room, it took only a momentary glance at each other to set in motion the plan we had long discussed. Each of us knew exactly what we had to do.

Packing our clothes had to wait. Clay and Percy dashed out of the room and ran as fast as they could go for our hot shower block. Clay had the key and although others were already there and trying to break in he had immediate entry to where he had hidden the two ice hockey goal-keeper sticks.

He and Percy returned triumphantly with the sticks to Bob Browning (my fellow New Zealander) and me as their co-partners and sledge builders. While they were away Bob and I had been ripping out the woodwork from our bunks to construct the framework. When the frame was completed we attached those two beautiful hockey sticks as perfect sledge runners.

And while all this was going on the remaining room members had the very important job of raiding the central distribution of Red Cross parcels and the camp exchange store. They were quick off the mark but still found themselves competing with a surging mass of other Kriegies.

However, the pre-planning paid off. Our group knew exactly what to take and what to leave. Heavy cans were kept to a minimum. Sugar was grabbed in quantity, as were chocolates and raisins. The key item that most overlooked in their panic was cigarettes. We had already figured out that these would have valuable purchasing power. So our foragers brought back many thousands of cigarettes.

By this time our sledge was taking shape with the final assembly being made outside the hut in the chill of a dark wintry night. Our efforts had taken considerably more than the hour but this didn't seem to matter, as there was utter chaos within the camp as Kriegies ravaged the stores and took everything, which they thought might have some use on the journey. Makeshift sledges seemed to be popping up all over the place.

Guards yelled at the top of their voices. In fact such was the noise that yelling was the only way to be heard. Every light in the camp was blazing and the searchlights moved backwards and forwards across the scene. What a great bombing target we would have made.

Our room group was extremely lucky to have secured some rope that had been used to surround the ice rink – another perk gained through the foresight of Clay in his role as hot shower superintendent. We loaded the supplies onto our sledge plus practically all of our own personal items and took a last look around the room at the shambles of what once had been our home.

Some had collections of photos to take off the walls. I had only one, the sole picture that had ever reached me in the camp. It was of two very special people, Jim and Jacky Dyson. This was carefully packed away with my small wartime logbook.

I can't recall whether Pete took his wonderful painting but am fairly certain I saw him carefully rolling it up into a cylinder. We also shouldered 'Kriegie-made' backpacks, empty but for a change of clothes. These had been made in anticipation of the very real possibility that we might not always have conditions which permitted the use of sledges.

Then the long journey began, an extremely depressing sight as members of our camp moved slowly out of those hated gates and onto the road. It looked like an endless stream. There were 2,000 of us in the North Compound alone, altogether well over 10,000 prisoners on the march. March is hardly the right word. It was more a painful and extremely slow shuffle as the cold began to chill hands and feet.

We had been on a rigid food ration for some weeks prior, with less than half of a Red Cross parcel per fortnight. Such an inadequate diet meant a generally poor level of health for most camp members, certainly not a fit state in which to face the rigours of the cold and exertions of the march.

For some time the pace seemed just bearable. We from our room were indeed an extremely fortunate group. We had very little weight on our backs and the sledge towed with relative ease. There were seven of us from our room at the moment of our exit from the camp so four took turns at pulling the sledge and three walked beside and behind carrying only their light loads.

Before many miles had passed we began to notice that the odd tin of food, particularly the heavier ones, was being discarded at the side of the road. Some poor devils were already suffering with the weight of their packs. We trudged on endlessly throughout the night at a pitifully slow pace. Ridges of ice on the road surface intermixed with snow made walking difficult, as did the slight camber of the road.

It was more comfortable in the centre but we couldn't stay there as occasional German transport came barging through, forcing us back to the churned-up verges. As the night dragged on the cold seeped into every fibre of our being. We were told that the temperature was more than twenty degrees below zero. The numbers were meaningless. We only knew that it was colder than we had ever known, an awful pain that sank to the bone and caused constant stumbles and falls.

One major problem that beset us throughout the entire time we were on the road was the extraordinary concertina effect of moving in such exceedingly long columns. Somewhere, miles away in the front, a halt would be called to give everyone a short rest. Those behind, tired and longing to stop, would plod on unaware. As they closed up with those ahead and gratefully stopped, they would barely have time to put down their packs and hunt out something to nibble on before being forced to move on. After putting up with this for mile after mile we woke up to the stupidity of it all and divided ourselves into shorter lengths with separate controllers.

Suddenly the column came to an extended halt in the freezing cold. The night was still pitch black and no one seemed to have much idea as to what was happening. The information filtering back was that they were trying to organise some form of shelter for what was left of the night. From where we were we had no idea what was going on so just stayed put, getting colder and colder.

Finally there was a slow shuffling forward and at last after rounding a bend we could see groups of Kriegies crowding into the entrance to a farm. Ever so slowly we moved forward in the bitter cold, still with no idea as to what was happening. Just as we got to the entrance we learnt there was no more room so we moved on through the night to another stop, another farm entrance and the slow process of squeezing in began again.

At last we reached the entrance of a huge barn-shaped building and finally found ourselves inside amongst straw and hay. There was a crush of humanity but oh the warmth was just wonderful. We lay back exhausted and felt the heat creeping back into our bones.

I have often thought back to that unique moment of pleasure with a lasting twinge of a guilty conscience, because I recall that I lay there not giving a damn for anybody nor offering to help anyone. I was delighted simply to have found enough space to just lie down, heedless that hundreds of others were still struggling to get in and find somewhere to rest and warm their weary bodies.

I can still today remember the voices of Canadian Red Noble and Welshman Shag Reece calling out to those still desperately trying to find a space, showing them with borrowed German torches where to go, helping others for hours after. We had some magnificent men amongst us and they were two such men. They probably had little or no rest that night.

The morning greeted us, promising another cold bleak day as we stumbled back onto the torturous road. Some were already suffering blistered feet. We from our room were extremely grateful for our soft leather, well waterproofed boots. There were no hot drinks to start the day and I found it interesting just how strongly my body told me what it wanted. Those cravings drove me to what I thought was the impossible. I sat down in the snow, opened a tin of margarine that someone had thrown away back there on the road, scooped it out, wolfed it down in large mouthfuls and left the can empty.

We started off again in that same slow shuffle along what the wintry daylight showed as the bleakest of roads, little more than a black, slush-filled track. We had hardly covered a mile or so when we reached a village called Halbrau where, thankfully, we were each given a bowl of hot soup.

It was a long queue and a long wait but was worth it when at last we got to gulp it down. Then we were on the road again – unwashed, unshaven and rapidly becoming very unclean.

The only difference was that this time we were trudging along in freezing conditions in daylight, so much for our protection from marauding aircraft theory. Limping along next to us was a German guard carrying full combat kit, which was about 60 lb. Quite a load for a fit youngster but most of these guards were of the older variety and some were already feeling the strain. He asked us if he could put his large knapsack on our sledge and offered to help pull the sledge. We told him to "get lost" or words to that effect.

He more or less pleaded but we ignored the poor devil. Soon after he collapsed and was picked up later on a truck. Rumour had it that he died but we never received confirmation of that. However it did make us feel bad about the incident. What we did have confirmed was that one of our guards lost a leg through frostbite while standing on guard during that first night.

With daylight the walking pace picked up a bit which helped us to generate a little heat and keep it circulating in our bodies. After about 20 miles we started to pass the odd small cottage indicating another village. Then we had the most unbelievable experience, almost like walking into fantasyland. As I trudged along I noticed a woman standing at a cottage gate with a small boy beside her. She was holding a steaming jug in her hand. When I rushed across to her the little boy shrank away but she held him tight and persuaded him to pass me a cup of hot soup.

I can't imagine what we must have looked like to the boy and indeed also to that kind lady who stood her ground as a considerable number of us crowded around her gate. To us she seemed almost angelic, magical, some quite different kind of being.

We moved on to what we could see was indeed an attractive little village. There was no sign of guards anywhere so two of us decided to see if we could buy anything with our cigarettes from a small store. Inside were two very elderly folk, a man and a woman. We started off in dreadful German asking for hot water but got a bit stuck when trying to tell them we would like to buy food.

They were a very pleasant couple and tolerant of our poor German but shook their heads sadly, said *"Kommen sie mit"* and took us into their kitchen to show that cupboard after cupboard was empty. They gave us a small loaf of bread and we gave them twenty cigarettes. You'd have thought we had given them a fortune. We didn't gain much but at least left someone a little happier.

The fantasyland experience continued. We had walked into an oasis of human kindness of the sort we had long forgotten existed, a kind of small point of sanity in a whole world gone mad. As we crowded into the centre of this village, a fairly large open space, we found a group of German women young and old – mostly old – handing out cup after cup of hot soup. There were also bowls of warm water for us to wash our hands and faces.

On the side of this village 'square' was a small church and nearby a public hall. The doors to both were thrown open so we could enter and seek shelter. Both buildings were already crowded. Some of our chaps with more fluency in German had already arranged private accommodation, probably anticipating the very best of home comforts for a hungry Kriegie. All this fraternisation with the enemy was staggering – but sadly we should have known it was just too good to last!

Into the midst of this pleasant place there suddenly drove carloads of black-garbed SS troops with weapons drawn. At gunpoint we were ordered to leave immediately. It was a brutal return to reality. We imagined that some cursed ardent Nazi had phoned headquarters about the disgraceful non-Nazi behaviour of the villagers of delightful Freiwaldau.

Some of the cynics said that we only received that welcome because of their terror of the advancing Russians. I don't agree. To me it was a wonderful impulsive action with an instinctive wish to help humans who were obviously in distress, and there were hundreds of our fellows in a very bad way. I never returned to Germany, but should I ever do so that is one village to which I owe many thanks for their touch of human kindness. The thought of its possible brutal treatment when over-run by the advancing Russian army doesn't bear thinking about.

The next town on our trudging journey was Muskau. On its outskirts a considerable number of us were diverted into quite large glass factory premises. We kept crowding into the place until it was crammed to the doors. The rest continued on to find shelter at a large horse riding school, a laundry, a cinema and at some breeding stables.

Our room contingent plus our valuable sledge found shelter in a low-ceilinged storeroom underneath the main building. Hundreds of us filled this confined area, many quite sick and all very cold. Dysentery was beginning to show up in increasing numbers of people. It was obvious that soon there would be a major hygiene problem.

We made an urgent request to the Germans for spades, picks and shovels so that latrines could be dug at various positions all around the premises. The Germans responded willingly. The local mayor or *Burgermeister* arranged for the furnaces of the glassworks to be lit to provide warmth. It was an amazing transformation.

From a bitterly cold, miserable, empty glassworks factory it suddenly became alive. The huge cylinder-type furnace in the centre of this spacious place slowly became red hot, then white-hot and all that wonderful glorious heat seemed to pour out directly into our bones.

We were allowed to stay there for a couple of days, a welcome break that helped most of us to recover. I shudder to think what sort of conditions would have developed without those latrines. Then it was back onto that long dreary journey and the shock of realising that a thaw had set in and the road was now pure slush.

We tried dragging our sledge for a short while but the effort was too great. We hated to leave what had become a faithful friend but realistically it was now more of a hindrance than a help. Regretfully we loaded our valuable possessions into our backpacks and left that beautiful sledge lying on the side of the road, conscious that we no longer belonged to a privileged class. We were now just stumbling, laden Kriegies like all the rest.

The next township we trudged through was Graustein, shuttered and empty by the look of it. Then we arrived at Spremberg to find a slew of railway trucks awaiting us. It was a toss-up whether we were relieved at the chance to get off our feet while travelling, or the horror of again being crushed like cattle into those appallingly ventilated modes of transport.

In the end it was a nightmare journey, which took us through to the huge German railway centre of Halle, a notorious target for RAF bombing raids. Whether by accident or design we were left to languish there on a siding apart from an occasional shunting for what seemed to be a couple of days. It's all too easy to lose any sense of time under those conditions. We were let out for obvious needs every now and then and after numerous requests were given hot water to mix our own drinks.

What we didn't realise until some of us became quite ill was that the guards had got hot water from the engine boilers which contained anti-corrosive chemicals. As a result there was considerable sickness in all the trucks.

Finally the unpleasant train journey courtesy of Nazi Germany began again, rumbling through the night to a place called Tarmsted, somewhere between Bremen and Hamburg but closer to Bremen. There we were offloaded to make our weary way to what was to be our next PoW camp.

This was run by German naval marines with guards now in pale green uniforms instead of the familiar pale blue of the Luftwaffe. But first we were forced to wait outside for hours in the pouring rain to be searched. God knows what they were looking for; it could hardly have been weapons. Some collapsed in the rain and lay where they fell.

At last we entered what at first looked as though it was a very similar type of prison camp surrounded with the same barbed wire perimeters and watchtowers. Almost too tired to be shocked, we found the insides of the huts were in an appalling condition. There were hardly any bunks and what few there were had been wrecked, as were all the stoves. Bedding was virtually non-existent. Most of the floors were of damp brick; there were no toilets in the huts, no showers and in fact no running water.

The one central latrine was a disgusting pit with slats of timber on which to sit with a very real risk of falling in. The plumbing in the huts was completely wrecked. There was indeed very little for the comfort of this large group of emaciated and very sick men. Almost too weak to protest we demanded an explanation. We were told the previous occupants were British soldiers who on being evacuated had deliberately wrecked everything in the belief the German military was going to move in.

We had multiple emergencies that had to be dealt with and all credit to the Germans they were fully co-operative. Our first and most urgent need was for spades to dig pits outside the windows of every room so that our fellow prisoners could just hunker out of the window to satisfy nature. Everyone had dysentery and that was about as far as they could move when the urge arose, which was frequently.

It is difficult to convey just how much we had deteriorated and how poor our physical state. Without exception every man was skeleton thin, listless and very dirty. But for all our problems we had an intense determination to rise above them. A quick count showed that over 70 of our number were missing. About half of these were left behind through illness and the other half just missing, perhaps escaped or possibly shot.

XXIII

Chaos

We had a Hell Camp in the making. Most of us were in poor shape and many were tottering on their feet. Some were suffering from frostbite and everyone was badly undernourished. Yet in spite of our weakened physical state and our miserable surroundings there was an indomitable spirit that would not accept this degradation.

On that score I had the greatest respect for the senior officers within our weary group who just would not permit any suggestion of lying down and accepting the inevitable. Heading this group was our very determined Squadron Leader Bill Jennens acting as adjutant. He stood at the gates; or rather he leaned on them and ranted at the poor German guards.

He kept an unending stream of demands and accused the guards of not taking action to meet them. His first demand was that they immediately bring to him the Camp Commandant. The Commandant, he told them loudly and clearly, must personally accept responsibility for this complete breakdown of all basic rights to British officers under the Geneva Convention.

He demanded washing facilities, beds to sleep on and adequate food – the list went on and on. Finally the Camp Comandant did come down and meet with our senior officers. He explained the impossible conditions but gave his assurance that he would do what he could.

The first achievement was modest. Water was laid on to one tap. Then after further requests we were given a long hose. This was led into the middle of an open recreational area where a sprinkler was fitted onto a rickety framework.

The guards watched, disbelieving, as we organised ourselves into groups based on hut occupancy and paraded in a long queue. Stripped of our clothes we stood under the icy cold spray of water and without soap scrubbed at our skin with bare hands.

It was still freezing winter conditions and yet each of us was willing to suffer the bitter cold just to get our bodies clean. It took a long time, spread over a couple of days or more, for all of us to be able to retrieve some self respect and a feeling of being clean, or at least less dirty than before.

A little more food mainly from Red Cross parcels began to build up health and morale. Further negotiations with our German naval marines achieved their agreement to provide carpenter's tools for us to make bunks. They also agreed we could pull down the alternate walls between our rooms in the huts to get sufficient timber. Amid the noise and the disorder bunks seemed to materialise miraculously.

The Germans also plundered, found or somehow produced quite a quantity of beds and squabs from a nearby hospital. Most of the plumbing for each hut was also restored. Without pots or pans cooking was a problem. We obtained permission to go out in guarded working parties to the nearby dump and collect piles of discarded tins from previous Red Cross supplies.

It wasn't long before we had improvised heating ovens, cooking trays, tin cups from which to drink and so on. The ranting and raving by Squadron Leader Jennens plus our own obvious determination must have impressed our naval captors. The next surprise was the arrival of truckloads of Red Cross parcels. This vast improvement lasted about two weeks.

Suddenly the harmonious relationship with our captors deteriorated. From one of relative trust the guards assumed an attitude of deep suspicion. We concluded that there could be only one reason for this sudden change – the tidy German mind again and the Teutonic need for attention to trivial detail. There had been a time lag after our sudden departure from Sagan and now all the paper work and administrative files had caught up with us. These would have included the inevitable summary of reports detailing what a bad and devious, escape-prone lot we really were.

The Commandant, we concluded, had read these with close attention and passed orders to the guards to "handle with care". The first impact was on the delivery of our Red Cross parcels.

Throughout the years and against our protestations the prison administration had always insisted on puncturing every can and opening every package in a Red Cross parcel. They insisted this was to stop us from hoarding them for escape purposes. All we could do was to cover the punctured holes in the cans with margarine, which did prolong the life of the contents to some degree.

Now our previously co-operating captors took radical action. Instructions were issued that the contents of all Red Cross parcels were to be opened and emptied in one single heap. That included cigarettes. The resulting mess was disgusting and insulting, so we simply refused to accept the parcels in this condition. It is hard to imagine a more unlikely situation than that of half-starved and convalescent PoWs flatly refusing to accept Red Cross food, messed up or otherwise, but refuse we did.

The stand-off continued for quite some days. We were fast getting very hungry and very concerned. Practically every prisoner was reduced to a slow walk, conserving energy just to be able to exist. Many just lay on their bunks without leaving them. All of us were well aware this was self-imposed starvation but felt united in our determination to be treated as humans rather than animals. The German Commandant came down and spoke to some of our senior officers, appealing to us to accept the opened conglomeration of Red Cross food.

We still refused and accused them of flouting the Geneva Convention. Finally when we had all began to wonder how long we could last, the Germans relented and the flow of Red Cross parcels resumed. The packets were as usual opened and cans punctured but at least delivered as separate components of our diet.

Our group from the room back in Stalag Luft III, the seven who had dragged that beautiful sledge for so many miles, was still together. We now had a new addition. He was British, very quiet and retiring, lying for hours on his bunk and saying very little. All we could discover about him was that he was not really in the RAF but was a civilian 'boffin' or backroom boy.

He had flown as an observer on a bombing mission to study the performance of some new high tech gadget. Unfortunately for him his bomber was shot down so he had to assume the guise of an RAF aircrew member. He was to prove a very useful member of the team.

After knocking out the alternate walls to make bunks, we now shared a larger space with 15 others. To make life more bearable we devised methods of sharing the stove and all the various utensils we had made. Operating as one unit of sixteen was a bit much so we stayed at eight. Bob Browning and myself, still operating as the 'tin-bashers' for our group, decided to make a chip heater.

This is a means of boiling water quickly, made up of an inverted cone with a central pipe or chimney. Water is placed in the cone and small pieces of combustible material, usually wood chips or paper, are dropped down the centre chimney and set alight. In a very short time the water is happily boiling.

Our chip heater, to be of any real use to our group, had to hold eight cups of water. The question arose as to how we would calculate the dimensions to be sure that the finished article would hold the required number of cups. We approached our newfound member and asked him if he had any idea how we could work it out. The result was utterly astounding.

It was as if Bob and I had given him the elixir of life itself. He sat up with alacrity, asked excitedly for pen and paper and set to work. Covering page after page with algebraic calculations, eyes bright and completely absorbed, he was a changed man. By the next day he smilingly gave us a very simple formula for the dimensions which he explained would give us exactly eight cups of boiling water, allowing for a limited amount of evaporation. All we had to do was abide by his measurements.

We did just that and, after about three days of bashing and crashing and soldering, we tried out his masterpiece. It worked exactly as predicted and we enjoyed eight cups of hot Canadian Red Cross coffee. And we also had a very happy and involved mathematics boffin. On reflecting back it was an utterly contradictory situation. While we focused all our concentration on making a chip heater to produce eight cups of hot water, practically all Europe was collapsing into devastation.

Survival was our paramount driving force. We were confident the war was in its closing stages. We could hear the artillery of Field Marshal Montgomery's British army shelling the major city of Bremen. We knew that Eisenhower's United States troops were now deep into the south of Germany and Russia was advancing into eastern Germany. We felt sure that very soon this sector would be over-run and we would be at last liberated.

Our camp was situated in a shallow valley. Less than a mile away was another PoW camp on the higher ground overlooking this valley. This camp, which held British merchant seamen, was quite close to a small village. We relished the comforting thought that the Germans would not bother moving us again unless the hostage card was played, a possibility which was growing less by the day.

That was our comparatively happy state until without warning or any previous hint of change the guards marched into our camp late one afternoon. Again the yelling and stamping and shouting of orders to pack up and move immediately. Our first thought was why the hell always at the end of the day, and more importantly why the hell now when the war was almost over.

Angry and frustrated we milled about. Out of our anger grew a general agreement: we would stage a deliberate go-slow. Each prisoner was to double back after leaving and create as much chaos as possible. For the next three or four hours this caused complete disorder.

By then only a few dozen prisoners had been moved out through the gates. More guards were mobilised. Menacing shots were fired into the air but still the go slow continued. Darkness had long since fallen before the mass of prisoners outside the gates began to build up into the semblance of a column and shuffle along the road. At that moment a rumour flashed around: the BBC had just announced the capture of Bremen by Monty's troops.

Bob and I had a quick discussion. We decided to escape immediately and hide somewhere until the British over-ran the area. A quick meeting with our friendly Canadian Red Noble, who was still our X contact, brought his agreement. Miraculously he produced a pair of wire cutters, a compass, a complete Red Cross box of food and wished us luck.

It was a night of high drama. Kriegies were wandering all over the place and guards were stomping about, yelling orders and holding their rifles menacingly. Interspersed with this was much laughter, which must have been irking the hell out of the Germans. We grabbed a few personal items for our improvised back-packs, I tucked the Red Cross box under one arm and holding the wire-cutters dashed out with Bob into the darkness having no particular plan at all.

We made for the opposite end of the camp, as far away as possible from the mob around the gates and the road. It was a nerve-wracking few moments as we had no idea how many guards were wandering about. The searchlights were flashing without any set pattern except that the concentration seemed to be towards the gate area so we decided to risk crossing the warning wire.

Once over, we crouched against the perimeter wires and started cutting through them in the dark. It was incredibly slow; in fact the progress we were making seemed hopeless. The wire-cutters were cutting poorly and jamming. We reconsidered and decided simply to scramble over the wire and hope we wouldn't be noticed in the confusion.

We both knew this was extremely risky but we decided it was worth the gamble. We clawed our way up the seven-foot high barbed wire and were balanced perilously on the top when a shot rang out. We jumped from the top into the dark, landed and then tried to find the Red Cross box I had thrown over the fence. In the pitch blackness all that could be found was one container that we later discovered held peanut butter.

Another shot rang out and we could hear guards running so we took off in a great hurry. Whether they were chasing us or someone else we had no idea and were not waiting to find out. It wasn't the most remarkable or smooth escape in the books but we were out of the camp and on the loose. As we moved off into the night we could still hear the sound of shouting coming from our recently vacated prison.

When we felt we'd moved a safe distance we stopped for a breather and to check our bearings. Of considerable concern was our complete lack of food. Then we discovered that our compass was missing. It must have fallen out of my pocket during our wire-jumping acrobatics. Navigation then was going to be of the follow-your-nose variety.

We could hear the artillery fire in Bremen thumping in the distance so we headed in that direction. The weather was cold but fine. But lack of moonlight caused us to trip over obstacles and step on twigs making a dangerous amount of noise. We slowed to a cautious amble.

Bob had a small container of water and we both had ample warm clothes but little in the way of waterproofing. During that first night we kept well away from the roads. Before daybreak we opted to hide in an area of untrimmed young pines whose branches grew very close to the ground.

We hadn't the faintest idea where we were or how close the nearest habitation was but slept soundly from sheer nervous exhaustion. The cold damp air of morning brought us shiveringly awake to a first glimpse of our surroundings. The view was reassuring. Peeping through our leafy cover we could see a small valley partly cultivated with vegetable gardens on the far side. Above these were small village type homes clustered on each side of what looked like a main road.

It wasn't long before small groups of women moved out into these vegetable gardens to work. We had expected to see some form of panic by citizens facing imminent invasion from the hordes of the attacking army. Instead all seemed calm and peaceful. Breakfast, a fingerful each of peanut butter scooped out of the can, was the first priority. Then on to our plan of action.

This was simple in the extreme: stay the hell out of the way and wait for the advancing British army, which would doubtless come along the road opposite. Instead as the morning progressed we could hear the singing of

German troops marching through the village – towards the front, not away from it. Their voices sounded like those of young boys. They seemed in good heart, singing for the love of the Fatherland.

What a madness the whole crazy situation had become – and what a frustrating lesson to us it was. We had seen the same stoic behaviour and undeniable bravery of the German people in eastern Germany. Their world was clearly falling apart around them yet acceptance of defeat didn't seem to be in their make up.

Our first day dragged on. We stayed as we were, as our position seemed reasonably secure. The rumble of distant guns continued unabated but there was certainly no sign of a retreating army. In fact all troop movement were clearly towards Bremen while the women continued to work in the fields. We sparingly scooped another odd finger of peanut butter, surveyed the valley below for a source of water and perhaps an edible vegetable or two, and waited for darkness.

If we had to bluff our way with the locals it was important that we try and stay reasonably presentable. That meant rehearsing our few Spanish words and finding water so that we could shave regularly with our one and only safety razor. After dark we carefully made our way down into the valley where we stumbled onto a shallow muddy pool. This had to do. We drank some, it tasted dreadful, and then each had a cold painful shave.

Our search for edible vegetables in the gardens found nothing but small plants. Not surprising, as it was early March. We noticed the silhouette of a small shed and felt our way inside. The nearby village was silent and in complete darkness. The door made some horrible creaks. Inside on a bench we found by feel a couple of round vegetables and carried them off triumphantly.

The next morning we anxiously examined our booty. To me they looked like two most unappetising turnips. Bob with his farmer's knowledge enlightened me. They were kohlrabi and if cooked well could be quite tender and pleasant. His information was not very encouraging but at least we had some possible sustenance however distasteful.

Some of our precious peanut butter was spread onto pieces sliced off with a table knife, which was part of our escape kit. We were hungry enough to find the result palatable, having long ago discovered that appetite when strong enough is very undiscriminating. The water quality of the previous night's muddy pool gave us some concerns but hunger and thirst had turned us into optimists who hoped it didn't contain too many bugs.

This routine of down for a shave and stretching our limbs during the night continued for five dreary days while we waited for Monty's men to come pouring down the road. But still the pounding of artillery continued. We knew it would be impossible to penetrate the nearby German defences and any attempt to cross the river Weser near Bremen would be suicidal.

Our only relief from the monotony was that on two occasions a very passionate and eager pair of lovers chose to relieve their tensions under a tree only a few yards from us. We were fortunate they didn't choose our position. As all the younger men were supposed to be at the front line we could only assume that this one was an 'oldie' in a state of rejuvenation. We didn't dare risk being seen so had no opportunity for a look at this remarkably eager beaver.

On the fifth day we felt it was time we reassessed our situation. We felt we'd been sold down the river by the optimistic BBC. There was no doubt that Monty would break through sometime but dire hunger was weakening us rapidly. There was no more kohlrabi, tough eating or not, and the peanut butter was almost gone.

What was our wisest plan of action under these circumstances? Were we certain the Germans had succeeded in moving our fellows onto the road or could they still be there? And if so did it mean the possibility of being held hostage was now eliminated? We batted the questions back and forth. To travel cross-country would be highly dangerous and there was a hostile population with which to contend.

After lengthy discussion hissed to each other in whispers we decided to return to our last campsite and check if our fellows had really moved on. The problem was that we had escaped in the night and without a compass so had only the vaguest idea of the direction. To travel back in the dark would have been hopeless. We were fairly certain that the road below along which the troops had been marching would lead us back to camp.

Hunger spurred the decision. Next morning early, before the workers appeared in the fields, we moved carefully back into the woods and found a well worn track. With packs on our backs we strolled out, across the valley and up onto the road just outside the village. There were the odd folk walking along the road towards us. We bid them *"Guten tag"*, received a similar reply and kept walking hoping like hell that none would want to make conversation.

One did say something so I just said, *"Ja das ist gut"*, pointed to myself and said *"Espano"* which brought a puzzled look. We kept walking. A few military vehicles passed in a hurry all going towards Bremen. We were in our Air Force battledress with wings and rank displayed. It would only be a matter of time before this run of luck would end.

As we turned a corner in the road the topography of the surrounding land took on a familiar look. Then we saw our camp below us in the distance. The problem now was to check that it was still occupied by our Air Force companions. Taking a chance we left the road and crossed over some fields towards a line of trees where we hoped to study the camp unobserved.

Our luck held. No one appeared to notice us. We sat for ages wishing we had binoculars, as it was obvious the camp was occupied with prisoners. There were guards around the perimeter and on the watchtowers. Somehow the inmates just didn't look like our chaps. Their dress looked different and even their carriage.

Further up the hill the other merchant seamen's camp could be seen. We felt it would be most unlikely they would also have been moved. They were known to fraternise and trade regularly with their guards so we decided to move up for a closer look. An hour later we were lying behind some shrubbery near this camp trying to decide how bold we might be when a convoy of three trucks pulled up outside the camp's main gates.

We could hardly believe what we were seeing. The trucks were laden with Red Cross parcels. This was a punishing sight. We threw all caution to the winds, decided that boldness or perhaps just plain recklessness was the only solution, and strolled up to the perimeter wires.

The guards looked at us casually so we went closer and called out to some types walking inside. We asked them if the Air Force prisoners had been moved from the other camp.

"Yes, they've all gone but there are quite a few of your friends in this camp," one seaman told us.

"You are crazy to be out there," another added. "The Commandant has been sending out search parties and posted notices warning those that escaped to return because of the hostile population."

We suggested they talk to the guards at the gates in the hope they could smuggle us back in. Hunger was ruling our every move. We who had longed for years to escape were now outside trying to break back into a PoW camp. In the end it wasn't even all that much of an effort. The guards at the main gates let us in without a fuss. They were then given instructions to take us for a hot shower and a meal. It was, we agreed, the soundest move we'd made in days.

After our shower and meal we entered the camp proper and were received by a welcoming committee made up of our own Air Force types who had avoided the march. They had feigned sickness and inability to continue further. Included in this group of malingerers was our own special Rhodesian friend and roommate, Ray Hill.

He explained with his delightful chuckle that he had acted out a very bad bout of malaria. So convincing was he that two German guards had carried him all the way to this camp on a stretcher while another had carried his gear.

Bunks were found for us with our own group. Food we discovered was plentiful. This seemed as good a place as any to wait for Monty and a hell of a lot better than Bob and I had chosen. Best of all we had avoided that last forced march to Hamburg, a trek that our fellows had to endure while uncertain of their ultimate fate.

XXIV

The Grand Finale

The Marlag prison camp proved to be a haven of almost forgotten creature comforts, at least in comparison to any of our previous camp experiences. Our merchant seamen hosts made us very welcome indeed and undoubtedly were well organised in trading with locals from the nearby village.

Ray Hill had the foresight to bring with him quite a stock of our cigarette currency. Rare luxuries such as whole chickens could be purchased for about thirty cigarettes. The chickens were passed through the wires on the end of our outside guard's rifles and payments made in a similar fashion.

I was staggered to see white bread in one of these transactions. This was a very rare commodity that came from some submarine base where it was eaten occasionally as a novelty but not highly valued by the U-boat men. To me it sparked memories of an almost forgotten age. We put our order in immediately but didn't in the end manage to get a supply of white bread because events overtook us. Trading conditions became intermittent and unreliable as all sorts of rumours flashed around of an imminent breakthrough by the British troops.

It rained for days after we talked our way into this PoW camp. I couldn't help thinking that we'd have been two cold, miserable and very hungry escapees if we'd still been sitting out in the open waiting for Monty and his troops. However, while still in this self-congratulatory mood I found there could be worse torments than death by kohlrabi. My roommate, Ray Hill, was the cause of this appalling experience.

"Don't go out, Jack. There are a couple of hell of a fine chaps coming around specially meet you." he told me one morning, sitting up in his bunk. Intrigued I asked what they wanted. Ray smoothly assured me it had something to do with my Scottish name of Rae. I was immediately hooked, and waited with interest.

Two tall Scotsmen arrived carrying what looked like large duffel bags. They shook my hand with enthusiasm, said they were delighted to meet me, opened their large bags and each produced a set of bagpipes. All the while they talked in broad Scots about their enthusiasm for the pipes and were obviously expecting some endorsement from my nonplussed self.

They asked for my choice of tune, looked a little puzzled when I shrugged, then they stood to attention with bags under arms and produced the most excruciating cacophony of sound I have ever heard in a small room. The noise was a threat to the eardrums but the players clearly enjoyed every minute of it as they marched up and down the room, cheeks puffed and perspiration beading on their brows.

As each piece came to an end they would momentarily stop, wait for my expected comments, announce the next piece and away they would go again. In the middle of this incredible torture I suddenly twigged. Once in a long forgotten conversation with Ray Hill I had told him I couldn't stand bagpipes except at a great distance.

When these "hell of a fine" Scotsmen finally stopped from exhaustion I thanked them although my ears were still ringing and I could hardly hear my own voice. They were obviously expecting some form of comment so I had to go further and praise their ability. Apparently that was the right thing to do as they parted in a great mood and promised to return any time I felt like a bagpipe session.

When they'd gone Ray Hill was almost in convulsions with laughter rolling about in his bunk. I gathered the other members of our room were also in on the joke as they had all kept well away. Ray, when he was finally able to speak, said he had told the Scotsmen that I was an expert on bagpipe music, renowned back in New Zealand as a judge in bagpipe contests.

I spent many hours planning revenge on that blasted super-humorist from Rhodesia but never did manage a comeuppance.

One morning news reached us that the British had indeed broken through in and around Bremen and were heading our way. The sound of artillery fire was certainly much closer. Then the Commandant entered the camp, called our senior officers together and told them he was going over to the British line under a flag of truce to arrange for our safe reception by the advancing army. For that reason we were all to pack our belongings and be ready to move.

Our camp, he said, was to become a major defence area. So he wanted to hand over all prisoners and keep them out of harm's way. This was quite conceivable as we were situated on the top of a rise that overlooked the road and valley. To the sound of the distant battle we rushed to the perimeter wires and watched his staff car set off down the road with a large white flag fluttering from it.

We could scarcely contain our excitement. Such was our joy that it could barely be put into words. Many of these men, prisoners for years, had hoped and dreamed about this day. Long after the car had disappeared from sight we crowded the wire and waited. The senior officers assembled at the gates in readiness for some kind of formal welcome.

Nothing happened, no car appeared and the road remained deserted. The day wore on and night came. Still there was no sign of the car and no messages were received. Only much later did we learn that a young British officer had ignored the flag of truce, arrested the Commandant, refused to believe his story and made no effort to check the locality of our camp.

Early the next morning our worst fears were realised. A ground-shaking rumble of noise announced the arrival of a huge Tiger tank from the opposite direction. It took up station at a point just behind the camp and overlooking the road. A group of German soldiers also appeared, towing a multi-barrelled pom-pom gun which they set up behind some trees. Then another Tiger appeared.

Meantime, down the road towards Bremen some Sherman tanks came into view, fronting small groups of troops who were fanning out into the fields on either side of the road. The nightmare began with a volley of shells from the Tigers and the pom-poms. Machine-gun fire joined in and the bullets whistled through our barbed wire, seeming to come from all directions.

We never imagined we could dig that fast. Using pieces of wood, tin cans and even bare hands we dug furiously. Shallow depressions and even slit trenches appeared as if by magic. We frantically formed any kind of shelter from this madness, and then hugged the ground for what seemed like hours while both sides blasted each other.

After a few hours we heard the Tiger tanks rolling away. A careful peep from our shelters showed two burning British tanks down the road and other smouldering ruins of smaller transports. Nevertheless the column was now moving slowly in our direction. Our ever-ready senior officers brushed off their now dirt-covered 'best blues' in readiness at the main gates for the official welcome.

But the pompous importance of the occasion was sadly lost to them as a small British tank burst through the back of our camp, rolled over the barbed wire and a broadly smiling Scottie popped out of the hatch. We welcomed him with a cheer. Other troops followed through the hole he had made in our camp perimeter.

For all of us, at long last, our days as prisoners of war had ended. Not long after we climbed happily into trucks and set off. Each of us with his own thoughts but all conscious that this stretch of road had been bought and paid for in the blood of those soldiers who had battled up the exposed approach to our camp.

My memories of those hours after leaving that prison camp and the days immediately after are strangely clouded possibly due to the release of months of built-up tension, but some sights I remember with graphic clarity.

Some I would prefer to forget as we drove down that road. All round were the signs of the price that had been paid just to reach the hill where our camp had been. The bodies of those on both sides of the conflict lay strewn around. And the countryside too showed the cost in dead cattle and other farm animals, mute reminders of the waste and horror of war.

We drove into a small township on the approaches to Bremen, passing a small aerodrome on the way. It had obviously been a Luftwaffe base, now marked by a huge pile of wrecked planes. It was a wonderful feeling to see those hated black crosses reduced to a pile of rubble.

I cannot recall where we were given accommodation or even how we were fed – an incredible blank in my memory. What I do remember vividly was my impatience to get the hell out of this shambles. We were again surrounded with 'bods', thousands of ex-prisoners all aimlessly wandering about.

Our best information was that as soon as possible we would be flown out of this area probably to Brussels. Something positive needed to be done to push this process forward.

"What say we take a walk into town and find the British who are in control here and see if we can jack up our own transport through the Army?" I asked Bob.

He agreed. Like me he felt that any action was better than just sitting around. Except for the odd military type the streets were deserted. Understandably the locals were keeping well out of the way with windows shuttered and doors closed.

It was a quiet cold evening as we strolled along looking for some centre of military operations. Near the outskirts of the town we saw a group of industrial-type structures on a rise above an imposing looking driveway. It looked like a possible place for a military administration centre. We were about to walk up this driveway when we were accosted by a very drunk and heavily armed Russian. At least we learnt he was a Russian after some garbled discussion with him.

He was holding a semi-automatic weapon, had a couple of revolvers slung from his waist and belts of ammunition draped over his shoulders. Obviously confused with our uniforms and unsure of our authority he decided to be friendly and produced a bottle, insisting that we drink with him.

We both pretended to take some of his concoction which smelt very much like methylated spirits or something equally unpleasant. After exchanging warm farewells we walked past this very loose cannon and up to the buildings. It certainly wasn't a hive of activity. Disappointed, we were about to leave when we noticed a chink of light under a door near to the main entrance.

Here was the place to make inquiries, we thought, hopefully not more drunken Russians. We knocked. No one answered so we opened the door and to our surprise found ourselves in quite a large room with a number of very frightened mostly young women. They were huddled together in groups with bundles of their belongings around them, looking as if they were ready to move.

Bob and I started to back away after the initial shock as this was not exactly "our cup of tea" but a rather regal lady from amongst them approached us and between garbled German and mixed up French we learnt that they were Polish forced labour women and this had been a forced labour camp. They were terrified for their lives. I think they were trying to tell us that there had already been attacks on women from the drunken

Russians who appear to have gone berserk.

After meeting our Russian we could well believe this. They pleaded for us to stay and defend them. This was a ridiculous proposal as we were unarmed and quite useless for any meaningful defence. After a quick discussion we decided that one of us would stay. The other would dash off, find the British military authorities and persuade them to guard the women and round up any problem Russians.

Somehow I found myself selected as the one to stay on guard. I'm not sure how that came about but Bob had the gift of persuasion. I stood by the door feeling quite inadequate in the knowledge that if it was kicked in by a fully armed drunken Russian I wouldn't be of much use. On that reasoning I decided there'd be more chance of defence by waiting outside and away from the entrance where the sight and closeness of their desired quarry would only inflame a wandering drunk.

Fortunately this proved to be the right decision because soon after moving to this new position another of those drunken armed-to-the-teeth Russians appeared. As with the one we had met before he was most confused by the RAF uniform, mumbling something that sounded like "Engleesh?" Using the effective words of *Heraus!* and *Verboten!* I persuaded him, albeit reluctantly and angrily, to move off. He did so, but not before firing a volley into the air.

That confrontation was fairly easy to handle I thought, but the bluff might not work next time. Where the hell was Bob?

It was now dark. Another drunk appeared or perhaps it was the same one. Hard to tell. Again the pantomime of another set of *Verbotens* and another reluctant withdrawal. The situation was becoming very dangerous. It would be very stupid to have survived this crazy war only to be shot full of holes by a drunken randy Russian.

At long last up the driveway came lights from a row of transports. Army types appeared with Bob in front. They assured us they would take over and arrest the troublemakers. I went back to the highly nervous womenfolk and told them the good news. The same gracious lady who first asked for our help indicated she wished to give me something.

Embarrassed, I tried to tell her it wasn't necessary but she insisted, rummaged through her belongings and passed me her gift. I thanked her and accepted it in the spirit that I am sure it was meant.

It was a Polish bank note, which long ago had lost its value but must have once meant something to her to be so carefully kept. I have no idea how much it had once been worth. All I could decipher was the number twenty. But I still have it amongst my memorabilia. And from time to time whenever I look at it I wonder what happened to that group of Polish women. Did they get back to Poland or were they transported to England? Wherever they went I hoped they were re-united with their loved ones and the homes from which the Nazis had displaced them. Bob and I were uncomfortably aware we were witnessing just a tiny part of the human toll of war.

This particular group of military were unable to help us with our own problem of getting back to Britain so we contained our impatience, went back to our crowded reception centre and waited. In a surprisingly short time, barely a couple of days, we were treated to the welcome sight of RAF transport arriving to fly us on the first leg of our trip to England.

The sheer numbers of PoWs involved must have been a logistical nightmare by itself, apart from the ongoing massive troop movements and supplies required for the front line, yet the RAF handled it all smoothly and efficiently. I suspect there were many matters to untangle in the background but to we ex-Kriegies everything was handled smoothly and with the minimum of fuss.

They flew us to Brussels where over a thousand of us were accommodated in a large hotel in the centre of the city. Again there was no fuss and little bother. We were fed without endless queues and our names were recorded together with our service numbers. Within 48 hours I was on a plane and flying back to beautiful England.

The plane touched down on 28 April, 1945, a fortunate return from that eventful day when I last took off from Biggin Hill on 22 August 1943. We were transported to Brighton where all New Zealand PoWs were being billeted in a large hotel of past grandeur. The rooms were modest but to us wonderfully comfortable after our recent deprivations. A glorious hot bath took it to the levels of undreamed of luxury.

A pleasant Waaf introduced herself as my "batman", apologising that she was terribly busy with a number of us to look after, checked as to whether I was OK and asked if my clothing had arrived from New Zealand House. I thanked her for her concern but assured her that my clothes had been transferred to a private home and I would collect them as soon as possible.

Once the euphoria of those first couple of days had passed we dashed off to the centre of London to kick up our heels and enjoy the delights we had been dreaming of for so long. Wine, women and song, we decided, that's what we've been missing all these months and years. The reality, alas, wasn't quite like that.

My first attempt to celebrate was in one of our old favourite pubs in London. It was filled with strangers. The world, I discovered, had not stood still while I was away. All my friends of those days were either somewhere in Europe or no longer with us. My next port of call was New Zealand House, always a great place to meet and greet. But no, not a familiar face to be seen.

The fallback position was to seek out some fellow ex-PoWs and see how they were celebrating. We weren't short of money as our service pay had been accumulating and we were bursting to spend it. The Crackers Club in Soho was the place, a favourite hangout for many of us but in particular the Canadians. There was nothing particular about either the decor or the service but it had always been a great place to meet, get in the mood and enjoy all that London had to offer.

Feeling somewhat flat, I climbed the stairs and walked into what I remembered as a laughter-filled room. But it was strangely quiet – not the usual volume of Canadian voices competing for attention. Then I saw them, quite a large number of mostly Canadian ex-PoWs sitting around a couple of tables, talking quietly. I could not recall the place having such a depressing atmosphere.

I joined them and discovered they were having the greatest difficulty in adjusting to being the way they were before becoming prisoners. The general consensus was that we, as a group of young people with enforced time on our hands, had been forced to evaluate life on a broader perspective, normally something achieved only in later years if ever.

We were no longer influenced by any given pattern of thought, propaganda or cultural restraints. Graphically aware of the suffering of women and children in Germany, the shocking carnage of war in general and the enormity of the destruction, we felt no need to be a part of all this. We felt alienated from the world around us. Perhaps if we'd had homes and families to return to immediately after our release there would have been a normality to sustain us but instead we were suddenly in a void.

Over the years since I've tried to analyse my feelings and those of many PoWs about that strange period of our lives. We listened mostly and said nothing, trying to readjust back to having a common outlook on the war and perhaps even feeling comfortable about the views we had before becoming PoWs.

Today's trendy approach would of course have had us rushed off for counselling. We, at least most of us, survived without it. The black mood did wear off as we slowly became conditioned and influenced by one side's point of view and gained enough social camouflage so that we at least talked and behaved like everyone else.

Ten days after our arrival the whole of Britain went wild at the news the war was over. May 8 was declared VE (Victory in Europe) Day. At long last, the end of this appalling conflict was official. I was in London that day and found the excited frenzy of the crowds hard to take, feeling completely unable to join in the celebrations. My one desire was to get out of that incredible crush of humanity and back to Brighton.

But for what seemed to be hours no one could move. Traffic was gridlocked. Even on foot there was little chance of reaching a railway station or Underground. Finally after being swept to and fro by the crowd interminably I found myself near a station, slipped in and succeeded in getting onto a train and back to Brighton. For that evening and all the next day I stayed inside the hotel, relieved at simply being clear of the crowds.

Fortunately I had a powerful stimulus to jolt me out of my depression. My great friend Jim Dyson, now a pilot, had just recently arrived in the UK from Canada. I was able to meet him near Blackpool and we celebrated together. This was a very special time for me. Jim, the proud father of a fine young son, brought news of his wife Jacky and my own family. As we talked, I could feel the blackness slowly lifting.

It was wonderful to see him, and to join with him in his excitement that at long last he was in the Air Force. We had once hoped that we would join together back in 1940 but circumstances decided otherwise. The war in Europe was over but Japan remained to deal with so the future was still uncertain.

Jim was still tied into the system and liable to be posted somewhere or other while I had a project of my own to keep me busy. During my pre-war time spent working for a meat company I was impressed by the attractive floor-coverings made by tanning woolly sheepskins and had often thought of producing them commercially. In prison camp I obtained some books about tanning and dyeing, and on returning to the UK was given a study tour of various tanneries in England. Before Jim and I went our separate ways we visited a mutual friend from our Auckland Grammar School days, Les Robertson, now a wing commander in charge of arranging postings back to NZ.

We decided that it would be much more fun to go back via the United States. After some discussion Les suggested I find a fiancée in the USA that I was going back to marry, and that I needed Jim there as my best man. With considerable plotting and planning, the details of which are still top secret, we managed to get a lovely American lady to send me a cable saying she was waiting for me.

All wedding arrangements had been made, said the message. I never met the lady but she must have been lovely to be so accommodating to a lonely serviceman. The authorities accepted the cable and approved the trip, leaving Jim and I feeling very smug about our arranged jaunt across the States.

However the best laid plans, and particularly devious ones, often go astray. About a week before we were due to leave other momentous happenings occurred, including the end of the war with Japan, VJ Day and the cancellation of American Lease-Lend finance to Britain.

This affected all British travel through the USA. Sadly, our trip was cancelled so Jim and I found ourselves on a ship called the *Andes* bound direct for New Zealand. She was a flat-bottomed ship built for trading along the South American waterways. She was also fast but not all that stable. In fact she rolled abominably. To add to the misery of the over-load of passengers jammed aboard, her skipper was determined to create a new record non-stop from England to Melbourne in Australia via the Suez Canal.

The *Andes* did break the record. I can't recall the details but I do remember the queasiness of that journey as she took the massive beam-on swells that sweep up from the Antarctic into the Great Australian Bight. The rise of the bow to dizzy heights and the corkscrew action as the ship slid down into the deep troughs left most passengers seasick, dizzy and very fed-up, not having set foot on land since leaving the UK. We had a one-night stopover in Melbourne then headed across the turbulent Tasman Sea.

At long last we neared our beloved New Zealand only to have another culture shock – our first broadcast from a New Zealand radio station for four years. I couldn't believe that what I was listening to was the New Zealand accent. To our unaccustomed ears it sounded like an exaggerated gabble from Donald Duck.

Naively, I had never considered that our delivery of the Queen's English was so accented.

The *Andes* seemed to be in the estrangement business. Its captain made few friends with his choice of Wellington as port of arrival. Hardly anyone on board came from that city. Nevertheless it was a momentous arrival.

Jim and I decided to bypass the troop train which wasn't due to leave for Auckland until long after our arrival. We got ourselves ashore and managed to short-circuit the red tape to secure places on a train leaving immediately.

As a result we had the thrill of surprising our loved ones by arriving totally unexpectedly. Words can never express those first moments with my parents, grandmother and my younger brother. And I'm certain Jim's reunion with Jacky, his young son and his mother Hedda would also have been of pleasure beyond expression.

We were home. The war in Europe and the Pacific was over and we could again get on with our lives. I knew the surf would still be rolling out at that beautiful Piha beach. The beach where Dad had toiled over many weekends to build a seaside bach, the place I had dreamed of so often over the past five years.

Emotions were overwhelming as at last I stood with my Dad inside that cosy little house. I gazed through an expansive set of windows framing the rugged scenery and the beauty of the surf below. My father had built this place with his own hands for my return. Hardly able to speak with the joy of the moment, I leaned my head against the cool glass and knew with certainty I was home.

Appendix

Service Record

1940

1 September	Posted GTS Levin enlisted LAC Pilot U/T.
27 September	2 EFTS New Plymouth, aircraft Tiger Moths.
23 November	3 FTS Ohakea, aircraft Hawker Hinds.

1941

27 February	Ceased flying training in New Zealand.
1 March	Promoted Sgt. Posted to UK.
19 May	Arrived at Uxbridge.
27 May	Posted to 53 OTU Heston.
11 June	First Solo in a Spitfire.
11 July	Posted to 485 Squadron Redhill (part of Kenley Wing 11 Group).
10 October	Promoted to Flt Sergeant.
21 October	Squadron moved to Kenley Base.

1942

12 April	Posted to 603 Squadron.
13 April	Embarked on USS *Wasp*, destination northern coast of Algiers.
20 April	Flew off USS *Wasp* for Malta. Arrived Takali air base Malta.
1 May	Shot down, baled out.
1 May	Promoted to Warrant Officer.
5 June	Transferred to 249 Squadron.
30 June	Received Commision to Pilot Officer.
17 August	Ceased operations in Malta, flown to Gibraltar.
22 August	Returned to England via Sunderland Flying Boat.
18 September	Posted to 57 OTU as an instuctor.
1 October	Posted to Castle Coombe for an FIS course.
6 November	57 OTU transferred to Eshott station (Northumberland).
30 November	Awarded the Distinguished Flying Cross.
29 December	Promoted to Flying Officer.

1943

3 May	Posted back to operations with 118 Squadron Coltishall.
25 May	Back with 485 (NZ)Squadron. at Merston.
1 July	Squadron transfers to Biggin Hill.
22 August	Engine failed during operation – became a POW.
	Awarded Bar to Distinguished Flying Cross.

1944

30 June	Promoted to Flt Lieutenant.

1945

28 April	Returned to the UK from Germany.

Successes

Following summary is a copy from Chris Shores' book *Aces High*, Grub Street 1994.

Date	Qty	Claim	Aircraft	Serial	Code	Location	Sqn
1941							
12 Aug		Bf109F Damaged	Spitfire IIa	P7438		Inland from Gravelines	485 Sqn
19 Aug		Bf109E Damaged	,,	P7621		Inland from Gravelines	485 Sqn
2 Oct		Bf109F Probable	Spitfire Vb	AD114		W Boulogne	,,
6 Nov		Bf109E Probable	,,	AD114		10m out to sea between Cape Gris Nez & Calais	,,
1942							
12 Feb		Bf109E Probable	,,			5m West of Ostend	,,
28 Mar		FW190 Probable	,,	,,		5m inland Cape Gris Nez & Calais	,,
28 Mar		FW190	,,	,,		20m inland Cape Gris Nez	,,
12 June		Bf109 Damaged	,,	BR 254	X-G	Malta	249 Sqn
27 June		MC202	,,	BR377	T-K	SW Sicily	,,
27 June		MC202 Probable	,,			,,	,,
4 July		Z1007	,,	BR233	T-Q	near Takali	,,
7 July		Bf109F	,,	BR323	T-S	Malta	,,
9 July	1/2	Ju88	,,			,,	,,
9 July		MC202 Probable	,,			,,	,,
13 July		Re2001	,,			,,	,,
13 July	2	Re2001 Damaged	,,			,,	,,
27 July		Bf109 Probable	,,	BR301	UF-S	,,	,,
27 July		Re2001 Damaged	,,			,,	,,
28 July	1/2	Ju88 Probable	,,			,,	,,
28 July		Ju88 Damaged	,,			,,	,,

1943

Date		Claim		Serial	Location	Sqn
15 July		FW190	Spitfire IX		Foret de Crecy-Berck	485 Sqn
15 July		FW190 Probable	„		„	„
27 July	1/2	FW190	„	JK979	SE Tricqueville	„
9 August		Bf109G	JK762		Lille-Merville area St Omer	„
17 August	2	Bf109Gs	EN560		S Desvres area	„
22 August		FW190 (a)	„		E Le Havre	„

TOTAL: 11 and 2 shared destroyed, 8 and 1 shared probable, 6 damaged.

(a) This victory was listed for Rae by returning pilots; there is no combat report due to his failure to return.

Index

The index is arranged alphabetically, except for entries under the author's name, which are in chronological order.

11 Group 23
53 OTU (Operations Training Unit) No. 4 Course 15, 17-20
57 OTU (Operations Training Unit) 77-79, 82-90
118 Squadron 90-93
249 Squadron 51-75
452 Squadron 25
485 (New Zealand) Squadron 20, 21-42, 76-77, 93-107
486 (New Zealand) Squadron 93
601 (County of London) Squadron 44
602 (City of Glasgow) Squadron 25
603 (City of Edinburgh) Squadron 44
611 Squadron (West Lancashire Squadron) 98

Abbeville 99-100
aircraft
  Airspeed Oxford 7
  Boeing Flying Fortress 103
  Cant 1007: 67, 68
  Focke Wulf Fw 190: 41, 78-79, 92, 93-94, 100, 102
  Hawker
    Hind 7
    Hurricane 36, 55
    Typhoon 94
  Junkers Ju 87: 68
  Junkers Ju 88: 54
  Messerschmitt Bf 109: 1, 54, 56-57
  Messerschmitt Bf 109F 32, 93, 104
  Miles Master 18, 80, 83
    spinning 87-88
  Miles Master III 80, 81
  Reggiane Re2001: 66-67
  Short Sunderland 74-75
  Supermarine
    Spitfire 1, 17-19, 24, 38

Spitfire Mark II 21-22
Spitfire Mark VB 32, 92, 93, 94
Spitfire Mark VC 43, 44, 56
Spitfire Mark IXB 96, 97-98
Spitfire (photo-reconnaissance – PRU Spit) 50, 62
airfields
   Biggin Hill, RAF 96-107
      Intelligence and Briefing Rooms 99
   Castle Combe, RAF 80
   Coltishall, RAF 90, 91-93
   Debert, Canada 13
   Eshott, RAF 83-90
   Hawarden, RAF 77-79, 81
   Heston, RAF 15, 17-20
   Hullavington, RAF 79-80
   Kenley, RAF 25, 34-42
   Levin, New Zealand 6
   Merston, RAF 93-94
   Ohakea, New Zealand 7
   Redhill, RAF 20, 21-34, 35
   Takali, Malta 52, 61
   Tangmere, RAF 94-95
   Uxbridge, RAF 15
American prisoner 139-140
Andes 170-171
Argus, HMS 95
Auckland Grammar School Old Boys rugby team 4, 26, 77

BSA motorbike 101
Baker, Pilot Officer (later Squadron Leader) Reg 10, 19, 93, 94
Barnett, Gary 101
Barry, 'Bottler' 8
Bateson, Henry 76
Beamish, Group Captain Victor 35, 39, 41-42
Beckingsale, Clay 129-130, 148
Beurling, Sergeant 'Screwball' 65-66, 73
'boffin', civilian 157
bomber escorts 103-104
Boucher, Hill 6, 7, 8
Bouchier, Group Captain C.E. 35
Brennan, Paul 51, 59, 76
briefings 24
Brighton, Sussex 168, 169
Brinsden, Frank 26
Brown, Doug 36, 101
Browning, Bob 148, 157, 158, 159, 166, 167
Brussels 168

Bull, Johnny 141
Bushell, Squadron Leader Roger (Big X) 123, 135, 141, 144

Calais 22
Carew, Edgar, and family 3
Carpenter, Sergeant Pilot Ted 10, 19
Channel Cover Patrol 22
Checketts, Johnny 96, 103-104, 105, 114
Churchill, Winston 64-65
Clark, Fraser 105
Cleary, Max 2
Close Escort Cover 24, 27, 33
Colbeck, Flight Lieutenant Harry 50
Collett, 'Pop' 129
Crackers Club, Soho 168-169
Crawford-Compton, Bill 27, 32, 36-37

Daddo-Langlois, Flight Commander Raoul 63, 65
Dargaville Bus Terminal 2
'Dawn readiness' 92-93
Dean, Sergeant Pilot Hughie 10, 12, 19
deck landings 95
deck landings, mock 94-95
Deere, Wing Commander Alan 96, 97, 104
Derbyshire 13
Douglas, Air Marshal Sir William Sholto 23
Douglas-Hamilton, Squadron Leader David 44, 45, 47-48, 51
Dulag Interrogation centre 112-113
Dunant, Henry 112
Dyson, Jim 2, 169-170, 171

Eagle, HMS 63
Empire Training School, Canada 10
engines, Rolls-Royce 93
Escort Cover 24, 33

'Fanny', Wing Commander 77-78
Feldwebel 110-111
Ferguson, John 'Fergie' 101
'Flossy', Wing Commander 77-78
Flying Instructors Course (FIS), 24 (3) 79-81
Ford, Sergeant Pilot Les 19
formations *see also* Close Escort Cover; Escort Cover; High Cover;
    Top Cover
    'Finger Four' 52, 97
    line abreast 52, 94, 97
    line astern 22, 23, 52, 94 *see also* 'Tail End Charlie'

Francis, Flight Lieutenant Gary 26, 32, 40, 77
Frankfurt am Main 112-113
Frecklington, Sergeant 'Freck' 34
Freiwaldau, Germany 151-152
French 'Alsace Squadron', Free 98, 99, 101

Garnham, Rex 12
Geneva Convention 112, 121, 155
George, Percy 145-146, 148
Gibbs, Bruce 104
Gibraltar 73, 74
Gneisenau 38, 39-40
Goodwin, Sergeant 34
Gracie, Squadron Leader 'Jumbo' 46-47, 51, 62, 83-84, 89, 90
Grant, Sergeant Pilot Reg 34, 37, 40, 76, 77, 89-90, 113
Grant, Squadron Leader Stan 51, 63
Gray, Bill 12
Griffith, Sergeant L.P. 'Griff' 27-28, 40-41
Gunn, Jim 96, 119

Halle, Germany 153
Harcourt-Jones, Flight Sergeant William 'Bill' 95-96
Haun, Major Jim 98
Heidrich (Alsatian dog) 135, 136
Hesslyn, Ray, DFM and Bar 51, 72, 73, 74, 76, 79-80, 114
High Cover 24, 27, 102
Hill, Ray 130, 162, 163, 164
Himmler, Heinrich 143
Hitler, Adolf 62, 143
Hume, Flight Commander Marty 41, 93, 94

Iceland 14-15
Italian Air Force (Regia Aeronautica) 65, 66

Jackson, Flying Officer, WAAF 87-88
Jennens, Squadron Leader Bill 143, 155, 156
Jones, Wing Commander 'Taffy', DSO, MC, DFC, MM 20
Jowett, Humphrey 131-132

Kent, Wing Commander J.A. 'Johnny', DFC, AFC 20
Kesselring, Field Marshall 45, 61, 62
Knight, Squadron Leader Marcus 26-27, 29, 32, 35
Kronfeld, Sergeant 34
Kulman, Lieutenant Keith 84-85

Laycock, Percy 2
Liken, Sergeant J. 40

Link Trainer 7
Lloyd, Air Vice-Marshal Hugh Pughe 46, 50-51
logbook, RAF Form 540: 28, 32, 34, 79
London 76, 168-169
Lowson, George 12
Lucas, Flight Commander Laddie 63, 67, 68, 86

Mae Wests 17
Malan, Squadron Leader (later Group Captain) 'Sailor' 96, 97
Malta 42,44, 45, 47-73
Malta, statistics for battle of 73-74
Marshall, Johnny 141
Massey, Group Captain 121
McElroy, Flying Officer 85
McIvor, Sergeant Pilot Jim 10, 19
McLean, Wing Commander J.S. 44
McNair, Flight Commander Buck 63
McNeil, Sergeant 'Tusker' 28-29, 34
Mdina, Malta 59
Middleton, Pilot Officer Bill 26
Mitchell, Bert 56-57
Monowai, SS 9, 10-11
Morrison 126
Mouchotte, Commandant René 98
Muskau, Germany 152

New Glasgow, Canada 13
New Zealand 2-5
Noble, Red 124-125, 150, 158

One More Hour 15
operations
   Bowery 63
   Fuller 39-40
   Harpoon 65
   Hercules 61-70
Oxted, Surrey 101

PoW camps *see* prison (PoW) camps
Paris 111
Park, Air Vice-Marshal Keith (later Sir Keith) 23, 51
Pattison, Flight Commander John 76, 77, 93
Pearce, Tom 4
Petersen, Bjelke 'Pete' 130, 145-146, 149
Phillips, Sergeant Pilot Ray 10, 19
Piha beach 2, 171
Piha Surf Life Saving Club 2

Pohe, Johnny 137, 144
Polawski, Flight Lieutenant 80
Polish forced labour women 166-167
Porter, Sergeant Pilot 21
Prinz Eugen 39-40
prison (PoW) camps
  Dulag Luft 115
  Marlag 161-165
    tank battle 165
  Stalag Luft III, Sagan 116-149
    cooler 138-143, 144
    description 120-121
    dirt, disposing of 124
    escape attempts by others 125-126
    escape ('X') organisation 119, 122-124, 132, 133, 134
    first impression 117-118
    food 129
    'Great Escape' 140-144
    musical entertainment 121-122
    showers 129-130
    sports played 122
    theatre 121, 132, 144, 145
    'tin bashing' manufacture 124
    tunnel, Dick 123-124, 127
    tunnel, George 144-145, 147
    tunnel, Harry 123-124, 127, 137, 140-142
    tunnel, Tom 123-124, 127-128
  Tarmsted 153-158
prisoners-of-war 131
Probert, Rex 133, 134, 135, 136, 137, 140
Pughe Lloyd, Air Vice-Marshal Hugh 46, 50-51

Rae, Flt Lt Jack D., DFC and Bar
  life in New Zealand 2-8
  joined Royal New Zealand Air Force 6
  Canadian interlude 10-13
  Atlantic crossing 13-15
  first Spitfire flight 18-19
  weather reconnaissance flight 37-39
  first combat flight in Malta 53-55
  baled out over Malta 58-59
  commission to Pilot Officer received 70
  DFC awarded 71-72
  infected leg problems 70-72
  return to England from Malta 73-75
  flying instruction 83-90
  forced landing in France 106-107

captured 109
interrogation 113-114, 115
arrival at Stalag Luft III PoW camp, Sagan 116
    see also prison (PoW) camps, Stalag Luft III, Sagan
escape attempt 133-137
march from Stalag Luft III 148-153
Tarmsted PoW camp 153-158
escape from Tarmsted PoW camp 158-162
Marlag PoW camp 162-165
liberation 165
return to England 168
adjusting to post-war life 169
return to New Zealand 170-171
Read, Flying Officer 18
Red Cross, International 112
Red Cross parcels 156-157
Reece, 'Shag' 150
Renown, HMS 44
Reykjavik, Iceland 14
'Rhubarbs' 33-34
Robertson, Les 170
Robson, Tony 36
'Ruby' 78-79
Russell, Sergeant 32
Russian Air Force officer 139

Sagan PoW camp, Silesia see prison (PoW) camps, Stalag Luft III, Sagan
Scharnhorst 38, 39-40
Scott, Des 15, 93, 94
Scottish bagpipers 163-164
Shand, Pilot Officer Mick 34, 117-118, 142
Sholto Douglas, Air Marshal Sir William 23
Singer car 3
Sliema, Malta 72-73
Smith, Jerry 64
smoking 118-119
Soho nightclubs 36-37, 168-169
Soukup, Lieutenant Herbert 58, 71
spinning in Miles Master 87-88
Stalag Luft III, Sagan see prison (PoW) camps, Stalag Luft III, Sagan
Stanford Tuck, Wing Commander Bob 132-133
Stenborg, Gray 80
Stenhouse, Dr, Gwen and family 86
Stower, Johnny 125-126
Strang, Flight Lieutenant Jack 27
surf-skiing 4
Sutherland, 'Mac' 105

Sweetman, Harvey 40

'Tail End Charlie' 22, 25 *see also* formations, line astern
Tartan Dive nightclub, Soho 36-37
Tawhai, Johnny 8
Thomas, Hal 22, 34
Top Cover 24, 33
Training Command, RAF 79
Travis, Lieutenant 98, 104
Tucker, Tommy 102, 104

VE (Victory in Europe) Day 169
VJ Day (Victory over Japan) Day 170

WAAFs (Women's Auxiliary Air Force) members 31, 87-88, 100-101
Walker, Captain 'Pappy' 98
Wartime Log, A 130-131
Wasp, USS 42, 43-46, 63
Watts, Sergeant 34
Wells, Flight Commander 'Hawkeye' 27, 32, 35, 40, 41
Welsh 126
Welshman, HMS 64
West, Flight Commander Ronnie 63
Westfield Freezing Co 2-3
White, 'Chalky' 105, 110
'Willie the Kid' 73
Wolseley car 101
Woodhall, Group Captain A.B. 'Woody' 47, 63, 66, 67

'X' organisation 119, 122-124, 132, 133, 134

Y Service 66
Yates, Alan 67, 73